JAPANESE IN MANGALAND
2

Basic to Intermediate Level

Marc Bernabe

Translation:
Olinda Cordukes

Cover illustration:
Nuria Peris

Inside illustrations:
Javier Bolado
Gabriel Luque
J.M. Ken Niimura
Barbara Raya
Studio Kōsen

Marc Bernabe (L'Ametlla del Valles, Barcelona, 1976) is a Japanese-Spanish / Catalan translator and interpreter, working mainly on manga and anime translations. Apart from his translation works, he also specializes in language and Japanese culture didactics for foreigners, with a master's degree by the Osaka University of Foreign Studies. His published works are: *Japanese in MangaLand* (Japan Publications, 2004), the Spanish adaptation of James W. Heisig's *Remembering the kanji* series, and other books on Japan and the Japanese language aimed at the Spanish speaking public.

Japanese in MangaLand 2
Basic to Intermediate Level
By Marc Bernabe

Published and distributed: *Japan Publications Trading Co., Ltd.,*
1-2-1 Sarugaku-cho, Chiyoda-ku, Tokyo, Japan.

First printing: *August 2005*

Overseas Distributors
UNITED STATES:
   Kodansha America, Inc. through Oxford University Press,
   198 Madison Avenue, New York, NY 10016.
CANADA:
   Fitzhenry & Whiteside Ltd., 195 Allstate Parkway, Markham,
   Ontario L3R 4T8.
AUSTRALIA and NEW ZEALAND:
   Bookwise International Pty Ltd.,
   174 Cormack Road, Wingfield, South Australia 5013, Australia.
EUROPE, ASIA and JAPAN:
   Japan Publications Trading Co., Ltd., 1-2-1 Sarugaku-cho,
   Chiyoda-ku, Tokyo, 101-0064 Japan.

ISBN-13:978-4-88996-186-7
ISBN-10:4-88996-186-0

Printed in Spain

前書き Preface

When *Japonés en viñetas* 1 (the original title of the book) was first published in Spanish in May, 2001, I never imagined it would have been received the way it was, even spawning English *(Japanese in MangaLand)*, German *(Japanisch mit Manga)*, French *(Le japonais en manga)* and Catalan *(Japonès en vinyetes)* versions, with other versions in Italian and Portuguese being prepared for publication even as I write this.

Japan is certainly a special country indeed: it has the overwhelming influence of its entertainment culture, which has spanned borders and invades us via manga, anime, videogames, and electronic gadgets, a fact which undeniably attracts the attention of the young (and not so young). Therefore, the idea of creating a Japanese teaching method using popular manga, a method aimed at such open-minded people, did not prove wrong by any means, as the first volume was very favorably received. I won't deny that this reception took me completely by surprise and made me extremely happy. Every email I get from a reader telling me how much they like it and how useful *Japanese in MangaLand* is for them encourages me to keep on going. Thanks to the Internet and emails, I have had the privilege of keeping in touch with readers and receiving their encouragement and suggestions.

The support of the readers has certainly helped me spur myself on in order to learn more and to keep a watchful eye for improvement. The effort I have made these past two and a half years towards learning and acquiring experience have allowed me to write the book you are now holding as well as a third one. These additional two volumes complement the first one, constituting, between all three of them, a Japanese course which guides you from zero level to an intermediate level. Also, I have continued working, with an increasingly large and select team of enthusiastic contributors at Nipoweb.com, an Internet web page on Japanese language and culture which grows by leaps and bounds, and which has become a reference in the world of Japanese studies in Spanish on the Internet. If you have any question or suggestion, you may submit them in English through the English section of this page: www.nipoweb.com/eng.

Nevertheless, this book would not have been possible without the support of many people, such as my inseparable **Verònica Calafell**, the genuine driving force behind this book, who revised it and supervised it and who is my official long-life sufferer in moments of desperation, as well as happiness, the whole team at **Norma Editorial** and **Japan Publications**, for backing the publication of the three volumes, the **Fundació La Caixa** and the **Japan Educational Exchanges and Services (JEES)**, for giving me the chance by means of a grant to vastly increase my knowledge, which has been directly poured into this book, professor **Sayo Tsutsui** 筒井佐代, for taking me in her seminar at the University of Foreign Studies in Osaka, **Luis Rodríguez** and **Josep Sadurní**, for patiently revising each and every one of the lessons as they were being written — so many months of work and patience!—, Itsue Tanigawa 谷川依津江, for revising the Japanese part in the book, **James W. Heisig**, for providing me with very valuable advise on typography and layout which have enabled me to give this book its actual form, and for supporting me at all times, the artists **Javier Bolado**, **Gabriel Luque**, **J.M. Ken Niimura**, **Bárbara Raya** and **Studio Kōsen** for creating the wonderful pictures that illustrate this book — over 200!—, my kind and patient translator, **Olinda Cordukes**, my friend and proof-reader **Daniel Carmona**, and, of course... all of you, the readers, and all of those who have shown affection and personally given encouragement. Undoubtedly, were it not for all of you and your support, this project would not have been possible. Thank you very much!

Marc Bernabe
March 20th, 2005
Osaka, Japan

目次 Index

本書の特徴 Introduction

This book you are holding is the direct continuation of the work *Japanese in MangaLand* (Japan Publications, 2004) and the lessons herein continue, in content as well as order, from the lessons in the first volume. In other words, it is advisable to study the first volume before you start studying this one. The only exceptions are those students who already have a basic knowledge of Japanese, and have mastered the *kana*, some kanji, and elementary grammar and vocabulary. If you belong to this group, you can start straight with this book, although it is still advisable to use the first volume for reference.

The entrance

Many readers used *Japanese in MangaLand* as the entrance to the world of Japanese language, since this book was planned as an enjoyable introduction to the language. No efforts were spared to make the study as easy and pleasant as possible: for example, the decision to always give the reading of the Japanese sentences in the Roman alphabet was taken to make the entry into the world of Japanese language as smooth as possible. The first volume is, then, some kind of "appetizer," thanks to which anyone can learn basic Japanese in an enjoyable way and with little effort. In other words, it's a type of "bait" to give people the itch to learn Japanese.

If, having studied the first volume, you are now reading this one, then it is safe to say that *Japanese in MangaLand* has achieved its intended aim. However, "playtime" is now over. Strap a headband with the rising sun on it around your head, just like the Karate Kid did, because you are about to fully enter the world of hard-core study. This time, you had better be prepared to do your work, because things are going to get serious.

Don't panic just yet, though: the book keeps its basic philosophy of "learning while having fun" and you have, of course, a good deal of humor and curiosities which will make your study as enjoyable as possible. Don't forget learning a language should be a recreational activity rather than an "imposition." This is why we use manga to illustrate our explanations and why we sometimes give funny examples: to get a few laughs out of you while you study. Forget spending hours learning by heart boring and never-ending lists of vocabulary, you are here to enjoy yourself, not to torture yourself!

Aims of this book

The main aim of this method is to establish the necessary basics in grammar and vocabulary so you can learn to read and, to a certain extent, write in Japanese. Obviously, listening and speaking cannot be dealt with in a written work, therefore, you should try practicing on your on.

One of the main aims of this work is to help you acquire enough ability to read manga, so you will have to do without the transcription in Roman letters, one of the bonuses in the first volume. This time, all Japanese words are written in *kana* and kanji, as it should be, although we will always lend a hand by providing you with the reading of each kanji in *furigana*. We also use kanji with medium-high difficulty in the example sentences — with their corresponding reading, of course — that way, when we read manga for children and teenagers in Japanese, we will find something similar to the example sentences in this book: sentences full of kanji, yet always with their reading shown in *furigana*. In the examples, we wanted to create a similar "atmosphere" to the one you would normally find in a manga. In this way you can get used to fast reading in Japanese with kana, kanji and *furigana*.

The lessons

This book has 15 lessons altogether, numbered from 31 to 45, chronologically following the numeration of the first volume. Of these 15 lessons, 11 are of a "grammatical" type and 4 are a "conversational" type. Let's see their characteristics:

Grammar lessons

Grammar subjects are chosen for these lessons, and they are thoroughly discussed, with many example sentences and clarifying tables or structure summaries which will make comprehension easier, and which you should be able to use as a basis when you want to review and study those expressions you find most difficult.

We present the various grammatical forms in a very different way to the usual one in "regular" Japanese classes. Since this is a book for self-taught study, we have preferred condensing grammatical patterns according to related subjects to make their association simpler and so that you can more easily link the relationship between them.

With regards to the manga-examples, these keep the same function they had in the first part. They will help you to see specific examples, in context, of those expressions studied in the theory pages. They will also help you to expand concepts, see some new constructions, and revise constructions seen in previous lessons. The manga-examples are a very important pillar of this book, so try not to skip them. Just like in the first part, manga-examples were originally taken from Japanese manga. For obvious copyright reasons, illustrations have been redesigned, even though the sentences themselves, which is what really matters here, remain the same. Therefore, you have real sentences taken from real manga created by Japanese, which guarantees that you are studying with "genuine" material.

Finally, every lesson has ten simple exercises which will help you, as a personal challenge, consolidate your knowledge and check whether you have understood what has just been explained. The right answers can be found in the first appendix, at the end of the book: you can use them to check whether you have solved the exercises correctly.

Conversational lessons

One of the defects in grammar lessons is their focus on formal aspects, which leaves the learning of new vocabulary aside to a certain extent. To solve this problem, a new concept was created: "Conversational lesson," which revolve around a contextual subject (At the airport, Shopping, In the restaurant, etc.). These lessons have four aims:

1. **Fostering the learning of new vocabulary.** With extensive theme-oriented vocabulary tables to make it easier to study or review vocabulary.
2. **Practicing previously studied grammatical concepts.** Example sentences are conceived in order to allow making best use of the knowledge you have acquired in previous lessons. We also indicate the lesson number where the grammatical pattern we have used appears, so you can review it if necessary.
3. **Providing you with a break between so many lessons full of grammar.** This way, you can clear your head learning something completely different and more enjoyable, but not less important, every three or four grammar lessons.
4. **Giving a conversation guide.** Very useful for possible trips to Japan or conversations with Japanese people.

These lessons include as well the so-called "Cultural Note," a one page section where a specific aspect of Japanese culture is discussed. You can use the Cultural Note to practice some vocabulary, and, of course, you can learn new things, often curious, about the Japanese culture and environment. As you know, mastering a language requires learning a lot more than words alone.

Appendixes

At the end of the book there are three appendixes with very useful extra information:

(1) **Answers to the exercises:** detailed answers to all exercises included in this book.

(2) **A compilation of kanji:** 100 new kanji, added to the 160 learned in the first part of the method, comprehensively explained and with examples.

(3) **Vocabulary index:** and index of more than 1,100 words with all the vocabulary in this book.

Japanese in MangaLand is conceived as a set of three books (this being the second one) which, apart from helping you learn Japanese in an enjoyable way, contain all the grammatical patterns, kanji and vocabulary required to pass levels 4 (elementary) and 3 (basic) of the 日本語能力試験 (Japanese-Language Proficiency Test), and can, thus, serve as a guide to exactly cover the specifications for these levels. We will give more details about this official test in book three.

On translations

There are many example sentences throughout the book, as well as many manga-examples, with their corresponding word for word translations into English, just like in the first volume. Sometimes, the sentences we offer may "squeak" for not being very natural, since we have chosen more literal translations for an easier understanding of their formation. Trying to create a more natural English translation of every sentence would be a good exercise: it would help you consolidate concepts, make and in-depth analysis of the Japanese sentence, and think about it as a whole rather than a mere group of words and grammatical patterns. Besides, it might help you discover the world and the complexity of the work of the translator.

Having said all this, we provide you with a glossary with all the abbreviations used throughout this book, and we encourage you to begin. Have you fastened that head-band around your forehead yet? You will need it!

略称集 Glossary of abbreviations

Excl.:	Exclamation.
Ger.:	Gerund.
Nom.:	Nominalizer.
Noun Suf.:	Suffix for proper names (people).
Soft.:	Sentence softener.
Suf:	Suffix.
CAP:	Cause Particle. *(why?)* Ex: から
CP:	Company Particle. *(who with?)* Ex: と
DOP:	Direct Object Particle. *(what?)* Ex: を
DP:	Direction Particle. *(where to?)* Ex: へ
EP:	Emphatic Particle. Most end-of-sentence particles state emphasis or add a certain nuance. (L.17, book 1) Ex: ね, よ, ぞ, etc.
IOP:	Indirect Object Particle *(whom?)* Ex: に
IP:	Instrument Particle. *(what with?)* Ex: で
POP:	Possessive Particle. *(whose?)* Ex: の
PP:	Place Particle. *(where?)* Ex: で, に
Q?:	Interrogative particle. Shows that the sentence is a question. Ex: か
SBP:	Subordinate sentence Particle. This particle is used as a link between a subordinate sentence and the main sentence. Ex: と
SP:	Subject Particle. *(who?)* Ex: が
TOP:	Topic Particle. Shows that the preceding word is the topic in the sentence. Ex: は ^{wa}
TP:	Time Particle. (When?) Ex: に

LESSONS

31 to 45

第31課：意志・願望

Lesson 31: The volitive form

Welcome to lesson 31, which opens this intermediate course of Japanese through manga. Throughout the book, we will refer to lessons and subjects already explained in the first part of the course. Therefore, we will take for granted that they have already been studied and learned. Having mentioned this, we can now enter the world of desiderative expressions in Japanese.

The volitive form, or desiderative expression, in Japanese, just like many other aspects of this language, has some special points. First of all, in Japanese you distinguish between "wanting to do something" and "wanting something," and there is also a big difference in the subtlety level when talking about your own wishes and when talking about what other people want, as we will now see.

	Simple f.	Meaning	Rule	-masu f.	Root	Rule	Volitive
Group 1 Invariable	教える	to teach	〜する ます	教えます	教え		教えたい
	起きる	to wake up	〜する ます	起きます	起き		起きたい
Group 2 Variable	貸す	to lend	〜す します	貸します	貸し	Root＋〜たい	貸したい
	待つ	to wait	〜つ ちます	待ちます	待ち		待ちたい
	買う	to buy	〜う います	買います	買い		買いたい
	帰る	to return	〜する ります	帰ります	帰り		帰りたい
	書く	to write	〜く きます	書きます	書き		書きたい
	急ぐ	to hurry	〜ぐ ぎます	急ぎます	急ぎ		急ぎたい
	遊ぶ	to play	〜ぶ びます	遊びます	遊び		遊びたい
	飲む	to drink	〜む みます	飲みます	飲み		飲みたい
	死ぬ	to die	〜ぬ にます	死にます	死に		死にたい
Group 3 Irregular	する	to do	*Irregular verbs: no rule*	します	し		したい
	来る	to come		来ます	来		来たい

To want to do something

The form "to want to do something" is quite easily constructed adding the 〜たい ending to the root of a verb. First, we need to conjugate the verb we wish to use into the *-masu* form (L.19). Next, we remove the ending 〜ます –so we now have the root of the verb– and we add 〜たい: with a little bit of practice you will easily pick this up. The verbal root will appear several times further on, so it is highly recommended that you study it carefully now (see table).

A verb in the 〜たい form (such as 買いたい, *to want to buy*) is no longer grammatically considered a verb and it becomes to all purposes an *-i* adjective. Therefore, all its conjugations (negative, past and past-negative) will function just like we saw in L.13 with *-i* adjectives. Have a look at this table:

		Affirmative	Negative
Present	General rule	〜い	〜ヰくない
	Example	行きたい	行きたくない
	Translation	*I want to go*	*I don't want to go*
Past	General rule	〜ヰかった	〜ヰくなかった
	Example	行きたかった	行きたくなかった
	Translation	*I wanted to go*	*I didn't want to go*

The direct object in 〜たい sentences can come either with the particle を or the particle が. There is only a difference of usage: using が implies a stronger wish than を. Ex: テレビを見たい | テレビが見たい. Both sentences mean *I want* (or *we want* or *they want*, etc.) *to watch television*. In the second case, with が, the wish is a burning one.

Finally, we will point out that if we add the verb です after 〜たい we obtain a formal sentence. Ex: テレビを見たいです *I want to watch television*.

The structure in this kind of sentences usually is "Subject は Direct object を（が）Verb in 〜たい form (+ optional です)."

● メタリカの新発売のCDを買いたかった *I wanted to buy Metallica's latest* CD.
● 私はあの本を読みたくない *I don't want to read that book*.
● 僕は弁護士になりたいです *I want to become a lawyer*. (formal)

Note: The verb なる *(to become)* always comes with the particle に (L.28).

To want something

In case we want to indicate we want "something," we will not use ～たい –which is used when we want "to carry out an action" –, but ほしい. After the direct object we will always have the が particle or, sometimes, は (we never use を in this case). Ex: マンガ が欲しい *I want a manga*. Remember that by adding です at the end of the sentence, we obtain a formal sentence. Ex: マンガが欲しいです *I want a manga*. (formal)

It is important to bear in mind that, just like ～たい, ほしい functions the same way as *-i* adjectives, and therefore it is conjugated like them: ほしい, ほしくない (neg.), ほしかった (past), ほしくなかった (neg. past.) Ex: マンガが欲しかった *I wanted a manga*.

● 新しい彼女が欲しい *I want a new girlfriend*.
● 私はパソコンが欲しいです *I want a computer*. (formal)
● コーヒーは欲しくない。コーラが欲しい *I don't want a coffee. I want a cola (drink)*.
● りんごは欲しくなかったです *I didn't want an apple*.

Another usage of ほしい, also explained in the table below, is in the formation of desiderative sentences of the sort "I want someone to do something." We will only use this kind of sentence in a very limited form, since it implies the speaker is, or at least feels, "superior" in hierarchy to his interlocutor.

These imperative sentences are formed with the verb conjugated in the *-te* form (L.24) plus ほしい. We will add です at the end to give the sentence a more formal tone.

● この文章を生徒達にわかってほしい *I want the students to understand this sentence*.
● この映画をあなたに見てほしいです *I want you to see this movie*.
● この人を愛してほしい *I want you to love this man*.

Usages of *hoshii* (欲しい)	
A: I want something Subjectは Thingが欲しい（です） 私は辞書が欲しい（です） *I want a dictionary.*	私：*I* 辞書: *dictionary* 田中: *Tanaka* 買う: *to buy*
B: I want someone (inferior to me) to do something Subjectは Someoneに Thingを *-te* verb+欲しい（です） 私は田中さんに辞書を買って欲しい（です） *I want Tanaka to buy (or "to buy me") a dictionary.*	

Another person

No one can truly know what other people want to do. You can guess or have a strong idea, but you can never be certain. Putting this subtle statement forward, we understand why we cannot use the 〜たい and ほしい forms in Japanese, the way we have just explained, when talking about other people.

There are, of course, strategies to overcome this hindrance, like, for example, the 〜がる form. With 〜がる, a sentence takes the meaning of "it looks like the other person wants to do x." To use this expression you only need to replace the last い in 〜たい or in ほしい with 〜がる. Thus, 彼は新しい車を欲しがっている could be translated as *It looks like he wants a new car*. An important point is that this form can only be used in the gerund (*-te* form, L.24), that is: 〜がっている. This sentence *彼は眠たがる is wrong, you must use the gerund for a correct one: 彼は眠たがっている *It looks like he wants to sleep*.

● あの男は子どもと遊びたがっている *It looks like that man wants to play with the child*.
● 彼は新しい彼女を欲しがっている *It looks like he wants a new girlfriend*.
● 三井さんはパソコンを欲しがっていました *It looks like Mr. Mitsui wanted a computer*.

The negative form of sentences with 〜がる is an exception to this rule, because both the normal negative form and the negative gerund are allowed.

● 彼は学校に行きたがらない *It looks like he doesn't want to go to school*.

Alternative strategies

However, using certain strategies, we can make sentences with the 〜たい and the ほしい forms, seen above, with another person as the subject. You don't need to study them now, but we can have a look at some examples:

I think, he says. Using と思う *(I think)* or と言う *(he says)* at the end of the sentence. These structures give the sentence a connotation of impersonality because, instead of a categorical statement, we are given a hypothesis (with と思う) or a quotation of somebody else's words (with と言う). We will study this in detail in L.41.

● あなたは韓国へ行きたくなかったんだと思います *I think you didn't want to go to Korea*.

It seems, apparently. Using forms such as みたい, ようだ or らしい at the end of the sentence, expressions with the general meaning of "apparently." We will study these expressions in L.43.

● 彼女は結婚したいらしい *Apparently, she wants to get married*.

I intend to…

つもり is a construction that doesn't exactly have a desiderative meaning, but it can be included in the same group. Using つもり we will give our sentences the meaning of "I intend to." The usage of this construction is very simple: you only need to make a normal sentence and add, after the verb in its simple form (L.20), the word つもり, always with the verb "to be" in the end. Remember the verb "to be" is conjugated だ in its colloquial form and です in its formal one (L.9).

- 新しいパソコンを買うつもりだ *I intend to buy a new computer.*
- 来年、日本へ行くつもりです *Next year, I intend (I want) to go to Japan.*
- 美穂と結婚するつもりです *I intend / I am going to marry Miho.*

We should stress that つもり is never conjugated, what we conjugate is the verb before or after it. Notice what happens when we conjugate the verb before つもり:

- 俺は戦わないつもりだ *I intend not to fight.*
- 美穂と結婚しないつもりです *I intend not to marry Miho.*

Notice now what happens if we use つもりはない (つもりはありません in its formal form), a negative after つもり. It is a rather strong negative:

- 君と結婚するつもりはありません *I don't intend (at all) to marry you.*
- 中国人と交渉するつもりはない *I am not going (don't intend) to negotiate with the Chinese.*

More about つもり

It is important to state that, just like with 〜たい and ほしい, the expression つもり cannot be used directly with other people. You must use the same strategies we saw in the subsection "Alternative strategies" *(I think, he says, apparently)*. The 〜がる form cannot be used with つもり.

However, つもり is not only used with the meaning of "I intend to." Very often, depending on the context, this expression is used to indicate the idea of "being convinced that" or "believing that."

- 母は元気なつもりです *My mother is convinced she is healthy (although I think otherwise)*. **Note:** When つもり functions with a -na adjective, that adjective keeps the な; it doesn't lose it as in other cases (L.14).
- 僕は偉い人のつもりではない *I don't believe I am an important person.* | *I don't think I am an important person.* **Note:** With nouns, we must use the particle の before つもり.

We have reached the manga-examples section. Let's see, through manga panels, some usages of the expressions we have learned in the previous pages. In this case, we will analyze how to use desiderative expressions in Japanese.

a) I want

J.M. Ken Niimura

> **Masao:** あなたと話^{はなし}がしたい。
> *you CP conversation SP want to do*
> **I want to talk with you.**

Our first example shows a very clear usage of the ～たい form to indicate one's own wish. The root verb, in this case, is the irregular する, *to do*, whose ～たい form is, as shown here, したい. As we saw in L.24, when we add the verb する to a noun (話, *conversation*), we obtain a verb (*to talk*).

We almost always use the particle を between the direct object (話 here) and the verb (する here), but in this case が is used. The reason for this, as we discussed earlier, is that using が implies more emphasis, a stronger urge. To conclude, we will comment that Masao must know his interlocutor well (or, either, he treats him as an inferior) because he doesn't add the verb です after ～たい. Adding です, the speaker would have formed a politer sentence.

b) I don't want to

Ueda: うるさいったら！ラグビーのことなんか聞きたくない！
noisy I say! Rugby POP nom. not even want to hear
Shut up! I don't want to hear anything about rugby!

二度と口に出すな！
twice mouth PP take out (prohibition)
Don't mention it again!

Ueda has hurt himself badly playing rugby and comes out with this sentence when teammates try to cheer him up. 聞きたくない comes from the verb 聞く *(to hear)*. Just as we saw earlier in the conjugation table, the 〜たい form of verbs ending in 〜く is Root + きたい. Therefore, we would have 聞きたい *(I want to hear)*. The negative is formed like the negative of *-i* adjectives, so we will replace the last 〜い with 〜くない. Thus: 聞きたくない *(I don't want to hear)*.

In L.17 we studied the end-of-the-sentence particles and we glanced at the particle な. As we see here, な after a verb in its simple form, at the end of a sen-

Javier Bolado

tence, functions as a negative imperative, that is, we use it to give orders such as "don't do x." A very clear example would be: 日本語を勉強するな！ *Don't study Japanese!*

c) I want something

Teru: やっぱり欲しいな... 決定的な証拠が...
of course I want EP... conclusive proof SP...
Of course I want... to find conclusive proof...

We find here the typical structure "Direct object + が + ほしい," but with reversed sentence order, something very common in spoken Japanese.
The nucleus of this sentence would be 証拠が欲しい *I want (a) proof.* Everything else just embellishes the sentence adding nuances. やっぱり is an adverb with no clear translation, that we have translated as *of course,* but in other contexts it can also mean *too, still, after all...*

Bárbara Raya

J.M. Ken Niimura

d) I want you to do something

Even though Shimane is talking to a stranger, in a rather formal way, he must collect the taxes owed by the taxpayers. Therefore, although he is using formal Japanese, he uses the expression "て＋ほしい," which, as we saw earlier, implies an imperative tone, as well as implying that the speaker feels superior to his interlocutor. Shimane's linguistic strategy is aimed at making his interlocutor feel embarrassed so that he pays, in a polite but firm and imperative way.

Shimane: で、金子さん、滞納している税金を払って欲しいんですが。
well, Kaneko (noun suf) fail to pay tax DOP pay want to be but
Well, Mr. Kaneko, I want you to pay the taxes you owe us.

自動車税、１２万３千円。
car tax 12 "man" three thousand yen
The automobile tax costs 123,000 yen.

e) It looks like he wants

When talking about somebody else's wishes, you cannot use the ～たい or ほしい forms directly, because it is impossible to know for certain if someone wants something or if it only looks like he does. Therefore, we use the ～がる form, which gives the connotation of "it looks like." This form is obtained replacing the last い of ～たい and ほしい with ～がる (～たがる, ほしがる). The resultant verb is conjugated in the gerund. In this panel we have the expression 会いたがっていました *Apparently, he wanted to meet somebody*. 会いたがっていました is nothing but past gerund (-te form) of 会いたがる, which comes from 会いたい (*I want to meet*), which in turn comes from the verb 会う (*to meet someone*).

Kyōko: あなたに会いたがっていましたよ。
you IOP meet apparently EP
Apparently, he wanted to meet you...

f) I intend to...

Bailey: 知るかよ　この性格を変えるつもりはない！
know Q? EP this character change intend there isn't
What do I know? I'm not going to change my character!!

Gabriel Luque

Here is a good example of つもり, which we use to say "I intend to." The negative is constructed conjugating the verb in the negative form and adding つもり, although, to obtain a flatter refusal we use the form つもりはない. In our example, then, the speaker's intentions are very clear.

Another aspect worth pointing out is the particle か in 知るか, which is a more colloquial and shorter form of ものですか. The connotation expressed by 知るか is *How do you expect me to know...?* Or *What do I know?*. We will see this construction in more detail in L.57 (book 3). Don't mistake it for the interrogative particle か (L.17).

g) I'm convinced that...

In this last example, we will see a different connotation of the つもり form, which has little to do with desiderative expressions. We saw earlier that つもり had the implicit meaning of "I intend to," in other contexts the expression can have the meaning of "I'm convinced that" or "I believe that." In this case, Sonia asks Jan to walk properly, that she's had enough of his halfhearted pose when walking. Jan's answer is, literally, "I believe I walk normally." That is, the speaker really believes his way of walking is correct, even though it isn't from Sonia's point of view.

Studio Kōsen

Jan: 普通に歩いてるつもりですがね。
normally walk I believe to be EP
I believe I walk normally.

1. Conjugate the present 〜たい form of the verb 買う *(to buy)*.

2. Conjugate the past negative 〜たい form of the verb 見る *(to see)*. Hint: this verb belongs to Group 1.

3. Translate into Japanese: "I want to drink sake." (to drink: 飲む, sake: 酒)

4. Translate into English the sentence: 去年、台湾へ行きたかった。(去年: last year, 台湾: Taiwan)

5. Translate into formal Japanese the sentence: "I don't want shoes." (shoes: 靴)

6. Translate into English the sentence: 彼女にお茶を持って来て欲しいです。(彼女: she, お茶: tea, 持って来る: to bring)

7. Translate into English: 小林さんは出張へ行きたがっていません。(小林: Kobayashi, 出張: business trip)

8. What strategies are there to indicate a third person wants to do something if we want to use 〜たい or ほしい?

9. Translate into Japanese the sentence: "I intend to learn Japanese." (to learn: 習う, Japanese: 日本語)

10. What function does the particle な sometimes have at the end of a sentence, after a verb in simple form?

第32課：可能・義務・許可

Lesson 32: Can and must

In this lesson we will study the potential and obligational forms in Japanese, that is, we will learn how to form sentences such as "I can do x" and "I must do x."

The simplest structure

We will now see how to form sentences such as "I can do x." Without a doubt, the simplest way to construct this kind of sentence is by using the pattern "sentence + ことができる" (which can be translated as *to be able to* or *can*).

The formation is as simple as making a normal sentence (with the verb in the simple form) and adding ことができる.

● 私はピーマンを食べる *I eat green peppers.*
● 私はピーマンを食べることができる *I can eat green peppers.*

The formal form, the past, and the negative are obtained by conjugating the verb in the same way we have already seen: past できた, negative できない, past negative できなかった. Very often we will find it in kanji: 出来る (formal way: 出来ます).

● 俺達は歌舞伎を楽しむ *We enjoy kabuki.*
● 俺達は歌舞伎を楽しむことが出来ない *We can't enjoy kabuki.*
● ここでおいしいパンを食べることができる *You can eat good bread here.*

With *suru* verbs (L.24) the verb する is left out and we just add できる.

● 彼女は飛行機を操縦する *She flies a plane.*
● 彼女は飛行機を操縦できた *She could / knew how to fly a plane.*

There are also some punctual cases where you can make potential sentences with only the help of the verb できる after a noun, using the particle が.

● 里美さんはスワヒリ語ができます *Satomi can (speak) Swahili.*
● 僕はギターができない *I can't (play) the guitar.*

A more complicated structure

The strategy of "sentence + ことができる" is more of a formal register. However, it is very practical for beginners, because all that is required to make a potential sentence is to add ことができる to the sentence. You can stick with the simple structure until you get used to the "authentic" way of making a potential sentence.

The above mentioned "authentic" way is obtained conjugating the verb you need into its potential form. As usual, conjugations are relatively easy, but not obvious, so you should study the following table carefully. Let's have a look at the conjugation rules:

● Verbs in Group 1 (if you don't remember them, you can review L.20), replace the last 〜る with 〜られる. Ex: 見る *(to see)* ⇒ 見られる *(can see)*.

● Verbs in Group 2, replace the last *-u* with *-e* and add *-ru*. Thus, *kau* ⇒ *ka-* ⇒ *kae-* ⇒ *kaeru* | *asobu* ⇒ *asob-* ⇒ *asobe-* ⇒ *asoberu*, etc. The only special conjugation is that of verbs ending in *-tsu*, which are conjugated *-teru* and **not** *-tseru*.

● As usual, irregular verbs must be learned by heart. Note the potential of する *(to do)* is できる *(can)*. Are you beginning to see how it goes?

	Simple f.	Meaning	Rule	Potential	Negative	Cond. negative
Group 1 Invariable	教える	to each	〜するられる	教えられる	教えない	教えなければ
	起きる	to wake up		起きられる	起きない	起きなければ
Group 2 Variable	貸す	to lend	〜すせる	貸せる	貸さない	貸さなければ
	待つ	to wait	〜すてる	待てる	待たない	待たなければ
	買う	to buy	〜すえる	買える	買わない	買わなければ
	帰る	to return	〜するれる	帰れる	帰らない	帰らなければ
	書く	to write	〜すける	書ける	書かない	書かなければ
	急ぐ	to hurry	〜すげる	急げる	急がない	急がなければ
	遊ぶ	to play	〜すべる	遊べる	遊ばない	遊ばなければ
	飲む	to drink	〜するめる	飲める	飲まない	飲まなければ
	死ぬ	to die	〜するねる	死ねる	死なない	死ななければ
Group 3 Irregular	する	to do	*Irregular verbs: no rule*	できる	しない	しなければ
	来る	to come		来られる	来ない	来なければ

The usage of the potential form

Let's have a look at some examples of this new grammatical form. So that we can get a clearer idea, we will try to transform the sentences seen in the first section.

The verb in the first sentence (私はピーマンを食べる) is, logically, 食べる. Since this verb belongs to Group 1, we must leave out the last 〜る and replace it with 〜られる. Indeed: 私はピーマンを食べられる *I can eat green peppers.*

In the second sentence (俺達は歌舞伎を楽しむ), the verb, 楽しむ, belongs to the second group, therefore, we must replace the last *-u* with an *-e,* and add 〜る. Thus: 俺達は歌舞伎を楽しめない *We can't enjoy* kabuki. Besides the potential form, we have also conjugated the resultant verb, 楽しめる, in the simple negative form. Remember that the resultant verb is, to all purposes, a normal verb (be careful, as it always belongs to Group 1), and can be conjugated as such.

Note: The only difficulty in this kind of conjugation lies in knowing when a verb ending in *-eru* or *-iru* belongs to Group 1 or 2 (for example, 食べる belongs to Group 1, but 帰る belongs to Group 2) Being aware of this will allow you to conjugate the verbs properly. However, you always have the strategy of using the practical structure "sentence + ことができる," with which we can successfully avoid this type of obstacle.

● 友達は論文を書けない *My friend can't write a thesis.*
● 悟くんは６０キロを走れる *Satoshi can run 60 kilometers* (Group 2).
● 私は６時に起きられません *I can't wake up at 6 o'clock* (Group 1).

On particles

In the example sentences we have seen that を, the direct object particle (DOP), remains unchanged in the sentence. In fact, we have explained it this way to make it simpler, even though in potential sentences you can use either が or を after the DOP. That is, these sentences could have perfectly been 私はピーマンが食べられる and 俺達は歌舞伎が楽しめない.

There are small nuance differences between the usage of one particle over the other, but they are so subtle and subjective that it isn't worth, at least not at this level, to go into this topic any further. Therefore, we can state to a certain degree that it makes no difference, at this time, whether we use particle が or を in this kind of sentences.

Need-obligation

The second kind of sentences we will learn to construct here are need or obligation sentences *(I must do x).*

There are many ways to construct this kind of sentence, most of which are illustrated in the adjoining table, ordered according to their degree of formality. The most basic and useful is ～ければなりません with its casual form ～ければならない. Knowing this form should be sufficient.

	Need	Obligation	
	Structure	**Example: "I must sleep"**
Formal	～ければなりません	寝^ねなければなりません
	～くてはなりません	寝なくてはなりません
	～ければいけません	寝なければいけません
Informal	～ければならない	寝なければならない
	～くてはならない	寝なくてはならない
	～ければいけない	寝なければいけない
	～ければだめだ	寝なければだめだ
Colloquial	～きゃならない	寝なきゃならない
	～きゃいけない	寝なきゃいけない
	～きゃだめだ	寝なきゃだめだ
Vulgar	～ければ	寝なければ
	～きゃ	寝なきゃ

To form sentences of this kind you must conjugate the verb into the negative form and replace the last ～い with any of the forms illustrated in the adjunctive table. In the table on page 23 we have seen exactly how to make those changes, so before going on, it would be better if you studied that table carefully once more.

● 夫^{おっと}は料理^{りょうり}を作^{つく}らなければなりません *My husband has to cook.*

● 本^{ほん}を読^よまなければだめだ *I (you, we, etc.) must read a book.*

● 猫^{ねこ}にえさをあげなきゃいけない *We (I, you, etc.) must feed the cat.*

● 部屋^{へや}をかたづけなきゃ！ *The room must be tidied up!*

Permission and prohibition

The third and last set of expressions we will see will allow us to form, on the one hand, sentences giving permission and, on the other hand, their opposite, sentences forbidding something. They are both constructed with the help of verbs in their *-te* form, which we already saw in L.24 and which you should review carefully to be able to make the most of this lesson. Let's have a look at how permission sentences are constructed.

Permission		
	Structure	**Example: «You can make it»**
Formal	〜てもよろしいです	作^{つく}ってもよろしいです
	〜てもかまいません	作ってもかまいません
	〜てもいいです	作ってもいいです
Informal	〜てもかまわない	作ってもかまわない
	〜てもいい	作ってもいい
Col.	〜ていい	作っていい

Permission

To give or ask for permission in Japanese we will add も and any of the following expressions: よろしいです, かまいません or いいです to a verb conjugated into the *-te* form. Take a look at the adjunctive table to find out about their usage and the formality registers of the various options. The basic form is 〜てもいい, followed by the verb です if we want to create a formal sentence. To turn the sentence into a question, that is, to make a request, we only have to add か after the sentence and give that か an interrogative intonation, a very easy construction studied in L.17. Let's go over some examples:

● ここに座^{すわ}ってもいいです *You (I/we, etc.) can sit here.*

● このケーキを食^たべてもよろしいですか？ *Can I eat this cake?*

● 辞書^{じしょ}を使^{つか}ってもいい *You can use the dictionary.*

Prohibition

To conclude this dense lesson, we will study prohibition sentences. Prohibitions are also based on verbs in the *-te* form, to which は (being a particle, pronounced *wa* here and not *ha*) and one of the forms in the adjunctive table are added. The most basic forms

Prohibition		
	Structure	**Ex.: «You can't make it»**
Formal	〜てはなりません	作^{つく}ってはなりません
	〜てはいけません	作ってはいけません
Informal	〜てはならない	作ってはならない
	〜てはいけない	作ってはいけない
	〜てはだめだ	作ってはだめだ
Col.	〜ちゃだめ	作っちゃだめ

are 〜てはいけない and 〜てはだめだ. Keep an eye out for the colloquial expressions which contract the ては form and replaces it with ちゃ; it is very common and we will run across it sooner or later (L.53, book 3).

● このケーキを食^たべてはいけません *You must not eat this cake.*

● 辞書^{じしょ}を使^{つか}ってはだめだ *You mustn't use the dictionary.*

Potentiality and prohibition expressions in Japanese are not excessively hard to assimilate due to the relative simplicity of the verbal conjugations. The manga-examples here will help us illustrate and expand on the lesson.

a) Can (Verbs in Group 1)

> **Client:** コクがあってとてもよそでは食べれないよ
> *body/taste SP have absolutely other place PP SP eat EP*
> **They are very tasty, you can't have them anywhere else.**

In this example, characteristic of one of the many typical cuisine mangas, we have the hero sitting at the counter of a *rāmen* noodle restaurant. Just then, the hero makes the remark we have emphasized.

The client declares these *rāmen* "can't be eaten" anywhere else, so he uses the negative potential form of the verb to eat (食べる). Take a look at the first table in this lesson to check how this verb is conjugated (it belongs to Group 1): you remove the last ～る and add ～られる, therefore, the verb should be 食べられる *(can eat)*, the negative form being 食べられない *(can't eat)*.

Still… haven't you noticed something strange in the manga-example? Indeed, the hero says 食べれない instead of 食べられない, which is the correct form according to the table. In fact, it is a relatively new phenomenon, but increasingly widespread: very

often, especially among the younger generations, the ら is omitted in the potential conjugation of verbs, giving us verbs like 見れる *(can see)*, 起きれる *(can wake up)*, or 考えれる *(can think)*, whereas their normal forms are 見られる, 起きられる and 考えられる, respectively.

b) Can (verbs in Group 2)

> **Yōko:** きっとまた会える！！
> *sure again meet!!*
> **I'm sure we'll meet again!!**

Studio Kōsen

We will now see an example of the conjugation of the verbs in Group 2, which, as we saw in page 23, are conjugated by replacing the last *-u* of the verb in the simple form with *-e* and adding ～る. With the verb we have here, 会う *(to meet/see somebody)*, the process would be *au* ⇒ *a-* ⇒ *ae-* ⇒ *aeru* (会える, *can meet somebody*). Once you get used to it, learning how to conjugate these verbs isn't difficult at all. The best way to learn them quickly is to practice with all those verbs we've been studying throughout the course, trying to put them in their potential form. There is a complete list in Appendix iii.

c) *Koto ga dekiru*

> **Gotō:** 彼らの人生は幸せだと断言する事ができますか…？
> *they POP life SP happy be SBP affirm do can Q?…?*
> **Can you affirm that theirs is a happy life?**

J.M. Ken Niimura

The main sentence in this manga-example is (あなたは) 断言する *((you) assert/affirm)*, which has been turned into a potential sentence via the useful expression ことができる. Notice how こと is written in kanji here (事). In fact, the expression we are now studying can be entirely written in kanji (事が出来る), although its use depends on one's own preferences.

What would be the potential form of this verb? 断言する being a *suru* verb (L.24) means that we only need to conjugate the する part. In the conjugation table in page 23 we see that the potential for する, as an irregular verb, is できる. Therefore, its potential form would be 断言できる *(can affirm)*.

d) A special case: *kikoeru* and *mieru*

Studio Kōsen

Title: 波が聞こえる
なみ　き
wave SP *hear*
I can hear the waves.

The potential form for the verbs 見る *(to see)* and 聞く *(to hear)* is somewhat special because in Japanese we distinguish between what one can see or hear unconsciously or passively and what one can see or hear because one specifically wants to. In the first case (unconsciously) the verbs 見える and 聞こえる are used and the particle が is compulsory. Whereas in the second case (consciously) the normal potential forms 見られる and 聞ける are used with が or を. However, both are translated as "can see" and "can hear."

In this panel, for example, we don't hear the waves (波) because we want to, but because the sound is there and it reaches our ears. Thus, we use 聞こえる. On the other hand, if we "can hear" a record because that is what we want, we will say レコードが聞ける. (See L.44 to expand on this.)

e) Must do x

We will now see an example of the need-obligation forms. As we saw in the theory section, there are many ways to construct these types of sentences, from formal expressions to colloquial and vulgar, although the most basic one is, without a doubt, 〜ければならない. In this case, we have one of the most colloquial expressions, 〜きゃ, its base being 〜ければならない, but it has contracted the first part (ければ), turning it into a simple きゃ, and left out the last part (ならない). The conjugated verb in this case is 助ける *(to save)*. To create the need-obligation form we must conjugate the verb in the negative (助けない), remove the last 〜い and add 〜ければならない, thus obtaining 助けなければならない *(must save)*. Just as we see in the example, the colloquial form is 助けなきゃ (L.53).

Gabriel Luque

Kim: 佐藤君　助けなきゃっ　ねえっ
さとうくん　たす
Satō (noun suf) help EP
We must save Satō! OK?!

f) Ask for permission

Here an example of is how to request something politely. Remember you must conjugate the verb into the *-te* form and then add もいい, adding です when creating a formal sentence. When requesting for permission, you must add the interrogative particle か at the end. In this case, we have the verb 壊す (to break), its *-te* form being 壊して, to which we add 〜もいいですか to form a request sentence: 壊してもいいですか (Can I break?/ Do you mind if I break?)

Mario: あの壁…壊してもいいですか？
that wall... break can Q?
Do you mind if I break that wall?

g) Prohibition

In this last example we see a prohibition sentence, the exact counterpart to a permission sentence. As we studied in the theory section, these sentences are also formed with verbs in the *-te* form plus 〜はいけない. Indeed: ほれる *(to fall in love)* ⇒ *-te* form ほれて ⇒ prohibition form ほれてはいけない *(you must not fall in love)*. In the colloquial register, contracting the ては part and turning it into a simple ちゃ (L.53), as in this example, is very common. We will now answer Mario, from the previous example, with the negative form. 壊す ⇒ *-te* form 壊して ⇒ formal prohibition form (he has made his request formally, so the answer should be a formal one) 壊してはいけません, or 壊しちゃいけません if we contract the ては part into ちゃ.

Ken'ichi: まゆこ、オレにほれちゃいけないぜ。
Mayuko, I IOP fall in love no must EP
Mayuko, you mustn't fall in love with me.

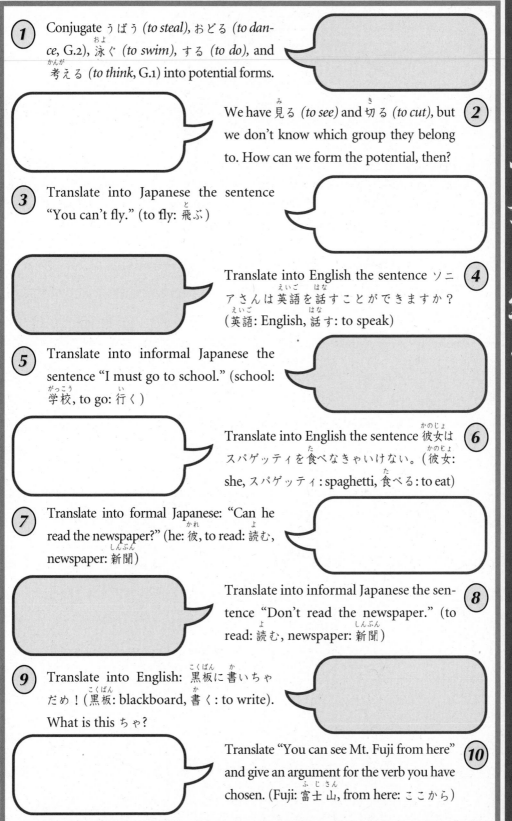

1 Conjugate うばう *(to steal)*, おどる *(to dance*, G.2), 泳ぐ *(to swim)*, する *(to do)*, and 考える *(to think*, G.1) into potential forms.

2 We have 見る *(to see)* and 切る *(to cut)*, but we don't know which group they belong to. How can we form the potential, then?

3 Translate into Japanese the sentence "You can't fly." (to fly: 飛ぶ)

4 Translate into English the sentence ソニアさんは英語を話すことができますか？ (英語: English, 話す: to speak)

5 Translate into informal Japanese the sentence "I must go to school." (school: 学校, to go: 行く)

6 Translate into English the sentence 彼女はスパゲッティを食べなきゃいけない。(彼女: she, スパゲッティ: spaghetti, 食べる: to eat)

7 Translate into formal Japanese: "Can he read the newspaper?" (he: 彼, to read: 読む, newspaper: 新聞)

8 Translate into informal Japanese the sentence "Don't read the newspaper." (to read: 読む, newspaper: 新聞)

9 Translate into English: 黒板に書いちゃだめ！(黒板: blackboard, 書く: to write). What is this ちゃ?

10 Translate "You can see Mt. Fuji from here" and give an argument for the verb you have chosen. (Fuji: 富士山, from here: ここから)

Lesson 33: At the airport

Now we will start a new kind of lesson, where we will choose a situation and develop possible conversational strategies. You can use these lessons to learn different options in the spoken language, to practice structures already seen, and finally, to learn a little bit about Japanese culture.

Some basic sentences

To be honest, airports and airplanes, even if they are Japanese, are the most "linguistically safe" places in the world, because almost everybody can speak English fluently and expects us (if our features are non-Japanese, of course) to speak in English, as well. Japanese, unfortunately for us students, will only be an unnecessary bonus, although it may come in useful in certain moments.

However, we will avail ourselves of this lesson to review grammatical structures and learn a lot of vocabulary. Let's start with the simplest and most useful sentences. As a rule, we will only use those grammatical expressions we already know from previous lessons, so you can take the opportunity to review as you study.

Vocabulary: airport	airplane				
airport	空港 (くうこう)	check in	チェックイン	passenger	乗客 (じょうきゃく)
aisle	通路 (つうろ)	counter	カウンター	pillow	まくら
arrival	到着 (とうちゃく)	delay	遅刻 (ちこく)	plane	飛行機 (ひこうき)
baggage	荷物 (にもつ)	departure	出発 (しゅっぱつ)	plane connection	乗り継ぎ (のりつぎ)
boarding	搭乗 (とうじょう)	economy class	エコノミークラス	plane ticket	航空券 (こうくうけん)
boarding gate	搭乗口 (とうじょうぐち)	emergency exit	非常口 (ひじょうぐち)	seat	座席 (ざせき) ｜ シート
boarding pass	搭乗券 (とうじょうけん)	excess baggage	超過重量 (ちょうかじゅうりょう)	seat belt	シートベルト
boarding time	搭乗時刻 (とうじょうじこく)	first class	ファーストクラス	takeoff	離陸 (りりく)
booking	予約 (よやく)	flight assistant	客室乗務員 (きゃくしつじょうむいん)	time difference	時差 (じさ)
business class	ビジネスクラス	landing	着陸 (ちゃくりく)	toilet	トイレ
captain	機長 (きちょう)	number x	X番 (ばん)	window	窓 (まど)

● 日本語が分かりません *I don't understand Japanese.*
● 日本語をあまり話せません *I don't speak much Japanese.*
● 英語で話してください *Could you please talk in English?*
● 英語ができますか? *Do you speak English?*
● 私はアメリカから来ました *I come from the US.*

Interrogatives	
how?	どう
how much?	いくら|どれほど
what?	何/何
when?	いつ
where?	どこ
who?	誰
why?	どうして

In this first lot of examples, some interesting things have appeared, such as a verb in the negative potential form (L.32, 話せません), a request of the *-te* form + ください kind (L.24, book 1), the verb できる (L.32)... There are a few new things, such as the word あまり, which means "not much" when it comes with a verb in the negative (L.45), and the word から, which means "from" and which we will study in depth in L41.

In the last sentence you can change the word "US" for the name of your own country using the list on the left.

From now on we will use (L.x) to indicate in which lesson you can find more information about the grammatical structures in each sentence.

Check in

Let's start (or finish) our trip safely checking in our baggage in Japanese:

Countries in the world	
Argentina	アルゼンチン
Australia	オーストラリア
Brazil	ブラジル
Canada	カナダ
China	中国 (ちゅうごく)
Chile	チリ
Costa Rica	コスタリカ
Cuba	キューバ
Cyprus	キプロス
France	フランス
Germany	ドイツ
India	インド
Ireland	アイルランド
Israel	イスラエル
Italy	イタリア
Jamaica	ジャマイカ
Kenya	ケニア
Malaysia	マレーシア
Mexico	メキシコ
New Zealand	ニュージーランド
Nigeria	ナイジェリア
Pakistan	パキスタン
Portugal	ポルトガル
Russia	ロシア
Singapore	シンガポール
South Africa	南(みなみ)アフリカ
South Korea	韓国 (かんこく)
Spain	スペイン
UK	イギリス
United States	アメリカ
Zambia	ザンビア

● チェックインをしたいんですが

I would like to check in. (L.32)

● 窓側の席をお願いします *A window seat, please.*

● お荷物はいくつですか?

How many bags do you have? (L.25)

● 搭乗時間は何時ですか? *When is boarding time?* (L.12)

● 搭乗ゲートは何番ですか?

Which number is my boarding gate? (L.5)

● 6番ゲートはどこですか? *Where is gate 6?*

On the plane

Well, we are on the plane and it is probably full of Japanese passengers, so one of these sentences could come in useful before, during or after the trip. By way of review, remember the words ありがとう *(thank you)*, どういたしまして *(you are welcome)*, ごめんなさい *(excuse me)*, and すみません *(I'm sorry / excuse me)*, which are essential (L.4, book 1):

● はじめまして、Xです *How do you do, my name is x.* (L.4)
● X番の席はどこですか？ *Could you please tell where seat number x is?* (L.9)
● 席を替わってください *Could you please change my seat?* (L.24)
● この荷物をここに置いてもいいですか？ *Can I put my bag here?* (L.32)
● シートを倒してもいいですか？ *Do you mind if I lean my seat back?* (L.32)
● すみません、トイレに行きたいんですが... *Excuse me, I need to go to the toilet...* (L.31)
● すみません、通してください *Excuse me, could you let me through, please?* (L.24)

Another very common situation in plane cabins is interaction with flight assistants, who, even though they always speak English, very often they will be surprised or amused if we talk to them in Japanese. At this stage, expressions with "please" (Xをください and Xをお願いします) which we glanced at in L.4, will be very useful.

Airplane food	
apple juice	りんごジュース
beer	ビール
chicken	鶏肉
coffee	コーヒー
fish	魚
ice	氷
meat	肉
milk	牛乳
orange juice	オレンジジュース
snack	おつまみ
sugar	砂糖
tea	お茶｜ティー
tomato juice	トマトジュース
vegetables	野菜
whisky	ウイスキー
wine	ワイン

● シートベルトを締めてください

Fasten your seat belt, please.

● お食事は何にしますか？ *What would you like to eat?*

● どんな飲み物がありますか？

What sort of drinks do you have? (L.18)

● ワインをお願いします *Wine, please.*

● コーヒーのおかわりをください *More coffee, please.*

● まくらと毛布をください

A pillow and a blanket, please.

● 大阪に何時に到着しますか？

At what time do we arrive in Osaka? (L.12)

● 次の乗り継ぎに間に合いますか？

Will we get there in time for the next flight connection?

● 気分が悪いので薬をお願いします

I don't feel well, could I have some medicine, please?

Flight connections and baggage claim

If we ever need to make a flight connection in a Japanese airport, this section should be helpful. We will also find useful sentences when claiming our bags.

● ＪＬ１２３便に乗り継ぎたいんですが… *I want to make a connection with flight* JL 123… (L.31)

● 全日空の乗り換えカウンターはどこですか？ *Where is the* ANA *counter for flight connections?*

● 乗り継ぎ便に間に合いませんでした *I have missed my flight connection.*

Useful information: There are two big Japanese airlines, which are Japan Airlines (JAL, 日本航空) and All Nippon Airways (ANA, 全日本航空 or abbreviated 全日空).

● 荷物の受け取り所はどこですか？ *Where is the baggage claim?*

● カートはどこにありますか？ *Where are the trolleys?*

● 私の荷物が見つかりません *I can't find my bags.*

Customs and money change

We will conclude by going through passport control and changing some money. Then, we will leave the aseptic airport and breathe the air of our destination, Japan! But, first, let's go to customs:

● パスポートを見せてください *Show me your passport, please.*

● 滞在予定は何日ですか？

How many days are you planning to stay?

● １５日間です *15 days.*

● 滞在の目的は何ですか？ *What is the purpose of your visit?*

● 観光です *Tourism.*

● 申告するものはありますか？ *Anything to declare?*

● あります | ありません *Yes. | No.*

Now, we can change money at any foreign exchange office:

● 両替所はどこですか？ *Where is the foreign exchange office?*

● 両替をしたいんですが…

I would like to change some money…

● これを円に替えてください *Change this into yen, please.*

● 手数料はいくらですか？ *What commission do you charge?*

Customs	
business	ビジネス
customs	税関
declaration	申告
entry card	入国カード
nationality	国籍
passport	パスポート
passport control	入国審査
stay	滞在
studies	留学
tourism	観光
visa	ビザ

Money change	
bank	銀行
bank note	紙幣
cash	現金
change rate	為替レート
coin	硬貨	コイン
commission	手数料
dollars	ドル
euros	ユーロ
money change	両替
traveler's check	トラベラーズチェック
yen	円

文化編：ビザ

Cultural note: the visa

A visa (ビザ) is a document issued by the embassy (大使館) or consulate (総領事館) of a foreign country, which guarantees the recipient an entry to that country for a certain period of time, as long as it is shown together with the passport (パスポート). As far as Japan is concerned, many foreigners can enter the country without previously obtaining a visa thanks to bilateral agreements.

For example, visitors from Austria, Germany, Ireland, Liechtenstein, Mexico, Switzerland and the United Kingdom are permitted a stay of up to 6 months without a visa, and visitors from Argentina, Australia, Canada, Chile, France, Hong Kong, Israel, Italy, New Zealand, Poland, Singapore, Spain and the United States, among others, are permitted a stay of up to 3 months without a visa; whereas visitors from Brazil, China, India, Russia and South Africa, among many others, require a visa. South Koreans always require a visa to enter Japan, except when they are part of a school group on a visit, and in that case they can only stay for a month*.

Japanese student visa, on a passport page

The visa is just a recommendation made by the relevant embassy or consulate to the Japanese Immigration Office (入国管理局) so that they may grant a residence status of x to a specific person. There are many kinds of status, and each of them has restrictions regarding the possibility or not of employment, as well as the activities allowed to the visa holder. Among these are work (teacher, journalist, doctor, etc.), study, temporary and special (permanent resident, child or spouse of a Japanese citizen, etc.)

*This information may have now changed.

漫画例　Manga-examples

We have already mentioned that airports and airplanes won't give us many chances to practice our Japanese, but there's no harm in seeing some typical and useful situations and sentences. We will now do this using the manga-examples.

a) Buying a ticket

J.M. Ken Niimura

Client: １５時００分発JAL１０５便大阪行きに乗りたいんですが...
じゅうごじ　ゼロ　ふんはつジャル いちゼロご びんおおさか ゆ　　　　の

15:00 hours departure JAL 105 number Osaka destination pp get on want be but...
I would like to get on the flight JAL 105 going to Osaka, leaving at 3 PM.

We start with a sentence full of specific airport vocabulary: this is what someone says when going to buy a plane ticket. In the sentence, our client specifies the departure time (１５時００分, *15:00 hours*), adding the suffix 発 –which means *leaving at*–, the flight number, code JAL 105, plus the suffix 便, which in this context has the meaning of *(flight) code*. He mentions the destination as well, Osaka (大阪), followed by the word 行き, which could be translated as *destination*, or, literally, *going to*, which is our best option here.

As you can see, there is a lot of information in just one sentence. You don't need to learn it all by heart, but hopefully this manga-example should help you review vocabulary. Other points we might notice in the sentence are the fact that it uses the 〜たい volitive form (L31) and the tag んですが..., very common in spoken language and used to tone down a sentence. Here, it would serve to make the desiderative expression less categorical, so as not to sound "harsh."

b) Checking in the baggage

Bárbara Raya

Woman: はい 搭乗券！あずける 荷物は？
here boarding pass! hand in bag sp?
Here is your boarding pass!
Any bags to check in?

Hideo: これです。すみません...
this be. Excuse me...
This is it. Excuse me...

This ground stewardess seems to be quite angry! The truth is Japanese are extremely kind when talking to customers. However, someone must have played a dirty trick on this woman for her to act in this way and to speak in such a short and colloquial manner to her customer (something inconceivable!) In the panel we see how she is brusquely giving Hideo his *boarding pass* (搭乗券 or 搭乗カード) and asking him if he wants to check in any *bags* (荷物). She uses the verb あずける, which means *entrust, hand in.* Take note of the word はい, a very versatile word which cannot only be interpreted as *yes* (the meaning we have seen until now), but also as *well, let's see* − when trying to call somebody's attention −, or *here you are* − when handing something in −, etc.

c) The boarding pass

Woman: JAL１０７便です。お気をつけていってらっしゃいませ。
JAL 107 flight be. be careful (formal)
It's flight number JAL 107. Have a good trip.

This is the standard way of giving a boarding pass, and not what we saw in the previous example... The ground stewardess gives the customer his flight number (ＪＡＬ１０７便) and wishes him a good trip. The expression she uses is (気をつけて), which we saw in L.4. It means *be careful,* but here it is basically *goodbye,* and, in this context, it can clearly be *Have a good trip.* Here, the stewardess has used the most formal expression there is (and

Studio Kōsen

the longest) お気をつけていってらっしゃいませ, because she is speaking to a customer, and in Japan "the customer is king," or, in their own words, "god."

d) Everything ready to board

Voice: じゅうよじ ゼロ ふんはつ タイペイ ゆ ゼロいちななびん しゅっぱつ かた
１４時００分発 台北行き０１７便で出発の方は
14:00 hours departure Taipei destination 017 flight PP, departure POP person SP
Passengers to Taipei on flight 017, with departure time at 14:00 h...

いまとうじょうてつづ おこな
ただ今 搭乗手続きを行っております。
now board procedure DOP make (humble)
...are now proceeding to board.

Here is another sentence full of airport terminology. The first part is very similar to what we have seen in the first manga-example. Therefore, we will point out the words 出発 *(departure),* ただ今 (which means *now*, in a formal context), the omnipresent 搭乗 *(boarding),* and 手続き, which means *procedure.*

We will also underline the form 〜ております, which means exactly the same as the gerund 〜ています (L.24). However, おります is used to lower the speaker's position, raising, thus, the interlocutor's position and showing "humbleness" when speaking (L.52). This is the treatment a customer deserves as the "god" he is.

Javier Bolado

e) Cabin service

J.M. Ken Niimura

Stewardess: しんぶん ざっし
新聞・雑誌いかがですか？
newspaper magazine how about be Q?
Would you like to read a newspaper or a magazine?

Once on the airplane, flight attendants will start offering us everything we need for the trip, ranging from magazines to food to headphones. In Japan, the most common sentence used is exactly the same as the one in the manga-example, 〜はいかがですか (in the example the particle は is omitted). The word いかが belongs to the formal register and means *Do you feel like...?* or *How about...?* In colloquial register we use the word どう to express the same, like in the sentence ビールはどうですか？ *(How about a beer?)* By the way, the air hostess in the example is holding 週刊誌, that is, *weekly magazines.*

f) Message from the captain

> Captain: まもなく着陸致します。シートベルトをお締めになって下さい。
> *soon landing do (formal). Seat belt dop fasten (formal) please*
> **We will be landing shortly. Fasten your seat belts, please.**

This is a typical message from the captain to the passengers. How many times have we heard that hackneyed "fasten your seat belts"? Well, in Japanese we say シートベルトを締めてください, whereas the very formal version is just like in the example: シートベルトをお締めになってください. The construction お+verbal root+になる (L.52, book 3) is part of the most formal Japanese. Although we see that 下さい can be written in kanji, we often find that it is written in hiragana. In the first part of the sentence, we see the word

Gabriel Luque

着陸 *(landing)* and the verb 致します, which is precisely the most formal version of the omnipresent verb する *(to do)*. Thus, 着陸 being a word that becomes a verb once you add する, we obtain the verb 着陸する *(to land)*.

g) Information sign

Our last example has not been taken from a manga, it is a real photograph taken at a Japanese airport. In the photo we see the already familiar words 出発 *(departure)* and 到着 *(arrival)* and many words in katakana which show the great influence English has

南ターミナル
South Terminal

4F	展望デッキ	*La SORA ラ・ソーラ*
	Obs. Deck	
3F	出発ロビー	
	Departure Lobby	
1F	チェックインロビー	
	Check-in Lobby	
1F	到着ロビー	
	Arrival Lobby	

Foto: Marc Bernabé

on Japanese: ターミナル *(terminal)*, デッキ *(deck)*, ロビー *(lobby)* or チェックイン *(check in)*. In an airport we will never have any orientation or comprehension problems, because all signs are (almost) always in English. Remember, though, that once outside of the airport, it's a whole other world!

To conclude, we will just mention the other words in the sign, 南 *(south)* and 展望 *(observation)*.

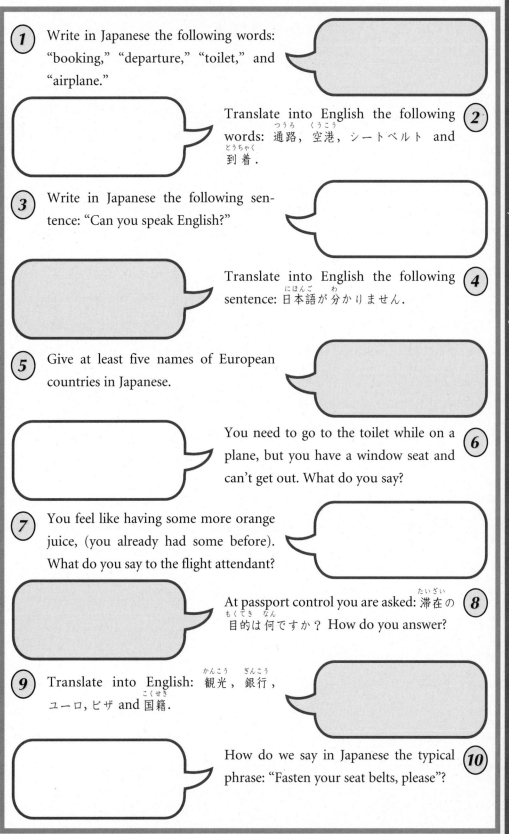

1. Write in Japanese the following words: "booking," "departure," "toilet," and "airplane."

2. Translate into English the following words: 通路, 空港, シートベルト and 到着.
   つうろ くうこう
   とうちゃく

3. Write in Japanese the following sentence: "Can you speak English?"

4. Translate into English the following sentence: 日本語が分かりません.
   にほんご わ

5. Give at least five names of European countries in Japanese.

6. You need to go to the toilet while on a plane, but you have a window seat and can't get out. What do you say?

7. You feel like having some more orange juice, (you already had some before). What do you say to the flight attendant?

8. At passport control you are asked: 滞在の目的は何ですか? How do you answer?
   たいざい もくてき なん

9. Translate into English: 観光, 銀行, ユーロ, ビザ and 国籍.
   かんこう ぎんこう こくせき

10. How do we say in Japanese the typical phrase: "Fasten your seat belts, please"?

第33課 練習 Exercises

第**34**課：疑問詞・非過去形

Lesson 34: Interrogatives and future

Until now, we have seen quite a lot of conjugations and different usages of verbs, the interrogative included. However, we have hardly talked about adverbs and interrogative pronouns, which are very useful when asking all sorts of things. We will also talk about Japanese having no future tense.

Interrogative

Here and there, throughout the course, we have seen how interrogative sentences are constructed, and we even have seen some of the words used when forming them, such as 何 *(what)*, どこ *(where)*, いくら *(how much)*, etc. This time, we will discuss these kinds of words in depth, to give our interrogative sentences a much wider dimension.

To review, we will remember that the basic interrogative construction consists of adding the particle か at the end of a sentence, and pronouncing it with a rising intonation (asking). At the colloquial level, the particle の is sometimes used. There are also times when we even do without particles altogether and directly pronounce the sentence in an interrogative way.

- 横浜は近いです *Yokohama is close.* (formal statement)
- 横浜は近いですか？ *Is Yokohama close?* (formal interrogation)
- 横浜は近いの？ *Is Yokohama close?* (informal interrogation)
- 横浜は近い？ *Yokohama is close?* (colloquial interrogation)

What, when, where, who?

Let's start with the typical *what?*, useful when asking all sort of things. All we need to do is replace the Direct Object (DO) with 何, very often pronounced 何 for phonetic reasons, and remember to add か at the end of the sentence.

- ここに何がいるか？ | ここに亀がいる *What is there here?* | *There is a turtle here.*
- 何が食べたいの？ | 魚が食べたい *What do you want to eat?* | *I want to eat fish.*
- それは何ですか？ | それはチーズです *What is that?* | *That is cheese.*

In the case of *when?*, *where?* and *who?*, the usage is the same: we only need to replace the relevant object. We will use いつ for *when?*, どこ for *where?*, and 誰 for *who?*.

Interrogatives	
何 | 何	what?
いつ	when?
いくら	how much?
いくつ	how many?
誰	who?
どうして	why?
どう	how?
どこ	where?
どの	which?
どれ	which?
どんな	what kind of?
どれくらい	how much?

● いつハワイへ行ったか？ ｜ 去年、ハワイへ行った

When did you go to Hawaii? | I went to Hawaii last year.

● 下着はどこにありますか？ ｜ 下着はソファにあります

Where is my underwear? | Your underwear is on the sofa.

● 誰がビールを飲んだの？ ｜ 美穂ちゃんがビールを飲んだ

Who drunk the beer? | Miho drank the beer.

How much?

There are several variations to express *how much?*. The two most basic expressions are いくら (when talking about an economic quantity), and どれくらい (basically, to ask about distance, weight, etc.).

● このキャベツはいくらですか？ ｜ このキャベツは２００円です

How much is this cabbage? | This cabbage is 200 yen.

● 新宿はどれくらい遠いですか？ ｜ 何キロも遠いです

How far is Shinjuku? | It's a few kilometers away.

The other way to express *how much* is related to "counters," which we have already gone over in L.25 (book 1), so you should review that lesson before going on.

● 本を何冊買いますか？ ｜ 四冊です *How many books are you buying? | Four.*

● パソコンを何台持っている？ ｜ 三台だ *How many computers do you have? | Three.*

Let's remember that practical ～つ, whose interrogative is いくつ. It will be useful when we don't remember the correct counter or when we don't know how to conjugate it properly.

● 柿をいくつ食べますか？ ｜ 三つです *How many persimmons will you eat? | Three.*

Why?

We will use どうして before an interrogative sentence to ask *why?*. The orthodox way to answer is by adding から *(because)* to the end of our reply. Therefore, we only need to construct a normal sentence and simply add から.

● どうしてアラビアに行きたいの？ ｜ アラビア語を勉強したいから

Why do you want to go to Arabia? | Because I want to study Arabic.

The *kosoado* group

In L.9 (book 1) we already learned about those words called "*kosoado*." They are pronouns which always share the prefixes *ko-* (close to the speaker), *so-* (close to the hearer), *a-* (far from both), and *do-* (interrogative). Ex: これ *(this)*, それ *(that)*, あれ *(that over there)*, and どれ *(which?)* Refer to the table for more information. Be careful with the semi-exceptions (in bold type): あそこ and ああ are not あこ nor あう.

Kosoado			
Close	**Transl.**	**Half-way**	**Transl.**
ここ	here	そこ	there
こちら	this way	そちら	that way
この	this	その	that
これ	this one	それ	that one
こんな	this kind of	そんな	that kind of
こう	like this	そう	like that
Far	**Transl.**	**Interr.**	**Transl.**
あそこ	here	どこ	where?
あちら	that way	どちら	which way?
あの	that	どの	which?
あれ	that one	どれ	which one?
あんな	that kind of	どんな	what kind of?
ああ	like that	どう	how?

Using the *kosoado* to make questions is extremely useful and simple: all you need to do is use the corresponding interrogative.

● 君のペンはどれですか？ | これです *Which is your pen?* | *It's this one.*
● 彼はどこですか？ | あそこです *Where is he?* | *Over there.*
● どんな音楽が好き？ | ヘビーメタルだよ *What sort of music do you like?* | *Heavy metal.*

Japanese has no fixed future tense

In the Japanese language there is no way we can concretely express the idea of future. This is because there is no specific conjugation: in English we have *will*, whereas in Japanese we must rely on other strategies to express the future. Very often, forming sentences in the present tense and getting the idea of the future tense from the context will be enough, other times we will add "time" adverbs implying the future tense (see table) to avoid misunderstandings.

Future time adverbs	
後で	after
これから	from now on
今度	later
～後	...in xx time
明日	tomorrow
あさって	the day after tomorrow
来週	next week
来月	next month
来年	next year
ある日	some day
将来	in the future
今後	after this

● 青森に行きます | 明日、青森に行きます

I go to Aomori. | *I will go to Aomori tomorrow.*

● 医学を勉強する | 来年、医学を勉強する

I study Medicine. | *I will study Medicine next year.*

In the last example, it would have been better to use つもり (L.31) as well, to strengthen the idea:

● 来年、医学を勉強するつもりです

I intend to study Medicine next year.

Let's...

Even though it isn't directly related to the future, we will take the opportunity to look at a verbal conjugation expressing invitation as well as volition (but in a subtler way than with the 〜たい, 欲しい and つもり forms, which we saw earlier in L.31). We are talking about the expressions "let's...," for invitation and "I'm going to / I mean to" to express one's will. This is how the conjugations work:

- **Group 1:** Replace the last 〜る with 〜よう. Ex: 見る *(I see)* ⇒ 見よう *(let's see)*.
- **Group 2:** Replace the last *-u* with *-ou (-ō)*. Ex: 急ぐ *(to hurry)* => ⇒ 急ごう *(let's hurry)* | 遊ぶ *(to play)* ⇒ 遊ぼう *(let's play)*. **Note:** Be careful with verbs ending in *-tsu*, they are conjugated *-tō* and not *-tsō*.
- **Irregulars:** As usual, we must learn these by heart.

In the case of the formal conjugation (in the *-masu* form) of these verbs, all we need to do is replace the last 〜す of the conjugation in the *-masu* form of the verb in question with 〜しょう, no matter what group the verb belongs to: 死にます *(to die)* ⇒ 死にましょう *(let's die)*. Now you should study the conjugations of the table below in depth.

	Simple f.	Meaning	Rule	Let's...	-masu f.	Let's... (formal)
Group 1 Invariable	教える	to teach	〜~~る~~よう	教えよう	教えます	教えましょう
	起きる	to wake up		起きよう	起きます	起きましょう
Group 2 Variable	貸す	to lend	〜~~す~~そう	貸そう	貸します	貸しましょう
	待つ	to wait	〜~~つ~~とう	待とう	待ちます	待ちましょう
	買う	to buy	〜~~う~~おう	買おう	買います	買いましょう
	帰る	to return	〜~~る~~ろう	帰ろう	帰ります	帰ちましょう
	書く	to write	〜~~く~~こう	書こう	書きます	書きましょう
	急ぐ	to hurry	〜~~ぐ~~ごう	急ごう	急ぎます	急ぎましょう
	遊ぶ	to play	〜~~ぶ~~ぼう	遊ぼう	遊びます	遊びましょう
	飲む	to drink	〜~~む~~もう	飲もう	飲みます	飲みましょう
	死ぬ	to die	〜~~ぬ~~のう	死のう	死にます	死にましょう
Group 3 Irregular	する	to do	*Irregular verbs: no rule*	しよう	します	しましょう
	来る	to come		来よう	来ます	来ましょう

Some examples

When the -ō form is used in the volitive sense, we will sometimes need the help of と思う (*I think, I believe*) to clearly express the idea of "intention," except in exclamations or sentences with a lot of "feeling." (We will see more about と思う in L.41.)

- 食べる (*to eat*) ⇒ うどんをたくさん食べようと思う *I will eat a lot of* udon.
- あげる (*to give*) ⇒ 哲さんにこれをあげようと思います *I mean to give this to Tetsu.*
- 読む (*to read*) ⇒ 今日は本を全部読もうぜ！ *I will read the whole book today!*

With the meaning of invitation, however, we can use the conjugated verb alone:

- 踊る (*to dance*) ⇒ 一緒にサンバを踊ろうか？ *Shall we dance the samba together?*
- 行く (*to go*) ⇒ 今度、一緒にコンゴへ行こう *Let's go to Congo in the near future.*
- 誘う (*to invite*) ⇒ 先生をパーティに誘いましょう *Let's invite the teacher to the party.*

Deciding on something

One of the example sentences in the previous lessons went like this: お食事は何にしますか？ (*What would you like to eat?*). What does the expression にします (or にする in its simple form) exactly mean? This expression is used when deciding on something, that is, to form sentences such as: "I choose x" or "I'm inclined to go for x."

It's usage is very simple, because we will always use にする after a noun or a nominalized sentence. In L.57 (book 3) we will see in more detail how a sentence is nominalized, but for the time being, adding こと should be all you need to know. Ex: 日本へ行く (*to go to Japan*) | 日本へ行くこと (*the fact of going to Japan*).

- お食事は何にしますか？ *What would you like to eat?*
  から揚げとラーメンにします *I'll have (choose) fried chicken and* rāmen.
- どんなセーターを買うことにしたの？ *What sort of sweater did you end up buying?*
  大きなセーターにしたよ *I chose (bought) a large one.*

To end this lesson, take a look at this miniconversation:

- A：来年、何を勉強するつもりですか？ *A: What are you going to study next year?*
  B：う～ん... 経済にしようかな？ *B: Hum... I might decide on Economics.*

In scarcely two lines, we have reviewed everything we saw in this lesson: a question with 何, a future time adverb (来年), the fact of deciding on something (にする), and, finally, a volitive form of the -ō kind (しよう). And we have even used つもり！

This lesson has been quite dense, so a few good examples with comic panels should clear up some of the ideas and concepts. Let's see, then, the "real" usage in context of interrogatives, lack of future and other things we haves been studying.

a) Who?

Keisuke: どなたですか？
who be Q?
Who is it?

Maiko: あんたのママのお<ruby>友達<rt>ともだち</rt></ruby>、マイコおねえさんだよ
you POP mommy POP friend, Maiko sister be EP
It's Maiko, your mommy's friend.

Just a few pages earlier we saw that to ask *who?* we use <ruby>誰<rt>だれ</rt></ruby>. Then, what is that どなた Keisuke is using, which, apparently, means the same?

We have already mentioned several times Japanese is a very hierarchical language and that the "politeness" with which one talks must reflect itself in the words one uses, words we must select carefully. So どなた is the "polite" way of <ruby>誰<rt>だれ</rt></ruby> and we use it

Javier Bolado

when asking a stranger *who is it?* in a formal situation. Likewise, there are formal and informal versions of other interrogative adverbs and pronouns. For instance, as we saw in the manga-example e) in the previous lesson, the formal version of どう (in its meaning of *how about?*) is いかが (L.33).

In the case of どうして *(why?)*, we have a formal version （なぜ） and even a colloquial version （なんで）. Finally, the word どんな *(what kind of?)* is really a contraction of どのような, a version which is used in formal situations.

b) Where?

Kōji: どこだ？ここは...
where be? here sp...
Where is... Here...?

In the theory pages we learned about *kosoado* words, which are "conjugated" via pronouns which indicate closeness or distance. In this case, we have two of the four conjugations (closeness and interrogative) of the *kosoado* indicating "place:" ここ (*here*) and どこ (*where?*). The two missing forms are そこ

Gabriel Luque

(*there*) and あそこ (*over there*). Remember this last one is slightly irregular. Mastering the *kosoado* is essential in trying to sound natural.

c) When?

Emi: ひとりで、生きてきて… 全てを失ったときに、あなたに会ったのですもの。
alone, live come, everything DOP loose when TP, you IOP meet be then
I had always lived alone..., I met you when I had lost everything.

Studio Kōsen

We will use this manga-example to do a very interesting exercise: forming a question from an answer we already know. What should we ask Emi, so that she gives us this answer? Since she replies with "when," we should obviously ask her *when?*. To do that, we will use いつ. For example, いつ私に会ったか？ (*When did you meet me?*) The answer is the manga-example. We can see Emi's sentence has a 時に (usually written in kanji). The word 時 (L.48, book 3) means *time*, but when it comes before a sub-ordinate sentence (like in this case), its function is to indicate *when* or *at that moment*; that is, a perfect answer when we are asked when something happened. The particle に after 時 is optional. Ex: いつ日本語を学びましたか？ *When did you learn Japanese?* 京都にいた時、日本語を学びました *I learned Japanese when I was in Kyoto.* / いつお風呂に入るの？ *When do you bathe?* 汚い時にお風呂に入る *I bathe when I'm dirty.*

d) Why?

Bárbara Raya

Boy: どうしてかえるの？
why go back Q?
Why are you going?

Taku: あまりにもくだらないからだ！
too much nonsense because be!
Because this is absolute nonsense!

Here is an example of a conversation where someone asks *why?* and the other person answers. This combination is easy to use: all you need to do is add the word どうして *(why?)* to an interrogative sentence. To answer, you just add から *(because)* at the end of the reply. Some examples: どうして日本語は難しいのですか？ *Why is Japanese difficult?* 漢字があるからです *Because it has kanji.* | どうして目が大きいのですか？ *Why are your eyes big?* 君を見たいから *Because I want to see you.* | どうして口が大きいの？ *Why is your mouth big?* 君を食べたいから！ *Because I want to eat you!*

e) In xx time...

Girl: 女の人が映って「おまえは一週間後に死ぬ」ってやつですけど
girl SP appear "you SP a week after TP die" say that one but
It's that one where a girl comes and says "you will die in a week."

A few pages above, we spoke about Japanese having no future tense and about the usage of time adverbs implying future to solve the problem.

A quite useful way to "create" future adverbs is by adding the suffix 〜後 *(in xx time)* to a temporal unit, like in this case, 一週間後 *(in a week's time)*. Thus, creating words such as 六時間後 *(in six*

J.M. Ken Niimura

hours' time), 三日後 *(in three days),* 五年後 *(in five years),* 二ヵ月後 *(in two months' time),* etc. will be very easy. **Note:** The character ヵ is only used to say "x months" and is read か: 一ヵ月 *(one month),* 四ヵ月 *(four months).* We can also use the character ヶ, with the same reading and meaning: 九ヶ月 *(nine months).*

The opposite of 〜後 is 〜前 *(x ago):* 一週間前 *(a week ago),* 六時間前 *(six hours ago),* 三日前 *(three days ago),* 五年前 *(five years ago),* 二ヵ月前 *(two months ago).*

f) Volitive

Man: おまえに渡そうと思ってたんだ...
you IOP give SBP think be...
I was going to give it to you...

J.M. Ken Niimura

We use the verbal conjugation *-ō* to a) express the idea of intention, or b) invite or suggest something. In the manga-example here, the expressed idea is clearly the first one: the old man "had the intention" of giving the ball to his interlocutor. When intention is expressed, using the tag と思う *(I think that...)* is very common to strengthen the idea. In this case, it has been conjugated in the past tense and gerund: と思ってた *(I was thinking)*. One more example: 車を買おうと思う *((I think) I'm going to buy a car)*. Had we done without と思う, the sentence would have been ambiguous: 車を買おう could be translated as *Let's buy a car!* (suggestion) or *I'm going to buy a car* (intention).

g) Deciding on

Bárbara Raya

Cat: 次はどれにしようかなァ。
next SP which "choose" (doubt)
Which one shall I choose now?

When deciding on something, we have a useful and easy structure: にする. In this case, the cat-man in the example is trying to decide which *sushi* dish he is going to eat among those passing before him on the conveyor belt (it is a 回転寿司 or "revolving sushi" kind of restaurant) and he uses にする to decide.

Curiously enough, this example is some sort of mixture of what we have seen in this lesson, since the にする is conjugated in the *-ō* form (にしよう) and there is even an interrogative of the *kosoado* kind (どれ, *which?*) We must stress the fact that the sentence どれにしようかな is very common when one has several options and doesn't know which one to choose. The かな in the end is a combination of the interrogative particle か, which we already know, and the emphatic particle な, which in this case has a connotation of "doubt." One more example: 彼は漫画家かな？ *Could he be a comic artist?*.

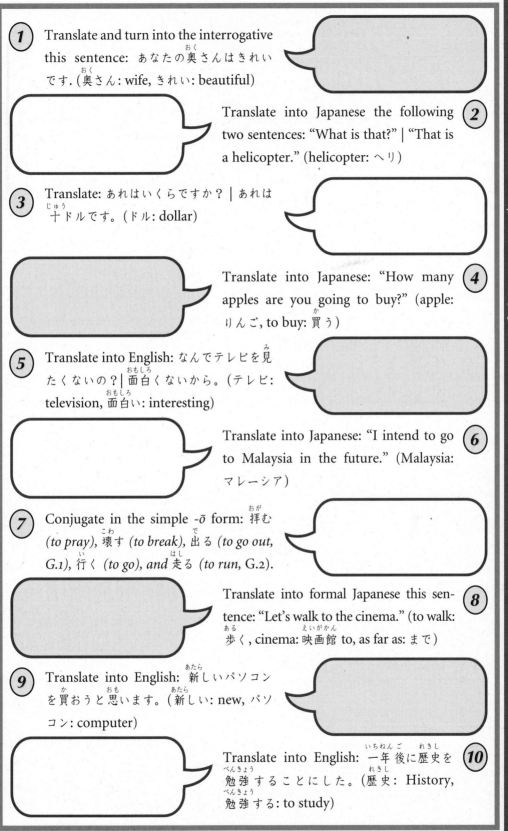

1. Translate and turn into the interrogative this sentence: あなたの奥さんはきれいです.(奥さん: wife, きれい: beautiful)

2. Translate into Japanese the following two sentences: "What is that?" | "That is a helicopter." (helicopter: ヘリ)

3. Translate: あれはいくらですか？ | あれは 十ドルです。(ドル: dollar)

4. Translate into Japanese: "How many apples are you going to buy?" (apple: りんご, to buy: 買う)

5. Translate into English: なんでテレビを見たくないの？| 面白くないから。(テレビ: television, 面白い: interesting)

6. Translate into Japanese: "I intend to go to Malaysia in the future." (Malaysia: マレーシア)

7. Conjugate in the simple -ō form: 拝む (to pray), 壊す (to break), 出る (to go out, G.1), 行く (to go), and 走る (to run, G.2).

8. Translate into formal Japanese this sentence: "Let's walk to the cinema." (to walk: 歩く, cinema: 映画館 to, as far as: まで)

9. Translate into English: 新しいパソコンを買おうと思います。(新しい: new, パソコン: computer)

10. Translate into English: 一年後に歴史を勉強することにした。(歴史: History, 勉強する: to study)

第34課 練習 Exercises

Lesson 35: -*te* form special

We have already studied the -*te* form in lesson 24 (book 1), and saw that it could be used when forming many different expressions. We are now going to study it in depth. Obviously, we recommend reviewing lesson 24 before going on.

Conjugation

In L.24 we saw how the -*te* form of several verbs was constructed, depending on their infinitive (dictionary form). If you take a look at the table, you will realize there is a new feature: the negative -*te* form, – obtained just by adding て to a verb's simple negative form (L.20, book 1) – and the -*te* form of a verb's negative conjugation – obtained by replacing the last 〜い in the verb's negative with 〜くて.

		Simple f.	Meaning	Rule	-*te* form	simple neg.	Neg. -*te* form	-*te* f. of the neg.
Group 1 Invariable		教える	to teach	〜る て	教えて	教えない	教えないで	教えなくて
		起きる	to wake up		起きて	起きない	起きないで	起きなくて
Group 2 Variable	A	貸す	to lend	〜す して	貸して	貸さない	貸さないで	貸さなくて
	B	待つ	to wait	〜つ って	待って	待たない	待たないで	待たなくて
		買う	to buy	〜う って	買って	買わない	買わないで	買わなくて
		帰る	to return	〜る って	帰って	帰らない	帰らないで	帰らなくて
	C	書く	to write	〜く いて	書いて	書かない	書かないで	書かなくて
	D	急ぐ	to hurry	〜ぐ いで	急いで	急がない	急がないで	急がなくて
	E	遊ぶ	to play	〜ぶ んで	遊んで	遊ばない	遊ばないで	遊ばなくて
		飲む	to drink	〜む んで	飲んで	飲まない	飲まないで	飲まなくて
		死ぬ	to die	〜ぬ んで	死んで	死なない	死なないで	死ななくて
Group 3 Irregular		する	to do	*Irregular verbs: no rule*	して	しない	しないで	しなくて
		来る	to come		来て	来ない	来ないで	来なくて

A brief review

So far, we have seen a few expressions where the *-te* form is used. Let's review them briefly. If you have any doubts, you can look up the corresponding lesson:

● **Gerund** (L.24): 本を読んでいます *I'm reading a book.*

● **"Please"** (L.24): 本を読まないでください *Don't read a book, please.*

● **Wish / order** (L.31): 本を読んで欲しいです *I want you to read a book.*

● **Prohibition** (L.32): 本を読んではいけません *You must not read books.*

● **Permission** (L.32): 本を読んでもいいです *It's OK if you read books.*

The combination of ～てもいい and the *-te* form of the negative conjugation of a verb (see table) will allow us to construct sentences such as: "you don't have to," that is, the lack of obligation. Ex: verb: 読む *(to read)* ⇒ negative: 読まない ⇒ *-te* form: 読まなくて ⇒ Sentence: この本を読まなくてもいいです *You don't have to read this book.* As you can see, the negative conjugation of a verb is considered like an *-i* adjective and its *-te* form is conjugated as such. One more sentence: 行かなくてもいいです *You don't have to go.*

● **Give / receive** (L.28): 本を読んでもらいます *Someone reads me a book.*

In L.28 we briefly saw the usage of the *-te* form plus the verbs あげる *(to give)*, もらう *(to receive)*, and くれる *(to receive)*. We will go over this subject in depth in L.45.

Connecting sentences

One of the most practical usages of the *-te* form is the possibility of joining two or more similar sentences and

	Infinitive	Meaning	Rule	*-te* form
-i adj.	高い	tall	~い くて	高くて
-na adj.	静かな	silent	~な で	静かで
Noun	先生	teacher	-で	先生で

giving, thus, a higher level of complexity to our sentences in Japanese.

● 彼女は掃除して、洗濯する *She does the cleaning and (then) the washing.*

● 私は遊んで、本を読みます *I play (have fun) and (then) read a book.*

We will see this way of connecting sentences again in L.46 (book 2), but now it is worth knowing adjectives and nouns can also be connected using the *-te* form. Check the adjunctive table for their conjugations, which are very simple.

● ***-i* adj:** この本は安くておもしろいです *This book is cheap and interesting.*

● ***-na* adj:** その電車は便利で速いです *That train is convenient and fast.*

● **Noun:** 父はサラリーマンで、友隆と言います *My father is an office worker and his name is Tomotaka.*

Finished action

Now we will study some very useful structures which are created with the *-te* form. Thus, allowing us to easily learn many new types of expressions.

The first expression we will see is 〜てある, which has the connotations of "a finished action" and "something has been done — and the consequence of this action remains unchanged—."

● 料理は作ってある *The meal is ready.*

● 盆栽はテーブルに置いてある *The* bonsai *has been put on the table (and it is still there).*

● パソコンはつけてある *The personal computer has been turned on (and is still on).*

Going and coming

Other common expressions are 〜ていく and 〜てくる. The first one, 〜ていく, has the connotation of "going" or "doing something (progressing)." It comes from 行く, *to go.*

● **To take:** 明日、マンガを持っていく *I'll take the comic book tomorrow.*

● **To go:** 駅まで走っていきます *I'm running to the station.*

● **To do something (constant):** 僕は経済を勉強していく *I study (and carry on with it) Economics.*

The second, 〜てくる, has several possible meanings, although all of them imply the idea of "coming." It comes from the verb 来る, *to come.*

● **To bring:** 明日、マンガを持ってくる *I'll bring the comic book tomorrow.*

● **To come:** 先生は歩いてきます *The teacher comes walking.*

● **To go (and the come back):** メキシコへ行ってきたよ *I went to Mexico (and came back).*

● **To come back:** ワインを買ってきた *I've bought wine (and have come back).*

There are many connotations here, so it may be slightly confusing. **Advice:** Think about the equations いく = *to go* and くる = *to come*, and it will be clearer.

After doing...

In the previous lesson we saw the lack of a future tense in Japanese and several strategies to express the idea of future. The 〜てから form can also help us in this context, since it means "after doing...," very useful when expressing future actions.

● テレビを見てからご飯を食べる *I eat (I'll eat) after watching* TV.

● 一杯を飲んでから寝ましょう *I'll go to sleep after having a drink.*

● 死んでから天国へ行くよ *After dying, you go to heaven.*

To try

The expression ～てみる (very common) has the connotations of "to try to do something" and "to do something just to try." These examples will help you understand:

● この本を翻訳してみます *I'll try to translate this book.*

● 刺身を食べてみたい *I'd like to try and eat sashimi.*

● カラオケへ行ってみよう *I'll try and go to karaoke.*

Note: Most of the expressions we are now seeing are compatible with other structures we have previously seen. For instance, example #2 combines ～てみる with the volitive ～たい (L.31) and #3 combines ～てみる with the -*ō* form (L.34).

Leave something done

The expression ～ておく, which comes from the verb 置く *(to place/to put/to leave)*, is used to give sentences a connotation of "doing something beforehand (so it is useful later)."

● ビールを買っておいたよ *I've bought beer (for later).*

● この本を読んでおこう *I'm going to read this book (in case it is necessary later on).*

● 日本語を勉強しておかなければなりません *I must study Japanese (it might be useful later on).*

Note: In the second example we have also used the -*ō* form (L.34) and in the third one, the form for need-obligation (L.32). In spoken language, ～ておく can be contracted into ～とく (言っておく ⇒ 言っとく, *I tell you*) or into ～どく (読んでおく ⇒ 読んどく, *I read it*).

Finish doing / regret doing

The expression ～てしまう has two very different connotations. The first one is "to finish doing something completely," "to get through something," and the second (very common) is "having done something one regrets," or "doing something with consequences."

● 一週間で教科書を読んでしまった *I read the textbook through in a week.*

● 日本語を全部 忘れてしまった *I have completely forgotten my Japanese.*

● 彼に「バカ」と言ってしまった *I called him an idiot (and now I regret it).*

● 僕は彼の不倫を見てしまった *I saw his (illicit) affair (and this could have consequences).*

Obviously, if we don't know the context, we could encounter ambiguous sentences:

● 私はケーキを食べてしまった *I ate (all of? / by mistake?) the cake.*

Note: ～てしまう can be contracted into ～ちゃう (言ってしまう ⇒ 言っちゃう, *I'll tell / blurt it out*) or into ～じゃう (読んでしまう ⇒ 読んじゃう, *I'll read it through*).

To be dying to

The last expression we will look at, ～てたまらない (formal version: ～てたまりません), is used to indicate the intensity of something, the feeling of unbearability, or that we have a very strong desire. It is exclusively used with the *-te* form of *-i* or *-na* adjectives, as well as with verbal conjugations which function as an *-i* adjective (like the volitive form ～たい).

● 今日は寒くてたまらないよ！ *I can't stand the cold today!*
● あの女性はきれいでたまりませんね *That woman is extremely beautiful.*
● 旅行に行きたくてたまらないよ *I'm dying to go on a trip.*
● 孫と遊びたくてたまらない *I'm dying to play with my grandchild.*

Conclusion

We have had the chance to review and study many usages of the *-te* form.

Hopefully, you will be able to profit from the study of the table in the first page of this lesson, since you have probably realized mastering the *-te* form is essential, as well as extremely useful.

To conclude the theory section, on the right you have a summary-table with those expressions using the *-te* form we have seen thus far (we have conjugated the verb 話す, *to talk*). We might see some more expressions throughout the book, but this lesson in itself constitutes a quite complete summary.

Grammatical summary of the *-te* form		
Form	**Meaning**	**Example**
～ている	gerund (L.24)	話している To be talking
～てください	please (L.24)	話してください Please, talk
～てもいい	permission (L.32)	話してもいい You can talk
～てはいけない	prohibition (L.32)	話してはいけない You must not talk
～てほしい	wish, order (L.24)	話してほしい I want you to talk
～てあげる	to do a favor (L.28, 49)	話してあげる I talk to you (doing you a favor)
～てもらう	receive something (L.28, 49)	話してもらう (I'll have) you talk to me
～てくれる	receive something (from someone close) (L.28, 49)	話してくれる You talk to me (doing me a favor)
(Connector)	(sentence connector)	話してだまる I talk and become silent
～てある	(finished action)	話してある It has been told
～ていく	to go to	話していく I'm going to talk (to him)
～てくる	to go and come back	話してくる I'll (go) talk (and return)
～てから	after doing...	話してから After talking...
～てみる	to try	話してみる I'll try to talk (to him)
～ておく	to do something before- hand, to decide on doing something	話しておく I'll tell it (for later)
～てしまう	to finish doing/ to regret doing	話してしまう I talked (and I regret doing it)
～てたまらない	to be dying to	話したくてたまらない I'm dying to talk

In the previous pages we have studied some of the many possibilities available once you master the -*te* form. Now, in the form of manga panels, we will see practical examples of some expressions which use this verbal and adjectival inflection.

a) "Please" in the negative

Girl: だけど甘く見ないでね
but sweet look EP
But don't underestimate me, OK?

One of most useful expressions we can construct with the -*te* form is the request "please." We already saw in L.24 (book 1) how it functioned: all you need to do is add ください (sometimes written in kanji: 下さい) to a verb conjugated in the -*te* form.

Therefore, in the case of the verb in this sentence, 見る *(to look)*, we must conjugate its -*te* form (it belongs to Group 1, so we will get 見て) and add ください to obtain the sentence 見てください *(look, please)*. In this lesson, we have learned a new feature: the negative of the -*te* form. To obtain this negative

Studio Kōsen

form, we must conjugate the verb we need in its simple negative (L.20, book 1) and then add で. Thus 見る ⇒ 見ない (simple negative) ⇒ 見ないで. Adding ください we will obtain a "negative please:" 見ないでください *(don't look, please)*.

If we do without ください, as in this manga-example, the sentence will have exactly the same meaning, but it will be a lot more colloquial (just like in English, since "come here, please" is not the same as just "come here").

Note: In this sentence we also have an -*i* adjective (甘い, *sweet*) transformed into an adverb (L.22, book 1). Besides *sweet*, 甘い can also mean *indulgent / optimistic*, therefore, the sentence would literally mean *don't look at me indulgently*, although here we have chosen a more natural version: *don't underestimate me*.

b) You don't have to

何も思い出さなくていい！

> **Fritz:** 何^{なに}も思^{おも}い出^ださなくていい！
> *nothing remember (don't have to)!*
> **You don't need to remember anything!**

In L.32 we saw the permission form 〜てもいい and here we have studied the *-te* form in adjectives and nouns. This takes us to the creation of sentences such as "you don't have to," which are usually constructed with the *-te* form of the negative conjugation of the verb (which functions as an *-i* adjective) plus 〜てもいい. In this case: 思^{おも}い出^だす *(remember)* => ⇒ 思^{おも}い出^ださない (negative: *to not remember*) ⇒ 思^{おも}い出^ださなくて (*-te* form of the negative) ⇒ 思^{おも}い出^ださなくてもいい (permission: *you don't need to remember*).

Javier Bolado

Notes: In the colloquial register, we tend to do without も in 〜てもいい sentences, like in this example. The word 何^{なに}も means *nothing*.

c) Connecting sentences

> **Kuraki:** ああ、うるさくて落^おち着^ついて食^くえんだろう
> *aah, noisy calmly eat can I?*
> **Argh, you are so noisy there's no way I can eat calmly, can I?**

In the theory section we saw sentences could be linked using the *-te* form. In this example we have two linkages, the first one with an *-i* adjective, and the second one with a verb.

The *-te* form of the *-i* adjective うるさい *(noisy)* is うるさくて, and the *-te* form of

ああ、うるさくて落ち着いて食えんだろう

J.M. Ken Niimura

the verb 落^おち着^つく *(to be calm / settle down)* is 落^おち着^ついて. Therefore, the sentence, formed by three elements would be うるさくて落^おち着^ついて食^くう *(to eat calmly with noise)*.

Notes: 食^くえん is the contracted form of 食^くえない, the negative potential (L.32) of the vulgar verb, primarily used by men, 食^くう *(to eat)*, which is synonymous of the standard 食^たべる *(to eat)*. だろう is the simple *-ō* (L.34) of the verb です (the formal would be でしょう). In this case it functions as a tag with a nuance of insistence or reassertion of what has been said.

d) To try

Helen: まだ使<ruby>使<rt>つか</rt></ruby>えるの？
still use (can) Q?
Is it still working?

Joey: さあ...やってみよう
(doubtful)... do (try)
I don't know... Let's try it.

Gabriel Luque

Another of the many usages of the versatile *-te* form is 〜てみる, which gives a sentence the meaning of "try to do something," or "do something just to try." This form is widely used, specially in spoken Japanese. In the manga-example we see it combined with the verb やる (a colloquial verb meaning *to do*), which belongs to Group 2 and, therefore, its *-te* form is やって. Therefore, やってみる would literally mean *to try to do*, that is, *to try*, as we propose here.

In the example sentence the verb is in the *-ō* form (with a connotation of invitation, L.34). Since the tag 〜てみる functions like any other verb, it can be conjugated in the same way. Note, as well, how in her sentence, Helen uses the potential form (L.32) of the verb 使<ruby>使<rt>つか</rt></ruby>う *(to use),* which becomes 使<ruby>使<rt>つか</rt></ruby>える *(can use)*.

e) Something irreparable

Studio Kōsen

Yuki: 食<ruby>食<rt>た</rt></ruby>べましょう、のびちゃうわ
eat (invitation), overcook (EP)
Let's eat, or they'll overcook.

We saw earlier how the expression 〜てしまう has the connotations of "finish doing something completely" and "do something with consequences." This last connotation can be used with actions performed by oneself as well as with voluntary or involuntary actions performed by other people. Here, Yuki remarks the (noodles) will overcook and she uses 〜てしまう to give the sentence the connotation of "and it would be a shame."

In the colloquial register, 〜てしまう is usually contracted into 〜ちゃう or 〜じゃう (〜ちゃった and 〜じゃった in the past), as in this case. のびる *(to overcook)* ⇒ のびて (*-te* form) => のびてしまう (〜てしまう form) => ⇒ のびちゃう (spoken contraction).

f) To go (and come back)

> **Sachiko:** 行_いってきます！
> *go (and come back)*
> **See you later!**

行ってきます！

Bárbara Raya

In L.27 (book 1) we already saw the fixed expression 行_いってきます, used when you are leaving home. This is the right time to explain where this expression comes from, since we have just studied it a few pages ago. The expression ～てくる has several meanings, but they all somehow imply the idea of *coming back / coming*. In the case of 行_いってくる, the sentence expresses the connotation —very common in Japanese—, of *I'm going (but I'll come back)*. The same connotations are found in very common sentences such as 東京_{とうきょう}へ行_いってきます *I'm going to Tokyo (and I'll come back later)*, and others which use the idea of *going (and coming back later)*.

g) It's a good thing...

恋をしていて…よかった。

Javier Bolado

> **Chiaki:** 恋_{こい}をしていて...... よかった。
> *love DOP do (ger.)... good*
> **Thank goodness I'm in love.**

To conclude, we will see a new usage of the *-te* form: the expression ～てよかった, which implies the idea of "thank goodness" or "just as well." In other words, it's a way to express relief. よかった is the past form いい *(well, good)*, so the literal translation of these expressions would be *It has been good that.*

In this example we have two *-te* forms. First of all, we have a gerund (which implies a continuous action): 恋_{こい}をしている (literally *to be doing love*, that is, *to be in love*). The resultant verb 恋_{こい}をしている is also conjugated in the *-te* form and then you add ～よかった to express the idea of "thank goodness:" 恋_{こい}をしていてよかった (literally, *lucky I have been doing love*, or, as we have translated here, *thank goodness I'm in love / lucky I'm in love*).

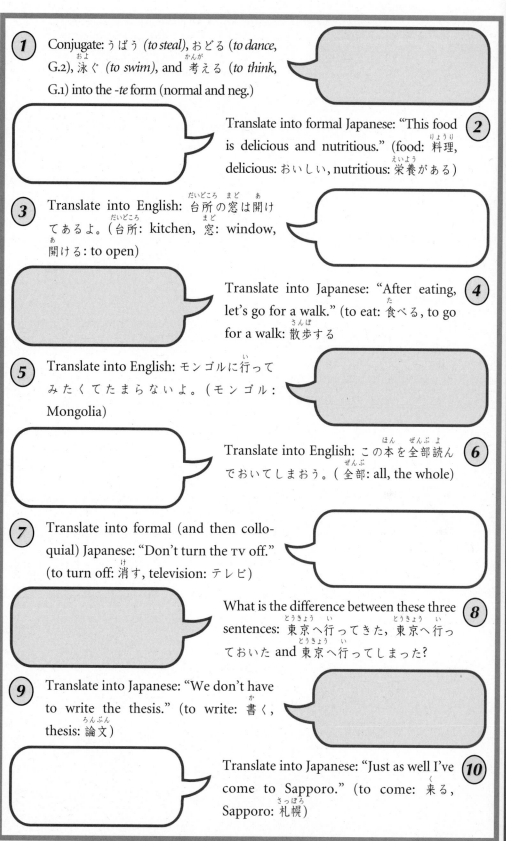

1. Conjugate: うばう *(to steal)*, おどる *(to dance, G.2)*, 泳ぐ *(to swim)*, and 考える *(to think, G.1)* into the *-te* form (normal and neg.)

2. Translate into formal Japanese: "This food is delicious and nutritious." (food: 料理, delicious: おいしい, nutritious: 栄養がある)

3. Translate into English: 台所の窓は開けてあるよ。(台所: kitchen, 窓: window, 開ける: to open)

4. Translate into Japanese: "After eating, let's go for a walk." (to eat: 食べる, to go for a walk: 散歩する

5. Translate into English: モンゴルに行ってみたくてたまらないよ。(モンゴル: Mongolia)

6. Translate into English: この本を全部読んでおいてしまおう。(全部: all, the whole)

7. Translate into formal (and then colloquial) Japanese: "Don't turn the TV off." (to turn off: 消す, television: テレビ)

8. What is the difference between these three sentences: 東京へ行ってきた, 東京へ行っておいた and 東京へ行ってしまった?

9. Translate into Japanese: "We don't have to write the thesis." (to write: 書く, thesis: 論文)

10. Translate into Japanese: "Just as well I've come to Sapporo." (to come: 来る, Sapporo: 札幌)

Lesson 36: In the hotel or *ryokan*

You probably remember we arrived in Japan in lesson 33: we concluded the lesson just as we left the airport. Our second conversational lesson is devoted to accommodations and the possible situations that can come up in a hotel, youth hostel, or *ryokan*. We will also study quite a lot of vocabulary.

The booking

Hotels with three stars or more, and youth hostels with international vocation are, like airports, usually quite "safe" places, linguistically speaking, since the staff almost certainly speaks English, at least at its most basic level. However, the same cannot be said about cheaper hotels, normal hostels, or *ryokan*, so you will probably have to make an effort to communicate in Japanese. The first step is calling to book a room, and these are the most useful sentences.

● 今夜、部屋を予約したいんですが... *I would like to book a room for tonight...* (L.31)
● 一泊、いくらですか？ *How much is it for a night?* (L.34)
● 朝食付きですか？ *Is breakfast included?*
● もう少し安い部屋はありますか？ *Do you have a cheaper room?*
● その部屋にします *I'll take that room.* (L.34)
● お名前と国籍をお願いします *Can I have your name and nationality, please?* (L.33)

Booking and check in					
bunk bed	二段ベッド	no rooms available	空室なし	reservation	予約
to cancel	キャンセルする	price	宿泊料	rooms available	空室あり
cash	現金	shared bathroom	共用トイレ	x nights	〜泊
curfew	門限	shared room	共同部屋	with bathroom	トイレ付き
credit card	クレジットカード	signature	署名	with breakfast	朝食付き
double room	二人部屋	single room	一人部屋	with shower	シャワー付き
nationality	国籍	triple room	三人部屋	youth hostel card	ユースホステルカード

Check in

As we have seen in the third example sentence in the previous point, as well as in some of the words in the vocabulary table, the suffix 〜付き after a noun means "included." Ex: ご飯付き *(with lunch)* | プレゼント付き *(with (a) present)*.

The opposite expression, that is, "not included" is 〜なし. Ex: 朝食なし *(without breakfast)* | シャワーなし *(without shower)*. It's worth memorizing these two expressions, for they are obviously useful.

Let's carry on with the subject of accommodation. You have arrived at the hotel or youth hostel and you want to check in. These sentences will help you:

● ケントと言いますが、予約を入れています *My name is Kent and I have a booking.*
● チェックインしたいんですが *I would like to check in.* (L.31)
● 国際ユースホステルの会員証で割引はありますか？

 Do I get a discount with my international youth hostel card?
● 部屋を見てもいいですか？ *Can I see the room?* (L.32)
● 今日から５泊の宿泊ですね *You are staying for five nights from today, aren't you?*
● 宿泊カードに記入してください *Could you fill in the registration card, please?* (L.35)

Services

Our next step will be to interact with the hotel staff, either to ask for some service or to ask how something works. We would like to stress that we are not only giving prominence to hotels in this lesson, but to youth hostels as well. So you should find some sentences here which should be very useful in this type of situation.

● 部屋番号は２０６です *My room number is 206.*
● ３１２号室の鍵をください *Could you give me the key for room number 302, please?*
● 貴重品を預けたいんですが... *I would like to put some valuable objects away...* (L.31)
● フロントの金庫を使ってください *Use the safe at reception, please.*
● ロッカーはありますか？ *Do you have any lockers?*
● 朝８時にモーニングコールをお願いします

 Could I have a morning call (tomorrow) at 8 AM, please?
● ドライヤーを貸してください *Could I borrow a hairdryer, please?*
● お風呂は何時から何時までですか？ *From when to what time is the bath open?*

Requests and problems

Lost keys, damaged air-conditioning or heating, noisy neighbors, accidents... All kind of problems can arise in a hotel, although in this lesson we will mainly deal with the most typical.

● すみません、ちょっと困っているんですが… *Excuse me, I have a problem...*
● 部屋の鍵をなくしてしまいました *I've lost my room key.* (L.35)
● 鍵を部屋の中に忘れました *I've left my key in the room.*
● 部屋がうるさくて眠れません *The room is so noisy I can't sleep.* (L.32/35)
● お湯が出ません *There is no hot water.*
● エアコン・電気・テレビがつきません *The air-conditioning / light / TV is not working.*
● 部屋の掃除をしてください *Could you clean the room, please?*

Check out

It's time to leave. On checking out, we pay our bill and... we say goodbye.

● チェックアウトをしたいんですが… *I would like to check out...* (L.31)
● お支払いは現金ですか、カードですか？ *Will you pay cash or credit card?*
● カードでお願いします *Credit card.* | 現金でお願いします *Cash.*
● いろいろお世話になりました *Thank you very much for everything.*

Hotel		Room			
bar	バー	air-conditioning	エアコン｜冷房	local call	市内電話
coffee shop	コーヒーショップ	alarm clock	目覚まし時計	morning call	モーニングコール
elevator	エレベータ	bath	バス	plug / socket	コンセント
emergency exit	非常口	bed	ベッド	sheet	シーツ
lobby	ロビー	chair	いす	sink	流し
to pay	支払う	door	ドア	sofa	ソファ
reception	フロント	faucet	蛇口	table	テーブル｜机
restaurant	レストラン	fridge	冷蔵庫	television	テレビ
safe	セーフ｜金庫	hairdryer	ヘアドライヤー	toilet	トイレ
stairs	階段	heating	暖房	toilet stool	便器
valuable objects	貴重品	international call	国際電話	towel	タオル
x floor	〜階	key	鍵	wardrobe	たんす
x room	〜号室	lamp	照明｜ランプ	window	窓

In the *ryokan*

A *ryokan*, or Japanese style inn, is a very special kind of accommodation with some rules and specific conventions that must be upheld (see the "Cultural Note" section). It will be very useful, then, to analyze some of the most particular situations in the *ryokan*.

To begin with, when we enter a *ryokan* we must take off our shoes and put slippers on instead. The check is carried out in your own room, having a cup of tea and following the detailed explanations from the staff member in charge, who will be there with us until we finish the proceedings.

Ryokan	
女将さん	landlady and owner of the *ryokan*
お風呂	Japanese style deep bath
障子	translucent rice paper placed on doors and windows
スリッパ (slipper)	slippers (to walk inside the *ryokan*)
畳	Japanese rice straw matting covering the floor
仲居さん	parlor maid or waitress
庭	garden
番頭さん	head clerk
ふすま	sliding door used as a partition between rooms
布団	mattress placed on the *tatami* to sleep
浴衣	light *kimono* used after the bath or to relax
洋式トイレ	Western style toilet (where one sits on)
露天風呂	aopen-air bath, usually a spa-bath
和式トイレ	Japanese style toilet (where one squats)
和室	Japanese style room (with *tatami, futon,* etc.)

● いらっしゃいませ。靴を脱いでください *Welcome! Take your shoes off, please.*
● この書類に記入してください *Could you fill in this document, please?*

When we have finished, the staff member in charge will tell us at what time dinner is served, where the communal bath is, and some other rules and regulations:

● 夕食は七時から八時までです *Dinner is from 7 PM to 8 PM.*
● お風呂は1階にありますが、露天風呂もあります

The bath is on the first floor, but we also have an open-air bath.

● どうぞ、浴衣を着て、くつろいでください

You may put your yukata on and enjoy your stay.

● 食事後に仲居さんは布団を敷きます *After dinner, the maid will lay out your futon.*

When we come back to our room after dinner and after having a relaxing bath, a soft *futon* will be waiting for us, just like the staff member in charge told us: お休みなさい！ *Good night! | Sleep well!*

文化編：旅館

Cultural note: the *ryokan*

The 漢字 that make up the word ryokan (旅館) give a clear hint about its meaning: travel (旅) house (館). Indeed, the 旅館 is what we could call a "Japanese style hotel or inn," radically different in character to Western style hotels. These are called in Japanese ホテル, an obviously foreign word which indicates this style of accommodation was only introduced in Japan in relatively recent times.

In the 旅館, we can enjoy the pleasure of traveling and staying at a typical Japanese inn, with all that this involves. We must comply with certain rules, such as taking our shoes off before entering the place, or bathing in the communal bath (お風呂) with other clients. However, the possibility of experiencing the pleasure of sleeping in a typical 和室, wrapped up in a light 浴衣, inside a soft 布団, placed on a floor covered with elegant 畳 mats is well worth it. The only inconvenience is that some 旅館 only have Japanese style toilets (和式トイレ), where one must squat. This is, though, changing at a fast pace, and at most of the

Picture of a traditional *ryokan* in Futami, Mie-ken (Photo: M. Bernabe)

旅館 you are now able to choose between Western-style or Japanese-style toilets.

Nowadays, many of the most traditional and genuine 旅館 are in rural tourist areas, especially in towns and villages with hot springs and natural spas, such as 箱根 (神奈川 prefecture), 熱海 (静岡 prefecture), 別府 (大分 prefecture), or 有馬 (兵庫 prefecture). The Japanese usually combine a stay at a 旅館 with visits to typical restaurants or with relaxing baths at spas (most of the 旅館 in these areas have their own hot springs facilities), specially open-air baths 露天風呂. Bathing outdoors, in hot water, is an unforgettable experience, especially when it's snowing!

In spite of its relatively high price, it is much recommended to go through the experience of staying in one of these delightful hotels. It is a true immersion in the Japanese ocean of culture. Don't miss it!

漫画例　Manga-examples

As usual, the manga-examples will help us see in practice what we have studied in the theory section. Let's see, then, how the real Japanese manage in hotels and inns, and let's learn from their experiences. If you study the sentences in this lesson, you should have no problem in Japanese hotels.

a) Before checking in

Tanaka: フィクション建設の田中で予約とってあるんですが。
Fiction Constructions POP *Tanaka booking take (finished action) (soft.)*
I'm Tanaka, from Fiction Constructions, and I have a booking.

Recepcionist: はい、田中さまですね。
yes, Tanaka (noun suf) be EP
Oh, yes, Mr. Tanaka, right?

Javier Bolado

Our first example illustrates how to introduce ourselves on arriving at a hotel where we have previously made a booking. This is a slight variation of the example sentence we saw in the second page of this lesson (ケントと言いますが、予約を入れています), although it has exactly the same meaning. Here, Tanaka first introduces himself as the member of the firm Fiction Constructions, and then with his surname, because in Japan the "group" one belongs to is given more importance than the person himself. Next, he uses the verb 取る *(to take)* after 予約 *(booking)*, while we used the verb 入れる *(to put)* in our example. The overall meaning of the sentences is exactly the same in this context.

We will underline, as well, the construction used by Tanaka (取ってある), which we saw in the previous lesson (～てある), and which you'll certainly remember meant "already finished action." On the other hand, we have already said the client is a "god" in Japan. Thus, receptionists use the honorific suffix ～様 (L.15) with the client's name.

b) "Seeing" the room

If we want to see the room before deciding on a hotel or a youth hostel, we will have to request it with the sentence we saw above (部屋を見てもいいですか？). In this scene the bellboy shows the room to some clients

Bellboy: こちらがバスとトイレになっておりますから…
here SP bath CP sink be (formal) because...
And here are the bath and the toilet, so...

Studio Kōsen

who are anxious to start "using" it. Poor thing, he is terribly embarrassed! The only remarkable point in this sentence is the construction なっております, a form which is more or less the "humble" equivalent of the verb *to be*. We will take a quick look at the usage of formal Japanese in L.51 (book 3).

c) The fearsome bill

Recepcionist: 昨晩のお食事代を含めまして、５７８５０円です。
last night POP meal price DOP include, 57,850 yen be
Including last night's meal, the total comes to 57,850 yen.
Client: ああ、支払いはカードで…
oh, payment SP card with...
Oh, I'll pay with credit card...

J.M. Ken Niimura

Here is a very interesting example which shows us how to check out and pay the bill. In the example, the receptionist uses the verb 含める *(to include)* to remark that the *price* (代) for *last night's* (昨晩) *meal* (お食事) has been included in the bill. Besides, he uses the already known *-te* form (L.35) to link the two sentences ("including last night's meal" and "the total comes to 57,850 yen") that form the composite sentence. The client, for his part, informs him he will *pay* (支払う) *with credit card* (カードで).

By the way, don't worry! A hotel in Japan is in no way as expensive as the one in this example. The cheapest ones range between 3,500 and 5,000 yen per person and night.

d) Asking for something at reception

Client: …カン切りお願い… そ、2903のスイートよ。
... can opener please... that's right, 2903 POP suite EP
Bring me a can opener, please... Yes, it's suite #2903.

Gabriel Luque

Most certainly, one time or other, we will have to ask for some object or service at the hotel. In this example we see how the client calls *reception* (フロント) asking for a *can opener* (缶切り).

The woman might appear to be treating the staff with too much familiarity which, in this case, indicates that as client of a suite, she feels superior to them. The standard sentence would be 缶切りをお願いします.

Typical things we can ask for are a *hairdryer* (ドライヤー), *soap* (石けん), or a *towel* (タオル).

e) Welcome to the *ryokan*

Landlady: いらっしゃいませ。私 ここの女将でございます
welcome. I here SP landlady be (formal)
Welcome, I'm the landlady of this *ryokan*.
荷物 お持ちしましょう
bags pick up (invitation)
Let me take your bags.

A *ryokan* is a completely different world. In the example we see the landlady, who introduces herself as ここの女将 *(the landlady here)*. The reading of the kanji 女将 – literally "woman-leader," that is "boss"– which should be read じょしょう, is what is called an *ateji* or "arbitrary kanji:" the reading of the kanji doesn't agree with the pronunciation it should have. The 女将さん, then, greets us with いらっしゃいませ, a word used to welcome clients at a commercial establishment (L27, book 1). Likewise, she talks to us very formally, using the verb でございます,

Bárbara Raya

(very formal equivalent of です, *to be*), and the formal sentence structure "お + verbal root + する." Notice, too, how she uses the invitation form *-ō* (L.34).

f) All full

Landlady: すみません、今日はもう満室でどこも空いてないんですよ。
I'm sorry, today SP already full all empty not be
I'm sorry, but today all the rooms are full and there are no openings.

The kids in the example arrive at the *ryokan* a little bit late, but they still decide to try and see if they can stay there for that night, so they ask the 女将さん if there are any rooms available. The owner of the 旅館 tells them all rooms are taken − 満室：満 *(full)*, 室 *(room)* − and then redundantly says *all* (どこも) are "*not empty*" (空いてない), or, in other words, "full." In Japanese, repeating the same idea in two different ways in one sentence is quite common.

g) In the communal bath

Kenji: おわ〜っいろんなおふろがある〜！！
wow! several bathtubs SP are!!
Wow, there are plenty of bathtubs!!
Shinji: 好きな所に行っていいぞ
like place go (permission) EP
You can go to any one you like.

The last example shows us some public baths like the ones we can find in a 旅館, an 温泉 *(hot spring)*, or in a 銭湯 *(public baths)*: many big bathtubs and people bathing in them. Be careful, because before getting in the water you must wash your body in the showers at the entry!

Regarding the sentences in the manga-example, we will point out the permission form てもいい used by Shinji, which we studied in L.32. Give it a good review.

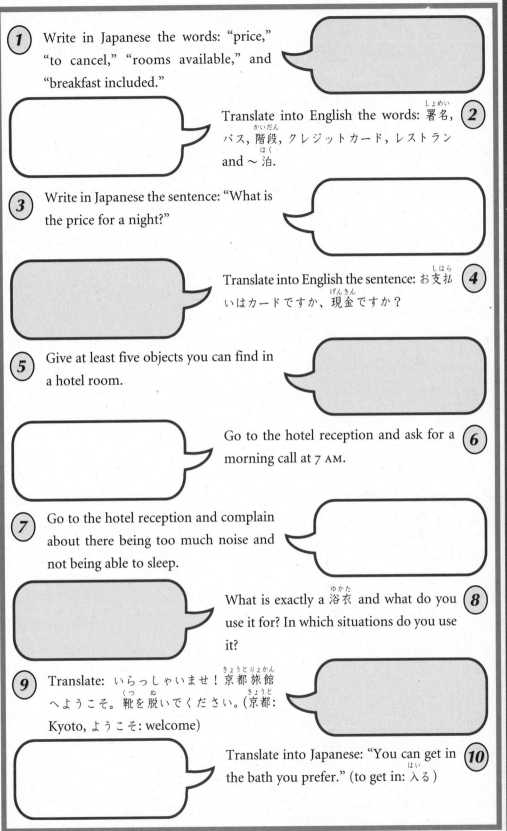

1. Write in Japanese the words: "price," "to cancel," "rooms available," and "breakfast included."

2. Translate into English the words: 署名, バス, 階段, クレジットカード, レストラン and 〜泊.

3. Write in Japanese the sentence: "What is the price for a night?"

4. Translate into English the sentence: お支払いはカードですか、現金ですか？

5. Give at least five objects you can find in a hotel room.

6. Go to the hotel reception and ask for a morning call at 7 AM.

7. Go to the hotel reception and complain about there being too much noise and not being able to sleep.

8. What is exactly a 浴衣 and what do you use it for? In which situations do you use it?

9. Translate: いらっしゃいませ！京都旅館へようこそ。靴を脱いでください。(京都: Kyoto, ようこそ: welcome)

10. Translate into Japanese: "You can get in the bath you prefer." (to get in: 入る)

第 36 課 練習 Exercises

第37課：助詞①は・が・も

Lesson 37: Particles (1) wa/ga/mo

In lesson 16 we gave a quick look at grammatical particles, but they are such an essential aspect of Japanese grammar that it is worth studying them in greater detail. This is what we will be doing in the following lessons. Now, we will begin with the two most difficult particles to master, は and が, and then we will top the lesson off with も.

The topic

Before properly starting with particles, the grammatical concept we call "topic" must be clear, since it is essential in Japanese. The ENCARTA dictionary description for "topic" is: "a subject written or spoken about."

Let's see some illustrative sentences: _John is eating the bread_ | _The bread, John is eating it._ The topic in the first sentence is "John" — talking about "John" who is eating the bread —. Whereas in the second sentence the topic is "the bread" — talking about "the bread" which John is eating —. In English, the topic is usually the grammatical subject of the sentence (as in the first sentence), and sentences like the second one are somewhat unnatural, or they belong to the spoken language. In Japanese it's different: the topic doesn't always coincide with the grammatical subject.

The particle は

The syllable は, which is read _wa_ and not _ha_ when it functions as a grammatical particle, is the particle indicating the topic of a sentence. Since most times the topic coincides with the grammatical subject, it is often mistaken for a subject particle; however, it isn't. So, we must commit this concept to memory: は = topic particle.

● この太郎は学生です "Talking about this Tarō," he is a student. (This Tarō is a student.)
● この学生は太郎です "Talking about this student," he is Tarô. (This student is Tarō.)

Notice how these two sentences are very similar but have different connotations. In the first one, the "topic" we are talking about is 太郎, whereas in the second one it is 学生.

は: basic usages

The structure which is possibly the simplest in Japanese, and which we have sufficiently mastered by now, is constructed with は. We are talking about "x は y です."

● 花子は学生です *"Talking about Hanako," she is a student. (Hanako is a student.)*
● 大学はつまらないです *"Talking about university," it's boring. (University is boring.)*

Besides this well known usage, the basic rule for は is that we use it to offer information the interlocutor already knows, either because we have just given the information in the previous sentence or simply because it's obvious. Examples of obvious information are identifiable names − sun, star, fire−, or generic names − house, truck, cat−.

● **Information that has just been given:** 池に亀がいます。亀はのろいです

There is a turtle in the pond. The turtle is slow.

Notice how the first time the word *turtle* (亀) appears, we introduce it with the subject particle が, and the second time, being information the interlocutor already knows (since it has become the "topic" in the conversation), we introduce it with the topic particle は. For the sake of simplicity, we may say that in English we have: が = *a* and は = *the*.

● **Proper names:** 美奈子さんは来ないの？ *Isn't Minako coming?*
● **Identifiable names:** 空は曇っています *The sky is cloudy.*
● **Generic names:** イルカは頭がいいです *Dolphins (generally) are intelligent.*

The interlocutor is supposed to know the "Minako" we are talking about. There's only one "sky," so there's no possible confusion. And, regarding the third sentence, we are talking about "dolphins in general." Therefore, all three sentences require は.

は: contrast and emphasis

The topic particle は can also be used to indicate contrast between two objects or ideas, both being marked by は:

● イワンは日本酒は飲めるけど、ウオッカは飲めない *Ivan can drink sake, but not vodka.*
● 夏子さんは優しいけど、麗子さんは冷たいです *Natsuko is kind, but Reiko is cold.*

However, the usage of は which is most difficult to grasp and contains more "implicit" or "not directly expressed" meaning is that as an emphatic marker: sometimes, は is used to reinforce a determinate idea. Let's see an example:

● 私はグッチは嫌いだ *I hate Gucci.*

In this sentence, the meaning implicit in は goes beyond a simple assertion of the kind "I hate Gucci (and that's it)." Using は, the speaker is implying that the brand Gucci <u>in particular</u> is what he doesn't like. This might make it clearer:

● 私はグッチは嫌いだ（けどプラダは好きだ）*I hate Gucci (but I like Prada).*

Let's see another group of sentences to clarify this usage of は. The dots on the words indicate the speaker is particularly emphasizing them:

● 私は昨日、日本語を勉強しなかった *I didn't study Japanese yesterday. (No emphasis)*

● 私は昨日は日本語を勉強しなかった *I didn't study Japanese yesterday. (Emphasis on "yesterday")*

● 私は昨日、日本語は勉強しなかった *I didn't study Japanese yesterday. (Emphasis on "Japanese")*

● 私は昨日、日本語を勉強はしなかった *I didn't study Japanese yesterday. (Emphasis on "study")*

As you can imagine, the second sentence implies "yesterday" I didn't study (but I did the day before yesterday or some other day). The third one implies I didn't study "Japanese" (although I studied something else), whereas the last one says I didn't "study" Japanese (but I did something else with the Japanese language, such as speak it, write it...).

The particle が

We have insisted that は is not a subject particle, but a "topic" one. The particle that indicates the subject in a sentence is が, and we will now see how to use it. We probably don't need to mention it, but if you have any doubts about what a particle is or how it works, you should thoroughly review L.16 (book 1) before going on.

が is used to mark the subject when it's introduced for the first time, as in the sentence こちらが美穂です *This is Miho*, or the sentence we have already seen 池に亀がいます *There is a turtle in the pond*. That is to say, when the subject is "new information."

● まだご飯が残っています *There is still some rice left.*

Generally speaking, verbs of existence, such as ある or いる (L.18, book 1), always require が to indicate the subject —as is the case in 池に亀がいます—, except when: a) we want to emphasize something, or b) the information is already known, when we will use は.

● **Normal:** 机に手紙がありません *There isn't a letter on the table.*

● **Emphasis:** 机に手紙はありません *There isn't a "letter" on the table (but something else).*

● **Known inf.:** 手紙は机にありません *The letter (we know which one it is) is not on the table.*

Usages of *ga* with certain verbs and adjectives		
Verbs and adjectives of ability		
出来る <small>でき</small>	to be able to L.32	英語が出来る <small>えいご　でき</small>
分かる <small>わ</small>	to understand	英語が分かる <small>えいご　わ</small>
上手な <small>じょうず</small>	skilled	英語が上手だ <small>えいご　じょうず</small>
下手な <small>へた</small>	unskilled	英語が下手だ <small>えいご　へた</small>
〜られる	(potential form) L.32	英語が話せる <small>えいご　はな</small>
Verbs of sense		
見える <small>み</small>	to see (involuntary)	海が見える <small>うみ　み</small>
聞こえる <small>き</small>	to hear (involuntary)	海が聞こえる <small>うみ　き</small>
Verbs and adjectives of need		
要る <small>い</small>	to be necessary	お金が要る <small>かね　い</small>
必要な <small>ひつよう</small>	necessary (2)	お金が必要だ <small>かね　ひつよう</small>
Adjectives of desire		
欲しい <small>ほ</small>	to want L.31	お金が欲しい <small>かね　ほ</small>
〜たい	to want L.31	英語が話したい* <small>えいご　はな</small>
Verbs and adjectives of emotion		
好きな <small>す</small>	like	海が好きだ <small>うみ　す</small>
嫌いな <small>きら</small>	dislike	海が嫌いだ <small>うみ　きら</small>
怖い <small>こわ</small>	frightening, scary	海が怖い <small>うみ　こわ</small>
悲しい <small>かな</small>	sad	海が悲しい <small>うみ　かな</small>

*Very often with を (L.31)
英語: English | 話す: to speak | 海: sea | お金: money

が: **further usages**

Let's describe briefly some more usages of が:

a) Interrogatives such as 何 <small>なに</small> *(what?)*, 誰 <small>だれ</small> *(who?)* or どこ *(where)* (L.34) always go with が. This is logical, since we are always asking about new information.

● 誰が来たの？ *Who came?*
<small>だれ　き</small>

● 何がおもしろい？ *What is interesting?*
<small>なに</small>

b) The subject in subordinate sentences is always introduced with が. We will expand on this in the manga-examples.

● ジョンが来た時、私は買い物に出かけていた
<small>き　とき　わたし　か　もの　で</small>
When John came, I had gone out shopping.

c) In conjunction with certain verbs and adjectives, the particle が is always used. Take a look at the table on the left to check which ones they are, and study the examples. An obvious exception is when we want to emphasize something, and, consequently, we use は.

● 牛乳が好きだ *I like milk* | 牛乳は好きだ *I like milk (but e.g. not cheese).*
<small>ぎゅうにゅう　す</small>

が: **but**

が has also another usage which has nothing to do with marking the subject. We can use this particle to link two sentences with the meaning of "but" (L.49, book 3):

● 私は本を読んだが、彼氏は読まなかった *I read the book, but my boyfriend didn't.*
<small>わたし　ほん　よ　かれし　よ</small>

● 河野君は金持ちだが、不幸です *Kawano is rich but unhappy.*
<small>かわのくん　かねも　ふこう</small>

Sometimes this が is used to connect sentences, and it doesn't necessarily mean "but:"

● 今日は外食するが、一緒に行きたいの？ *I'm going out for lunch, will you join me?*
<small>きょう　がいしょく　いっしょ　い</small>

And finally, we use が at the end of a sentence (in spoken language, formal or not) to soften a sentence, especially when making a request:

● 先生の本を借りたいんですが… *I'd like to borrow your (the teacher's) book, but...*
<small>せんせい　ほん　か</small>

は vs. が

As we have seen, particles は and が are closely related and very often can even appear together in the same sentence, like in the construction "x は Y が z," one of the most characteristic sentence patterns in Japanese.

- 象は鼻が長い *The elephant's (x) trunk(Y) is long (z).*
- サムは背が低い *Sam's (x) height(Y) is short (z). (Sam is short.)*

Likewise, many of the sentences formed with verbs or adjectives in the previous table also have the structure "x は Y が z."

- 彼はサッカーが下手だ *He (x) at soccer (Y) is unskilled (z). (He isn't good at soccer.)*
- 田中さんは猫が怖い *Tanaka (x) cats (Y) are frightening / scary (z). (Tanaka is afraid of cats.)*

The particle も

Let's leave は and が aside for a moment, and introduce another particle, with a much simpler and clearer usage. We are talking about も, whose meaning is "also, too, as well," or "neither," if it is a negative sentence. も can totally substitute particles は, が and を.

- 池に亀がいる。魚もいる *There are turtles in the pond. There are fishes too.*
- 彼は先生ではない。私も先生ではない *He is not a teacher. I'm not a teacher either.*
- 靴を買ったが、シャツも買った *I bought a pair of shoes and I also bought a shirt.*

も is also used to emphasize an idea of time or quantity, as well as to emphasize a number, when it indicates "very much, very many" or "no less than..." In negative situations, the meaning of this last kind of sentence is "not even."

- 私は彼女を何時間も待っていました *I waited for her for many hours.*
- 彼は本を2万冊も持っている *He has no less than 20,000 books.*
- 彼女は本を5冊も持っていない *She doesn't even have 5 books.*

The words 何も (*nothing*), 誰も (*nobody*), as well as the expression "not one," which is formed by " 一 +counter+も " (L.25, book 1), ex: 一枚も (*not one page*) | 一人も (*not one person*), always go with negative sentences.

- 映画館には誰もいない *There is nobody in the cinema.*
- あの人はテレビを一台も持っていない *That person has not even one television set.*

The words いつも (*always / never*) and どこも (*everywhere / nowhere*) can go with affirmative or negative sentences. We will see an example in the manga-examples.

You are probably able to understand by now the differences and similarities between particles は and が. We, Westerners, always have trouble learning to use them properly, because in our languages the "topic" and the "subject" in a sentence are usually the same. Let's study some examples...

a) The most basic usage of *wa*

Yamazaki: きょうふ　にんげん　こわ
恐怖は人間を壊す
fear TOP *people* DOP *destroy*
Fear destroys people.

As we have already said, は is the particle for "topic." Until now we had identified it in the manga-examples as SP (Subject Particle), to simplify matters. However, now that we know exactly how it works, we will call it TOP (Topic Particle). In this lesson we have studied the general guidelines for the usage of particles は and が, which will help us use these particles with relative confidence, knowing most times we won't be wrong. Anyhow, don't despair if you can't fully understand some of their usages or if you do make a mistake every now and then. It's quite normal, and only time and practice can correct it. We will now show some specific examples that will give you a better understanding of the "real" usage of these particles.

In this first example, we have seen a relatively simple sentence where we find the most basic usage of は: its function as the topic particle. In this sentence, "the topic" Yamazaki is talking about is *fear* (恐怖), which is, moreover, an identifiable concept (there is only one concept called "fear" and we all know it). It is natural, then, that the particle は is to go with 恐怖, because it indicates that this word is the "topic" and that it is an identifiable or generic concept as well. In other words: *"Talking about what we all know, fear,"* it destroys people.

b) Emphatic usage of *wa*

Gabriel Luque

Yaguro: 解放はしてやる
release TOP *do (give)*
I will release you (but)...

Another much more subtle usage of the topic particle is its function as an emphasizing particle. は can replace particles が and を or combine with particles に and へ (L.38) to emphasize the word it is identifying.

In this example, the "neutral" sentence, with no implicit nor special meaning, would be 解放を してやる *I will release you.* However, replacing the DO particle を with は we emphasize the word 解放 *(to release).* Thus, the implicit meaning of our sentence comes to be something like *I am going to release you, but I can't guarantee anything else*, or, as we suggest in the translation, *I will release you (but)...*

c) A typical *wa* - *ga* sentence

You can probably imagine by now that the distinction between は and が can fill in pages and more pages of magazines, books and doctoral theses on Japanese linguistics. One of the clearest usages is the combination of both particles in sentences

Studio Kōsen

Hide: オレは大人っぽい女が好きなんだよな
I TOP *adult (seem) woman* SP *like be* EP EP
I like more mature girls.

called *"wa-ga* sentences," where the topic is introduced first with は and then a characteristic or feeling related to this topic is developed using が. In this sentence, the topic is *I* and the feeling described is *like mature girls*. Besides, we know the noun modified by the adjective 好きな (here, the word 女, *woman*) always requires が. It is, then, a very clear example.

Note: One of the usages of the (rather colloquial) desinence っぽい, which is added to nouns and adjectives, is indicating the meaning of "liable to" or "seems." 怒りっぽい *(he is liable to get angry / irritable)*, しめっぽい *(dampish)* (L.44).

d) A subordinate sentence

We mentioned earlier how in subordinate sentences, that is, sentences inside another sentence, the subject will always be indicated with the particle が. It is quite logical, then, that since the "topic" (what we are talking about) will <u>always</u> be in the main sentence, there can't be any possible confusion as to what the "subject" of the sentence is. In our example, the main sentence is あんたは怖くてしょうがないんだ *You are terribly afraid.* The topic is obviously あんた *(you)*. The subordinate sentence is ボクが生き延びる *I survive.*

Other points: the particle の functions here as a nominalizer: it turns the whole sentence preceding it into a noun (L.40 / 57, book 3). The particle が follows this

J.M. Ken Niimura

nominalized sentence −ボクが生き延びるの−, because the adjective 怖い always requires this particle, as we already saw in the corresponding table in the theory section.
Note: The construction 〜てしょうがない means *very much* or *it can't be helped that...*

e) Usage of *ga* with the meaning of "but"

Javier Bolado

One of the cases where が cannot be confused with は is when the former goes after a sentence, giving it an adversative meaning; that is, to indicate *but* or *however*. In this example we have two sentences, いい手だった (sentence A) and 甘かったな (sentence B), linked by が in a "sentence A が sentence B" structure, that is, "sentence A, <u>but</u> sentence B." Words with the same meaning −*but, however*− and usage are けど, けれど and けれども (L.49).
Notes: 手 usually means *hand*, but here it has the connotation of *try*. Regarding 甘い, we already saw in manga-example a) of L.35 its main meaning is *sweet*, but it can sometimes mean *naive* or *indulgent*, like here.

f) The word «always»

Ako: いつものママじゃな〜い！！
always POP *mommy not be!!*
This is not my usual mommy!!

Bárbara Raya

In the theory pages we studied the most common usages of も, although we have also mentioned that sometimes も is combined with interrogative pronouns like 誰 (*who?*) or 何 (*what?*) to form words with a new meaning, such as 誰も (*nobody*) or 何も (*nothing*), which always go with negative sentences. The case of いつも, which, as you can guess, derives from いつ (*when?*), is somewhat special, because it can function both in affirmative and negative sentences alike with the meaning of *always:* いつも陽気です *He is always happy.*

g) A new usage of *mo*

Studio Kösen

James: 新しいお父さん、嫌いなの？
new father, dislike Q?
Don't you like your new father?
Hikari: べ〜つに、好きでも嫌いでもねえよ
particularly, like not dislike neither EP
I don't particularly like him nor dislike him.

Here we have a new usage of the particle , which expresses lack of definition or, as in this example, to evade the issue when asked a question one doesn't want to answer clearly: we are talking about the "A も B も ない" structure, which can be translated as "neither A nor B." This construction is used in a somewhat special way:

-i **adjectives.** Replacing the last い with く: 小さくも大きくもない *Neither big nor small.*
-na **adjectives.** Replacing な with で: 安全でも危険でもない *Neither safe nor dangerous.*
Nouns. Adding で: 先生でも学生でもありません *Neither teacher nor student.*

In our example we find the structure we have just studied with two *-na* adjectives: 好きでも嫌いでもない *I neither like nor dislike.*

Notes: James does without the particle が in his sentence (it should be 新しいお父さんが嫌い). This is quite common in spoken and colloquial language. The ねえ Hikari uses is a contraction of ない. In this context, べ〜つに (別に) means *specially, particularly.*

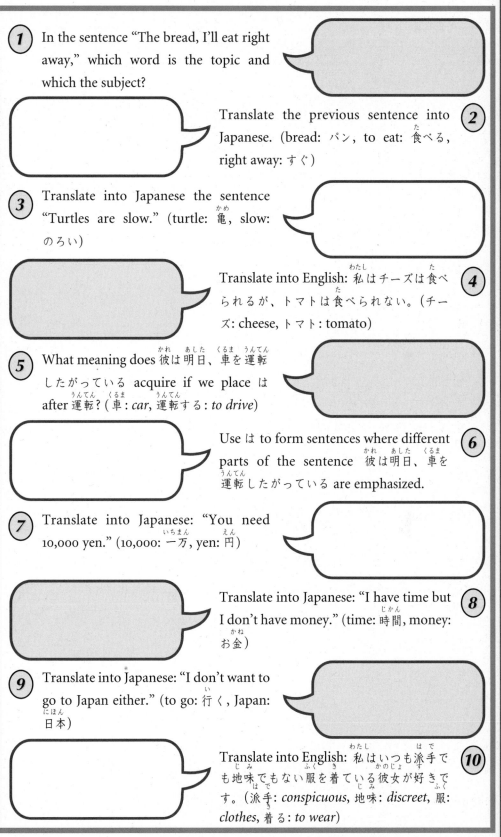

1 In the sentence "The bread, I'll eat right away," which word is the topic and which the subject?

2 Translate the previous sentence into Japanese. (bread: パン, to eat: 食べる, right away: すぐ)

3 Translate into Japanese the sentence "Turtles are slow." (turtle: 亀, slow: のろい)

4 Translate into English: 私はチーズは食べられるが、トマトは食べられない。(チーズ: cheese, トマト: tomato)

5 What meaning does 彼は明日、車を運転したがっている acquire if we place は after 運転? (車: *car*, 運転する: *to drive*)

6 Use は to form sentences where different parts of the sentence 彼は明日、車を運転したがっている are emphasized.

7 Translate into Japanese: "You need 10,000 yen." (10,000: 一万, yen: 円)

8 Translate into Japanese: "I have time but I don't have money." (time: 時間, money: お金)

9 Translate into Japanese: "I don't want to go to Japan either." (to go: 行く, Japan: 日本)

10 Translate into English: 私はいつも派手でも地味でもない服を着ている彼女が好きです。(派手: *conspicuous*, 地味: *discreet*, 服: *clothes*, 着る: *to wear*)

Lesson 38: Particles (2) ni/de/e

As in the previous lesson, we will keep the tone of an in-depth study for our next batch of particles: に, で and へ. We recommend that you review lesson 16, in the first book of the *Japanese in MangaLand* series, where we gave an introduction to grammatical particles.

The particle に

We will start this dense lesson having a look at the different functions of に, a particle with several usages which you may find a little bit difficult to assimilate. We will try to present those different functions of に in a simple and organized way so that you won't get lost.

Perhaps, the clearest usage of に is as a marker of Adverbial Complement of Place (ACP), that is, the word that indicates "the place" where something is. In this category there are two usages: existence and permanence.

① <u>Existence:</u> The verbs of existence いる and ある, both meaning "to be" (L.18, book 1), always require the ACP to be marked with に.
- 池に亀がいる *There is a turtle in the pond.*
- 姫路に白い城がある *There is a white castle in Himeji.*

② <u>Permanence:</u> Verbs indicating a long stay in a place, such as いる and ある – when they indicate permanence instead of existence–, 住む *(to live in)*, or 残る *(to remain)*, among others, also require に with their ACP.
- 直美ちゃんはそのぼろいアパートに住んでいる *Naomi lives in that rundown apartment.*
- 僕は居酒屋に残りたい *I want to stay in the pub.*

However, you must be careful with this usage, because に indicates "existence" or "relatively long stay" in a certain place, never indicating something which "happens" or "is done" in that place (even though this is also a ACP for us). In this second case, we use the particle で, which we will study shortly.

Direction, contact and time

③ <u>Direction:</u> に is used to indicate the Adverbial Complement of Direction (ACD) with the meaning of going "to / towards" some place. This usage is identical and inter-changeable with that of the particle へ, which we will also see in this lesson.

● 来週、沖縄に行きます *Next week, I'll go to Okinawa.*
● 武文くんは家に帰りたがっている *It seems Takefumi wants to go home.*

④ <u>Direct contact:</u> We need に to mark those ACP which indicate "surface over which something happens or an action is performed." It is also used with verbs of "direction," such as 入る *(to enter)*, 乗る *(to ride / get on a vehicle)*, 上る *(to go up)*, etc.

● いたずらっ子は壁に落書きをした *The naughty boy drew graffiti on the wall.*
● 社長は新幹線に乗りました *The president got on the Shinkansen (bullet train).*

⑤ <u>Specific time:</u> We use に to mark Adverbial Complements of Time (ACT) which indicate a specific point in time, such as a date, the time or a year.

● 6時半に待ち合わせをしている *I have an appointment at half past six.*
● アメリカは 千四百九十二年 に発見された *America was discovered in 1492.*

However, に is never used when the ACT cannot be determined with a specific date or time. The words 今日 *(today)*, 昨日 *(yesterday)*, 明日 *(tomorrow)*, 来年 *(next year)*, and 最近 *(lately)* go either on their own or with は (L.37). The days of the week – 月曜日 *(Monday)*, 火曜日 *(Tuesday)*, etc.– are an exception to this rule and can go with に.

Indirect object, change, and grammatical constructions

⑥ <u>Indirect Object:</u> に is used to mark the IO, that is, the object receiving the conse-quences of the action indicated by the verb: in other words, "whom."

● 依津江ちゃんは友達にアドバイスした *Itsue gave his friend some advice.*
● 先生は生徒たちに数学を教えます *The teacher teaches mathematics to his pupils.*
● 国王は科学者にノーベル賞を与えた *The king gave the scientist the Nobel Prize.*

⑦ <u>Change:</u> The verbs of change, such as なる *(to become)*, 変わる *(to change)*, or 変化する *(to vary)*, require the complement to be identified with に. In L.28 (book 1) we have already seen how なる functions, so we recommend that you review that lesson before going on.

● 将来、サッカー選手になりたい *In the future, I want to become (be) a soccer player.*
● 信号が赤に変わった *The traffic light turned red.*

⑧ Grammatical constructions: To conclude, we will also mention に is used in many grammatical constructions we have already seen or will see in future lessons. Here's a short list:

⇒ Constructions of the "to go to" or "to come to" sort (L.28). 買いに行く *To go to buy.*

⇒ Conversion of *-na* adjectives into adverbs (L.22). 上手に書く *To write skillfully.*

⇒ Constructions with あげる (*to give*), もらう (*to receive*), and くれる (*to receive*) (L.28, book 1 and L.49, book 3). 本は父にもらった (*I received the book from my father*).

Usages of *ni*	
Existence	母は京都にいる My mother is in Kyoto
Permanence	母は京都に住んでいる My mother lives in Kyoto
Direction	母は京都にいく My mother goes to Kyoto
Direct contact	母はキャンバスに絵を描く My mother paints on a canvas
Specific time	母は６時に来る My mother will come at 6 o'clock
Indirect object	母は父に絵をあげる My mother gives my father a drawing
Change	母は変になった My mother has become strange
Gramnatical const.	母は私に絵を描かせた My mother made me paint

母はは: mother | 京都きょうと: Kyoto | 住む すむ: to live | 来るくる: to come
絵え: drawing | 描くえがく: to draw | あげる: to give | へんな: strange

⇒ Passive and causative sentences (L.60, book 3). 友達に料理をさせた *I made my friend cook.*

⇒ Fixed constructions, such as 〜ために (*for*, L.48, book 3), 〜に違いない (*undoubtedly*), 〜によると (*according to*), 〜にかわって (*in exchange of*), or 〜に基づいて (*based on*).

The particle で

The usages of the particle で don't usually overlap with any other particle, except when indicating ACP, when it can be confused with に. We will first examine this more "problematic" usage, and then we will go over its other usages.

① **Place:** We can say there are two kinds of ACP in Japanese, because it distinguishes between the "place where one exists or remains" and the "place where one performs an action." The first type of ACP (existence / permanence) requires に, as you have just seen in the previous pages. Whereas, the second one always uses で.

● 彼は日本でテレビ出演している *He is on TV in Japan.*
● 千鶴さんはいつも家で勉強しなければならない *Chizuru must always study home.*
● 私は横浜のオフィスで働いていました *I worked at an office in Yokohama.*

Be careful with the verb ある, because it doesn't always indicate "existence." It can also indicate the place where something "happens" – a public event, for example –, in which case, its ACP must be indicated with the particle で.

● 明日、ロスで弁論大会がある *There is a speech contest in Los Angeles tomorrow.*

Time and manner

② <u>Time</u>: The particle で is used after an ACT which indicates "end of the action."

● 宿題は今週で終わりたい *I want to finish my homework this week.*

● あの人は６月で刑務所を出られる *That person will be able to leave prison in June.*

に can also be used here. The differences are mainly connotative.

● 契約は３月３日で/に終わる *The contract expires on March, 3.*

If we use に, we simply indicate the exact expiry date of the contract. With で, however, it has a nuance of "the contract is valid until March, 3, and then it expires."

③ <u>Required time</u>: This usage is closely related with the previous one in that it indicates the "time spent" in doing something. However, で cannot be replaced with に here.

● 彼は一年半で本を書いた *He wrote a book in a year and a half.*

● ６時間で仕事を終わらなければならない *I must finish this job in 6 hours.*

④ <u>Manner / Instrument / Material</u>: The particle で is also used to indicate the Adverbial Complement of Manner (how), as well as of Instrument (with what), and of Material (from / of what).

● 僕は船で韓国に行きたい *I want to go to Korea by boat.*

● 泥棒は人をナイフで襲った *The thief attacked someone with a knife.*

● 日本の家は木で作ってあります *Houses in Japan are made of wood.*

⑤ <u>Cause / Reason</u>: で also marks the Adverbial Complement of Cause (why), although it's rather weak — we don't place much emphasis on the "reason" for something.

● 理絵ちゃんは病気で仕事を休んだ

Rie didn't go to work because she was sick.

● 竜くんは趣味でホームページを作る

Ryū makes web sites as a hobby.

⑥ <u>Quantity</u>: The last usage of で we will see indicates the Adverbial Complement of Quantity (how much / many).

● あのおもちゃは３０００円で買える

You can buy that toy for 3,000 yen.

● 車は１０人で持ち上げることができた

We managed to lift the car between the 10 of us.

Usages of *de*	
Place	学生は寮でケーキをつくる The student makes a cake in the dorm
Time	学生は一日でケーキをつくる The student makes a cake in one day
Required time	学生は３時間でケーキをつくる The student makes a cake in 3 hours
Manner / Instrument	学生はオーブンでケーキをつくる The student makes a cake in the oven
Material	学生はいちごでケーキをつくる The student makes a cake with strawberries
Cause	学生は義務でケーキをつくる The student makes a cake as an obligation
Quantity	学生は一人でケーキをつくる The student makes a cake alone

がくせい: student | ケーキ: cake | りょう: dorm | いちにち: one day
オーブン: oven | いちご: strawberry | ぎむ: obligation | ひとり: alone

The particle へ

After the great number of usages and functions of the particles に and で, we'd better take a rest. This is just what we will do then, with the particle へ, one of the easiest to learn, because it only has one function. へ – pronounced *e* and not *he* when it functions as a grammatical particle– is only used to indicate the Adverbial Complement of Direction (where to).

● 日本へ行きたがっている人が大勢います *There are many people who want to go to Japan.*
● 空港へ妹を迎えに行った *I went to the airport to welcome (to meet) my sister.*

Note: へ and に (when they mean "direction") can be used in a practically identical and interchangeable way in most cases; there are almost no exceptions.

● 彼はドイツへ / に勉強しに行く *He is going to Germany to study.*

Usage of two particles at once

One of the peculiarities about particles is that two of them can sometimes be combined and appear together. This happens, for example, with the topic particle は, which can be combined with に, で and へ to indicate "topic / emphasis + something" (L.37).

● 池には亀がいる *"Talking about the pond," there is a turtle in it.*
● 中国へは行きたいが、ちょっと怖い *I do want to go to China, but it scares me a little.*

Note: は can never be combined with が and を because it directly replaces them.

Other possible particle combinations are での (広島での仕事はおもしろくない *The job in Hiroshima is not interesting*), への (日本への飛行機は少ない *There are few planes flying to Japan*), にも (家にも犬がいる *There is a dog at home too*), へも and でも.

The usage of でも

The combination でも can have two completely different meanings. The first is a mere combination of both particles (で = AC + も = also / neither).

● 電車の中でも勉強できる *You can study in the train too.*

The second でも has nothing to do with particle combinations, and means "even." We will see more about で＋も in the manga-examples.

● 子どもでもこの文章が分かる *Even a child can understand this sentence.*

Note: The words 誰でも *(anybody)*, 何でも *(anything)*, いつでも *(any time)*, and どこでも *(anywhere)* also use the combination でも.

漫画例　Manga-examples

As usual, we will now see a few examples in panels which will help us clarify the different usages of particles に, で, and へ. Nothing better than a few situations with real usage to clear up ideas and see Japanese language being used in different situations.

a) *ni* as place particle (existence)

Christine: このパーティーにはいなかったわ。仕事は終わりよ。
this party PP TOP *not be* EP. *Work top finish* EP
He wasn't at this party. Work is over.

Studio Kōsen

このパーティーには
いなかったわ。
仕事は終わりよ。

Here is an example of the usage of the particle に as an indicator of the Adverbial Complement of Place in its "existence" mode. It's the first usage of に we studied in this lesson.

In her sentence, Christine tells us the person she was looking for "was not" or, in other words, "did not exist" (いなかった) at the party. いなかった, as you know, is the simple past-negative form of the verb いる (*to be*, with animate objects, L.18, book 1). Indeed, both verbs of existence in Japanese, いる and ある, require the particle に to indicate the ACP that goes with them.

The second point to mention in this first manga-example is the simultaneous usage of two particles, the particle of existence for ACP に and the topic particle は. When adding は after に, we stress the ACP in the sentence, turning it into the "topic" we are talking about (L.37). Here, and exaggerating the example, the sentence would be literally translated as: *Talking about this party, (he / she) was not there.* It is very common to use は after particles に or で when the complement marked by them becomes the topic in the sentence.

b) *ni* as place particle (direct contact)

> Kenji: ここに書_かいてある
> *here* PP *written (perm.)*
> **It is written here.**

Here is a new example of the usage of the particle に, this time as the indicator of the ACP expressing direct contact, refer

Gabriel Luque

to #4 which we saw in the theory section. The action of "writing" must obviously be done "on" some surface, be that paper, wood, metal, or any other thing. In this example, we are not told on what kind of surface the writing is, we are just told where it is with the word ここ (*here*, L.34, obviously an ACP), which must be marked with the particle に. Another, perhaps even clearer, example would be: 紙_{かみ}に書_かいてある *It is written on the paper.*

Note: Notice how the construction 〜てある is used here. This construction was studied in L.35 and you probably remember it indicates "finished action (and it continues unchanged)."

c) *ni* as Indirect Object particle

> Locutor: サァこのボールはM・F大島_{ミッドフィールダーおおしま}くんにわたった！
> *oh this ball top midfield player Ōshima (noun suf)* DP
> **Well (now), the ball has gone over to midfielder Ōshima!**

Here we have a good example of the usage of に as a particle marking the Indirect Object, that is, "whom," "who for" the action is performed (usage #6).

In this case, it is the ball (ボール) that goes over to Ōshima. We all learned at school that to identify the IO we must ask "whom." Thus: "Whom did the ball go to?"

Javier Bolado

Answer: "Ōshima." Therefore it is obvious that the IO is Ōshima and that it must go with the particle に.

Note: In this example we find as well the usage of the particle は (L.37) as topic particle (here, "the ball"), and この, a word of the *kosoado* kind (*this*, L.34).

d) *de* as a cause particle

Yumiko: あたしは受験勉強で忙しいんだからねっ。
I TOP exam study CAP busy be because EP
Let me tell you I'm busy studying for the exams.

Javier Bolado

Here we have an example of the usage #5 of particle で, as a marker of the Adverbial Complement of Cause.

The particle で is used to express cause or reason (why?) but in a rather weak manner. In other words, these are cause-effect sentences which could almost be considered a pure "link of two sentences," since their causal relationship is hardly stressed. In this case, the effect is "I'm busy" and its cause (marked with で) is "I'm studying for the exams."

In lesson 41, and in lesson 48 of book 3, we will see two cause-effect connectors, から and ので, with a much stronger meaning than this で. But remember we've already had a glance at the usage of から as the answer to どうして *(why)* in L.34.

e) Two combined particles

Mayeen: 地球の美人がここでは化け物…
Earth POP beauty SP here PP TOP monster...
Beautiful women of Earth are monsters here...

A new example of the combination of two particles, で and は here. The particle は, as we are well aware of by now, is used to indicate the "topic" in the sentence.

The で we see here corresponds to the first studied one, that is, to its usage as the marker of ACP. If the ACP indicates "existence" or "permanence" it is indicated with に, but if it only indicates "place where the action is performed," we always use で. In this example, the "action" is the fact of "being monsters" (it isn't existence nor per-

J.M. Ken Niimura

manence, therefore its ACP will go with で), and its ACP is the *kosoado* word ここ *(here,* L.34), indicated, indeed, by the particle で.

f) The particle *e*

We will now study the usage of the Adverbial Complement of Direction particle, that is, "where to" or the place the subject is going to. へ is only used with verbs of movement such as 行く (*to go*), 来る (*to come*), 移動する (*to move*), and other similar verbs. In our sentence, the verb is 行く (*to go*) and the place the subject

Studio Kōsen

Hiyama: 優勝してブラジルへ行くんだ！
win do Brazil DP go be!
I'll win and I'll go to Brazil!

is going to is ブラジル (*Brazil*), which is marked with へ. The particle に (refer to #3 in the theory section) could also be used here. **Note:** Notice the connection between the two sentences "win" and "go to Brazil," which is formed with the *-te* form (L.35).

g) A different usage of *de+mo*

Tokurō: トイレでもこわれたのかな？
toilet or something broken Q? Q?
Is the toilet or something out of order?

Bárbara Raya

でも can have several usages, like the mere combination of meanings of the particles で (AC) and も (*too*), and other usages that have nothing to do with particles. For example, in the theory section we saw that でも has the meaning of "even," or that added to an adverb or an interrogative pronoun, it indicates "any." Likewise, in L.49 (book 3) we will see でも can also mean "but." However, でも in this example does not fall into any of these categories. In this case, でも has the connotation of indicating an undefined possibility: in the example, Tokurō doesn't specifically say "the toilet is out of order" (where the subject particle が would be used), but he ventures that the "the toilet or something" may be out of order. We will get a clearer idea by analyzing the ultimate Japanese sentence "to ask someone out": お茶でも飲みにいこうか？ *Why don't we go have a tea or something?* This でも can include things like tea, coffee, a soft drink, an ice-cream..., whatever.

1 Translate into Japanese the sentence: "In the university there is a bookstore." (university: 大学, bookstore: 本屋)

2 Translate into Japanese the sentence: "I go into the shop." (shop: 店)

3 Is the sentence 来年に経済を勉強するつもりだ correct? Why? (来年: next year, 経済: economics, 勉強する: to study)

4 Translate into Japanese the sentence: "Tarō gives Hanako a flower." (Tarō: 太郎, to give: あげる, flower: 花, Hanako: 花子)

5 What is the difference between 道に絵を描く and 道で絵を描く, and why? (道: road, 絵: drawing, 描く: to draw)

6 Translate the sentence: "Naoko cut a cake with a knife." (Naoko: 直子, to cut: 切る, cake: ケーキ, knife: ナイフ)

7 Translate the sentence: "I want to go back to LA." (to go back: 帰る, LA: ロス) What particle have you used, and why?

8 Turn into the sentence topic the part of the sentence "in the university," which you formed in question 1.

9 Translate into English: 誰でもこの文章を読める。(文章: sentence, 読む: to read)

10 What different usages can でも have? List them and give an example for each of them.

第39課：日本の交通手段

Lesson 39: Transport in Japan

Here we have another conversational lesson, with which we can learn lots of vocabulary, and where we have the chance to practice and make the best use of the grammar points we have learned up to now. Here we will focus on the means of transport we will probably be using when we go to Japan: train, subway, taxi and bus.

Taxi

Let's start the lesson having a look at a few sentences we can use when taking a taxi. It is worth mentioning that Japanese taxis are very expensive and, therefore, we probably won't be using them too often. A curiosity about Japanese taxis is that they all have automatic doors; that is, they open by themselves right in front of the passenger. Don't try to open one or you'll get a surprise!

● タクシー乗り場はどこですか？ *Where is the taxi stop?* (L.34)
● 浅草ホテルまでお願いします *To Asakusa Hotel, please.* (L.33)
● この住所に行ってください *Go to this address, please.* (L.24/35)
● 次の角を左に曲がってください *Turn left on the next corner.*
● ここで止めてください *Stop here, please.* (L.34)
● いくらですか？ *How much is it?* (L.34)

Transport		Taxi and bus			
bicycle	自転車	basic fare	基本料金	stop button	下車ボタン
bus	バス	bus stop	バス乗り場	straight ahead	まっすぐ
car	自動車｜車 bike	(loose) change	両替	taximeter	メーター
motorcycle	バイク	change	お釣り	taxi stop	タクシー乗り場
ship	船	corner	角	(to the) left	左 (へ)
subway	地下鉄	crossing	交差点	(to the) right	右 (へ)
taxi	タクシー	door	扉｜ドア	traffic light	信号
train	電車	driver	運転手	vacant	空車

Bus

We most probably won't be using municipal buses, because there is a great number of lines and using them can be very complicated, although in some rural areas we'll have no other option. As regards to long-distance services, if we have the JR Pass (see "Cultural Note"), we won't even consider getting on anything that is not a train. However, let's see some sentences that can be helpful when we are touring.

- 金閣寺行きのバス乗り場はどこですか？ *Where is the bus stop for buses heading to Kinkakuji?*
- このバスは鎌倉大仏へ行きますか？ *Does this bus go to the Great Buddha in Kamakura?*
- 大阪駅までいくらですか？ *How much is it to Osaka Station?* (L.34)
- 空港行きのバスは何時に出ますか？ *At what time does the bus to the airport leave?*
- 次のバスは何時に出ますか？ *At what time does the next bus leave?* (L.34)
- 宮島までどれくらい時間がかかりますか？ *How long does it take to Miyajima?*
- 日光東照宮に着いたら教えてください *Please, tell me when we arrive at the Tōshōgū in Nikkō.*
- 次で降ります *I'll get off at the next (stop).*

Note: You have probably noticed there are two words for "change" in the vocabulary table. The first one, 両替, is the "loose change" we are given when exchanging a note for coins. The second one, お釣り, is the "change" we are given when paying for something.

Subway and local trains

In Japan, trains rule, and we will certainly be using them very often, especially in large cities. In fact, Tokyo's subsoil has been bored for twelve subway lines... And these don't include the eighteen railway lines which cross the city above ground. The most famous railway line in all of Japan, the Yamanote (山手線), is a JR (Japan Railways) circular line with stops at most key centers in Tokyo, such as 東京, 池袋, 新宿, 原宿, 渋谷, 恵比寿, 品川... If you go to Tokyo, sooner or later you'll get on the Yamanote, as well as on the subway and on the many private railway lines which run all over the city.

First of all, we will need to buy a ticket. We will do this from special ticket vending machines. There will be a fare chart above the machines, telling us the price for the journey we want to make. In Japan, you pay depending on the distance, there isn't a standard price; if we are going further, we'll pay more. Besides, the concept of "multiple-journey subway pass" is almost non-existent, so buying a ticket for each journey is advisable.

We'll start, then, buying the ticket, perhaps one of the most difficult challenges facing the foreign visitor who is on his own.

● ここから一番近い地下鉄の駅はどこですか？ *Where is the closest subway station?*

● 切符はどこで買えますか？ *Where do you buy tickets?* (L.32 / 34)

● 渋谷までいくらですか？ *How much is it to Shibuya?* (L.34)

● 切符の自販機の使い方を教えてください

Could you please show me how the ticket vending machine works?

More situations

We will now see more possible situations on our trip by local train or subway. It's worth mentioning that most sentences can also be applied to trams, although these only exist in cities like Hiroshima, Nagasaki, and a few others.

● 地下鉄路線図を一枚ください *Can I have a subway map, please?*

● 時刻表をください *Can I have a timetable, please?*

● 一日乗車券はいくらですか？ *How much is a one-day pass?* (L.34)

● 梅田行きのホームはどれですか？ *Which is the platform for Umeda?* (L.34)

● この列車は秋田に止まりますか？ *Does this train stop at Akita?*

● 中央線に乗り換えたいんですが、何番線ですか？

I'd like to change to the Chūō line, what is the platform number? (L.31/34/37)

Beware of the ticket gates in stations! Almost all stations in large cities have automatic ticket gates which will open once the ticket has been put in, both going into the station and coming out. The machine automatically calculates if we have paid the right fare for our journey and, if we haven't..., the gates slam shut! Not letting us out! Not to worry though, aside from a little embarrassment, no harm will be done. If this happens, all we need to do is go to a machine called 清算機 *(fare adjustment machine)*, put our ticket in, and pay the remainder. Only then will we be able to leave the station.

● 南改札口はどこですか？ *Where are the south exit gates?* (L.34)

● 清算機はどこですか？ *Where is the fare adjustment machine?* (L.34)

● 清算機の使い方を教えてください

Please, show me how the fare adjustment machine works.

● 歌舞伎町の出口はどこですか？ *Which is the Kabukichō exit?*

● １１番出口です *It's exit number 11.*

Train					
bullet train	新幹線	going to x	〜行き	station	駅
change / transfer	乗り換え	last train	終電	subway map	路線図
coin locker	コインロッカー	non-smoking car	禁煙車	super-express train	特急列車
conductor	車掌	one-day pass	一日乗車券	terminal	終点
entrance	入口	ordinary train	普通列車	ticket	切符
exit	出口	platform	ホーム	ticket gate	改札
express train	急行列車	platform #x	〜番線	ticket office	切符売り場
fare	運賃	reserved seat	指定席	ticket vending machine	切符自販機
first class	グリーン車	seat for senior citizens	シルバーシート	timetable	時刻表
first train	始発	smoking car	喫煙車	unreserved seat	自由席

Long-distance trains and the Shinkansen

Finally, we will take a look at some situations which can happen on long-distance trains and on the famous and extremely fast bullet train, the Shinkansen.

- 切符売り場はどこですか？ *Where is the ticket office?* (L.34)
- 広島までの片道切符を一枚ください *A one way ticket to Hiroshima, please.*
- 仙台行きの新幹線を予約したいんですが *I'd like to reserve a seat on the Shinkansen to Sendai.*
- 次の京都行きの新幹線は何時発ですか？ *At what time does the next Shinkansen to Kyoto leave?*
- 禁煙席にしてください *A non-smoking seat, please.*
- 札幌行きの特急列車は何番線から発車しますか？

  From what platform does the express to Sapporo leave?
- ここに座ってもいいですか？ *May I sit here?* (L.32)

Problems of various kinds

Now we will see sentences that can be helpful when facing the most frequent problems.

- 切符をなくしてしまいました *I have lost my ticket.* (L.35)
- どこから乗りましたか？ *Where did you get on the train?* | 姫路です *In Himeji.*
- 乗り越ししてしまいました *I've completely past my stop.* (L.35)
- 列車を間違えました *I've got on the wrong train.*
- 乗り遅れてしまいました *I've completely missed my train.* (L.35)
- 予約を変更したいのですが... *I'd like to change my reservation, but...* (L.32/37)
- 払い戻ししたいのですが... *I'd like to get a refund (for my ticket), but...*

文化編：新幹線
Cultural note: The Shinkansen

Literally, the word 新幹線 means *new* (新) *trunk* (幹) *line* (線), although it is really the name given to the modern Japanese network of bullet trains. The first 新幹線 line, the famous 東海道線 –which links the capital, 東京, with the second most influential city in the country, 大阪 – was opened on the 1st of October, 1964, on the occasion of the Olympic Games celebrated in Tokyo that same year.

However, long before that, in 1939, there were already plans to build a network of high-speed trains. The then militarist Japanese Empire intended to link 東京 with 下関, south of the main island, 本州, to make it go all the way to Europe, via Korea and north

The stylish and aerodynamic Nagano Shinkansen (Photo: M. Bernabé)

China, which were Japanese possessions at the time!

Obviously, this plan was never realized, but handed down to the future builders of the new line a few half-finished tunnels which sped up the execution of the project.

Nowadays, there are several 新幹線 lines which cover the country from the city of 八戸 (north of 本州) to 鹿児島, the most southern city in the southern island of 九州. There are also plans to make bullet trains go as far as 札幌, in the northern island of 北海道.

Since its opening in 1964, the 新幹線 has never had a serious accident –except for a derailment with no victims in 2004, due to a very severe earthquake–, and has been amazingly successful, probably due to the strict application of the "3 S" and the "3 C," which were the slogans during its construction: *Security, Speedy, Surely* and *Cheap, Comfortable* and *Carefully*.

The aerodynamic 新幹線, which can reach 300 km/h (with an average speed of 200 km/h), transports a daily average of 700,000 people through thousands of kilometers of railroad tracks. If you are a tourist in Japan, it is highly recommended that you buy a Japan Rail Pass, a pass allowing you to get on all JR trains, including most of the 新幹線, for one, two, or three weeks. You can find more information in www.japanrailpass.net.

Let's see now a few examples in panels which will allow us to see some dialogues and situations related with the Japanese means of transport. The star in the lesson is, undoubtedly, the train, the true king of Japanese transport.

a) Announcement at stations

Sign: せんげん台駅
Sengendai station
Sengendai station.

Announcement: 準急浅草行きがまいります。
local express Asakusa direction SP come
The local express to Asakusa is entering the station.

We have lots of information in this first example. First of all, we will see a station name: せんげん台. We have already learned that "station" in Japanese is 駅. All stations are called 〜駅, like 東京駅 (Tokyo station), 石橋駅 (Ishibashi station), etc. Then, we have the word 準急 (local express). Generally, there are three kinds of trains, from the slowest to the fastest: 普通 or 各駅停車 (normal), 急行 (express), and 特急 (super-express), even though these names may vary depending on the railway company. The 準急 in the example is probably equivalent to an express train 急行.

Bárbara Raya

Finally, we have part of one of those frequent announcements we can hear in a Japanese station. They are always accompanied by very characteristic and curious melodies, which vary depending on the railway company. The complete version could be: 間もなく、X番線に準急浅草行きがまいります。危ないですから白線の内側までお下がりください *Presently, the local express to Asakusa will arrive at platform x. Because it is dangerous, please step back (and wait) behind the white line.*

Notes: 〜行き means *bound to x*. まいる is the humble version of 来る *(to come)* (L.52).

b) In the taxi

Rie: 太田の〇〇町まで
Ōta pop xx suburb to
To the suburb of xx in Ōta.

Gabriel Luque

Here is an example of what you say when you get in a taxi and you tell the driver where you want to go. It would be better to add お願いします *(please)* at the end, of course. 太田 is a city in the prefecture of 群馬, and 町 is a suffix which we add to a proper name and which means either "suburb of" (片倉町, *suburb of Katakura*), or "town of" (磯部町, *town of Isobe*). Here, the author has not wanted to make the name of the suburb clear, and has used two circles which are used when we don't want to specify. The Japanese use these circles – which they call まるまる – just like we use the x: 〇〇 さん *Mr. x.* 〇〇市 *The city of x.* Usually each circle replaces one kanji.

Note: The driver answers へぃ, which is a twisted way of saying はい *(yes)*.

c) Bus stop

Emi: あなたは？   **Miho:** すいません、バス乗り場がわからなくて…
you TOP?   *I'm sorry, bus stop SP not know...*
You?   **I'm sorry, I couldn't find the bus stop and...**

Studio Kōsen

Here is a sentence we can use as an excuse if we are late for an appointment. The word we will point out is バス乗り場, *bus stop*, which we already studied in the theory section. Let's analyze the rest:

Notice how Emi only says あなた (*you*, L.7, book 1) and は (topic particle, L.37). The sentence is cut, but obviously means *(Who are) you?* Leaving out parts of a sentence and assuming it is understood in the context is very frequent in spoken Japanese. すいません is a spoken distortion of the word すみません (*I'm sorry*). Now take a look at the ～がわ からなくて... As you know, the verb わかる *(to know)* requires the particle が (L.37). And here it is in the negative *-te* form, indicating the sentence is incomplete.

d) Ticket gates at train stations

J.M. Ken Niimura

Man: ありゃ期限切れの定期入れちゃったよ。
(excl.) period finished POP *pass put in* EP
Damn! I've put in my expired pass.

In this example we see how the wickets at train stations work: you put in your 切符 *(ticket)* or your 定期券 *(monthly pass)* – used by almost all Japanese サラリーマン *(office workers)* to go to work – and the small doors open. If the pass has expired, like in this case, or if the fare we've paid is not enough, the doors will slam shut. This is exactly what happens to the guy in this example.

Note: The man says 入れちゃった, which is the colloquial form of 入れてしまった. The verb 入れる means "to put in" and the form ~てしまう, as you will remember from L.35, gives the sentence the meaning of "doing something one regrets" or "doing something by mistake."

e) Inside the train

Kazuo: あは〜満員電車っていいもんだなァ
ooh full train good thing be EP
Ooh, I love jam-packed trains.

As you probably know, Japanese trains 電車 are world famous for being jam-packed with passengers (満員) at rush hour, just like in the example. However, some people, like our friend Kazuo, enjoy it more than others!
No kidding, the fact is that the Japanese railway network's quantity and quality are impressive – delays hardly exist, and the numerous trains arrive almost miraculously

Bárbara Raya

on the second –. Were we to compare it to the human circulatory system, the Japan Railways (JR) Shinkansen network would be the main arteries and veins, the main JR railway lines would be the secondary arteries and veins, and the numerous private railway and subway lines would be the capillaries. In metropolitan areas, you can go almost anywhere exclusively by train and subway.

f) The Shinkansen

The Shinkansen bullet train is the most popular means of transport for long distances in Japan. Fast, safe and comfortable, its network stretches to most main cities in the Japanese archipelago, as we saw in the "Cultural Note." In this example we have a lot of information, like the words 〜発 (departing from), 〜行き (bound for), the expression 〜番線ホーム (platform for line x), or the verb 発車する (to depart, in terms of a train, a car...).

Gabriel Luque

All 新幹線 trains have proper names. In this case, it is the あさひ going from 東京 to 新潟 on the 上越 line. In the case of the famous 東海道〜山陽 (from 東京 to 博多) line, the trains are called, from the slowest to the fastest, こだま (echo), ひかり (light), and のぞみ (wish).

Annou.: 東京発新潟行あさひ３３３号、２１番線ホームから発車します
Tokyo departure Niigata going to Asahi 333 numb., 21 numb. platform from depart
The Asahi 333 from Tokyo to Niigata will depart from platform 21.

g) Ticket prices

J.M. Ken Niimura

In this last panel, which illustrates the ticket vending machines (below) and the fare chart (above) that tells us how to determine our ticket price. The board represents the 東京 monorail (モノレール線) which goes from 羽田 airport to 浜松町 station, where you can change onto the JR company's famous and practical 山手線 circular line.

To check the price, we must first find in the board the station where we are (marked with 当駅, *this station*). Then, we must look for the station we are going to and check the price it shows. Imagine we are going to 大井競馬場前: in this case, from our station (整備場), the adult (大人) fare will cost us 260 yen and the child (小人) fare 130. At first, it may seem complicated, but don't worry, it's just a matter of getting used to it, and almost all price boards are also in English.

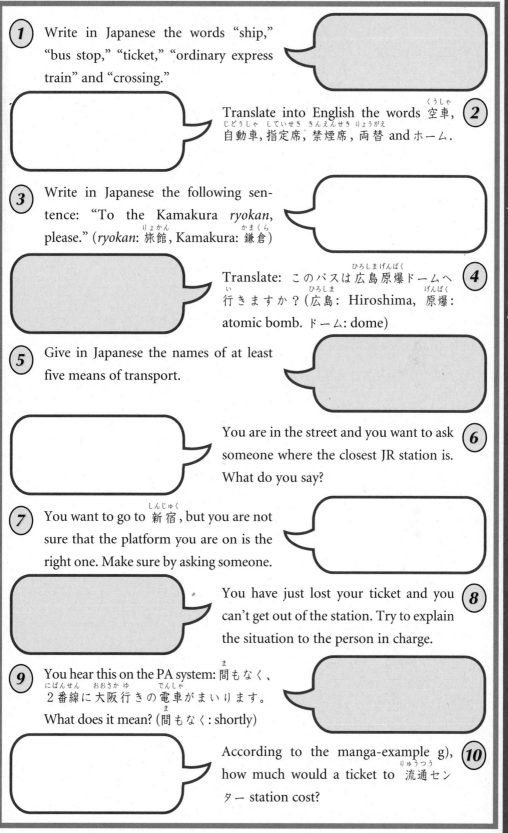

1. Write in Japanese the words "ship," "bus stop," "ticket," "ordinary express train" and "crossing."

2. Translate into English the words 空車 (くうしゃ), 自動車 (じどうしゃ), 指定席 (していせき), 禁煙席 (きんえんせき), 両替 (りょうがえ) and ホーム.

3. Write in Japanese the following sentence: "To the Kamakura *ryokan*, please." (*ryokan*: 旅館 (りょかん), Kamakura: 鎌倉 (かまくら))

4. Translate: このバスは広島原爆ドームへ行きますか？ (広島 (ひろしま): Hiroshima, 原爆 (げんばく): atomic bomb. ドーム: dome) (広島原爆 ひろしまげんばく, 行 い)

5. Give in Japanese the names of at least five means of transport.

6. You are in the street and you want to ask someone where the closest JR station is. What do you say?

7. You want to go to 新宿 (しんじゅく), but you are not sure that the platform you are on is the right one. Make sure by asking someone.

8. You have just lost your ticket and you can't get out of the station. Try to explain the situation to the person in charge.

9. You hear this on the PA system: 間もなく、２番線に大阪行きの電車がまいります。 What does it mean? (間もなく (ま): shortly) (にばんせん, おおさかゆ, でんしゃ)

10. According to the manga-example g), how much would a ticket to 流通センター (りゅうつう) station cost?

Lesson 40: Particles (3) no/o

After the "rest" we took with the previous lesson, we are going back to the harder grammar lessons, where we'll study in depth two more particles. With this lesson and the next one, we will have seen most usages of the Japanese grammatical particles.

The particle の

We mentioned in lesson 16 (book 1), when we gave a very general view of particles, that the particle の is used to mark the "possessive:" this statement was made hoping to simplify and generally introduce this particle. However, now that our knowledge is greater than 24 lessons ago, this is the perfect time for a rigorous and in-depth study of the various usages of の.

Before going on, it's worth defining what a "noun modifier" is. A noun (L.11, book 1) can be on its own or it can come with other words that describe it or complement its characteristics. These words are called "modifiers." Thus, it isn't the same saying "house" as opposed to saying "red house" or "Akira's red house." The adjective "red," as well as the proper noun "Akira" – connected by the genitive "'s"– modify the noun, giving more information about it or complementing it.

の as modifier

①　Noun modifier: The particle の is, then, the Japanese way to mark the noun modifier when this modifier is either another noun or a noun phrase. In short, we use の to connect two or more nouns.

If we simplify, we can distinguish up to five kinds of modifiers in Japanese: possessive, descriptive, positional, that of a creator, and appositional.

1-1 Possessive: it is the usage of の we already knew. It obviously indicates "possession."
● 私の家は広いです *The house of I (my house) is roomy*
● 筒井さんの車は小さくて赤いです *Mr. Tsutsui's car is red and small.*

1-2 Descriptive: It simply describes the noun, giving more information about it.

● これは鉄のパイプです *This is a steel pipe.*

● これは果物の店です *This is a fruit store.*

1-3 Positional: It describes the place where the modified noun is located.

● 木の下で休みたい *I want to rest under a tree.*

● 明はフランスの大学で勉強している *Akira is studying at a French university.*

1-4 Of a creator: It indicates the creator of something.

● 夏目漱石の小説を読んでください *Read Sōseki Natsume's novels, please.*

● アイヌの文化は興味深いです *The Ainu culture is interesting.*

1-5 Appositional: An apposition, in English, is a construction which isn't explicitly connected to any word — it is usually separated by comas— but which refers or explains something relative to a noun. In Japanese, however, it is connected to the noun it modifies.

● はじめまして。部長の田辺です *Pleased to meet you. I'm Tanabe, the head of the department.*

● 友達の広美ちゃんは結婚しました *Hiromi, my friend, got married.*

Indefinite pronoun and nominalizer

We will now see two usages of の, different to those we have studied until now: the indefinite pronoun and the nominalizer.

② **Indefinite pronoun:** の replaces a noun when the interlocutors know from the context, or the situation, what they are talking about.

● a) どんな映画が好きですか？

What kind of films do you like?

● b) アクションのが好きです

I like action ones.

We clearly see here how the の in the second sentence replaces the word 映画.

● どんなパンにする？

Which bun will you choose? (L.34)

● 甘いのが食べたい

I want to eat a sweet one.

Usages of *no*		
Possession	これは先生の本です	This is the teacher's book
Description	これは経済の本です	This is a book on economics
Positional	机の上に本があります	On the desk there is a book
Creator	ゲーテの本を読みたい	I want to read a book by Goethe
Appositional	私は先生の岡本です	I'm Okamoto, the teacher
Indefinite pronoun	これは私のです	This is mine
Nominalizer	本を書くのは難しいです	Writing a book is difficult
Question (colloquial)	本を書くのは難しいの？	Is it difficult to write a book?
Soft statement (feminine)	ゲーテの本を読みたいの	I'd like to read a book by Goethe
Explanation (manga-example d)	本を書いているのです	I'm writing a book

せんせい: teacher | ほん: book | けいざい: economics | つくえ: desk
うえ: on top of | よ,P: te read | か,-: to write | むずか,fl,M: difficult

(3) <u>Nominalizer</u>: To "nominalize" a sentence is to turn it into a noun phrase so that it works like a noun. For example, in the sentence "*riding a motorcycle* is difficult," the part in italics functions like a noun. Notice how this part can be replaced with a noun, for example, "*chemistry* is difficult." This hint will help you identify a verb or a sentence which has been nominalized.

In Japanese, then, の is used to nominalize sentences. We can also use the word こと, but we will go into this in depth in L.57 (book 3).

● バイクを運転するのは難しいです *Riding a motorcycle is difficult.*
● 水泳をしに行くのは楽しいです *Going swimming is fun.*
● 私は広子がどんな音楽が好きなのか知らない *I don't know what kind of music Hiroko likes.*

At the end of a sentence

We saw in L.17 how の functions as an end-of-the-sentence particle with the meanings of informal question and softened statement, as well as a soft command.

(4) <u>Question</u>: In the informal register, の replaces か (L.34) to indicate "question." It is worth mentioning な must be placed between の and -na adjectives (as well as nouns).

● 明日、何時に京都へ行くの？ *At what time are you going to Kyoto tomorrow?*
● あの人は本当に先生なの？ *Is that person really a teacher?*

(5) <u>Statement / Soft order</u>: This is used basically by women and children.

● 私はね、パリに何度も行ったの *As for me, I've been to Paris many times.*
● しんちゃん、それに触れないの！ *Shin, don't touch that!*

The particle を

As we briefly studied in L.16 (book 1), the particle を — which is always pronounced *o* and never *wo* — is used to indicate the Direct Object (DO), that is, "what" receives the verb's action. However, it has other usages as well.

(1) <u>Direct Object</u>:

● 太郎はパンを食べます *Tarō eats bread.*
● 哲治くんはスペイン語を勉強しています *Tetsuharu is studying Spanish.*

Note: There are certain constructions which we consider DO but which are not marked with を, as is the case among those verbs requiring が (L.37).

● 私は日本語が[notを]分かりません *I don't understand Japanese.*

Usages of o	
Direct Object	私(わたし)はりんごを食べます I eat an apple
Place of passage	私は橋を渡る I cross a bridge
Place from which one parts	私は電車を降りる I get off the train
Time passed	冬をハワイで過ごしたい I want to spend winter in Hawaii

りんご apple | 食たべる: to eat | 橋はし: bridge | 渡わたる: to cross | 冬ふゆ: winter | ハワイ: Hawaii | 過すごす: to spend | 電車でんしゃ: train | 降おりる: to get off

Other usages of を

② <u>Place of passage:</u> を can also be used to indicate the space where a movement is done.

● 鳥(とり)は空(そら)を飛(と)びます

Birds fly through the sky.

● 彼(かれ)はいつも街(まち)を歩(ある)きます

He always walks around town.

This usage of を requires, of course, that the verb be one of movement, such as 歩(ある)く *(to walk)*, 走(はし)る *(to run)*, 飛(と)ぶ *(to fly)*, 通(とお)る *(to pass)*, 渡(わた)る *(to cross)*, etc.

③ <u>Place where a movement starts:</u> を marks as well the Adverbial Complement of Place which indicates the origin of a movement "outwards" (be careful, though, the "movement" may be abstract). It is usually used together with the verbs 出(で)る *(to go out)*, 降(お)りる *(to get off a vehicle)*, 離(はな)れる *(to part from)*, and similar ones.

● 里奈(りな)さんは6時(ろくじ)に家(いえ)を出(で)た *Rina left home at 6.*
● 電車(でんしゃ)を降(お)りる時(とき)、注意(ちゅうい)してください *When you get off the train, be careful.*
● 社長(しゃちょう)は大学(だいがく)を卒業(そつぎょう)していないよ *The director has not graduated from university.*

④ <u>Time period:</u> Finally, を can be used as well to indicate the passing of periods of time, although this is a minor usage and not very frequent.

● 私(わたし)は夏(なつ)を沖縄(おきなわ)で過(す)ごした *I spent all summer in Okinawa.*
● 彼(かれ)は3ヶ月間(さんかげつかん)を無駄(むだ)にした *He wasted three months.*

A few adverbs

We hope you have understood well the different usages of the particles の and を. You have already seen, in these few last lessons, particles can have many different usages and may seem really difficult. However, the fact is that they are indispensable to making grammatically sound sentences in Japanese, and the student must get used to dealing with them as soon as possible. Don't worry if you get confused right now: with time and practice you'll soon master them.

We will now take a little well-deserved break, studying a few time adverbs, widely used in Japanese.

The adverbs もう and まだ

The adverbs of time もう — which has nothing to do with the particle も, and which is pronounced *moh*, with a "long" *o* — and まだ are usually studied together. Their relationship is obvious, since もう can be translated as "already" and まだ as "still."

もう indicates something is not in the same state as it was before.

● 山田さんはもう昼ご飯を食べた *Mr. Yamada has already eaten his lunch.*
● 利香はもう宿題をしました *Rika has already finished her homework.*
● リックはもう中国語を勉強していない *Rick doesn't study Chinese any longer.*

Whereas まだ expresses the opposite idea of もう: it indicates something is still in the same state as it was before.

● カレーはまだ残っていますか？ *Is there still some curry left?*
● まだ何もを食べていないよ *I still haven't eaten anything.*
● 私はまだ日本人のことを理解できない *I'm still unable to understand the Japanese.*

The adverbs くらい and ごろ

The adverbs くらい and ごろ are usually both translated as "approximately" or "more or less." However, their usage is very different, so we must be careful not to confuse them.

くらい and ぐらい are used to indicate an approximate quantity, be it either of volume, money, time, or any other thing. When having this nuance of "aproximate something," くらい and ぐらい have almost no difference of usage or meaning.

● この間、梨を２キロぐらい買ったよ *The other day I bought more or less two kilos of pears.*
● そのバイクは２百万円くらいです *That motorcycle costs about two million yen.*

Be careful, as くらい is sometimes used in contemptuous tone, meaning "at least."

● 一点ぐらい入れろよ、お前！ *At least put one point in, kid!*

Whereas ごろ refers to an approximate "period of time:"

● １０時ごろに家を出ますよ *We will leave home at about ten.*
● 日本は６月ごろに梅雨があります *In Japan the rain season is some time in June.*

Last of all, take a look at these sentences to get a clear idea of the difference between ごろ and くらい:

● 私は５時間ぐらい働きました *I worked for about five hours.*
● 私は５時ごろに働きに行った *I went to work at about five.*

Now let's go on to analyze, through practice, some of the usages we have studied in the previous pages. Generally speaking, の and を are among the least difficult particles to master. However, a few examples should help us set in what we've learned.

a) *o* in DO and nominalizing *no*

Gerne: この星でぜいたくなたべものをたべているのは旅行者だけ...
ほし　　　　　　　　　　　　　　　　　　　　りょこうしゃ
this star PP luxurious food DOP eat (nom.) TOP traveler only...
On this planet, only travelers can eat sumptuous food...

Studio Kōsen

Let's start the manga-examples with a double example, since we have both an を and a の in the same panel.

Before going straight into the subject, notice, too, how there is a で of place (L.38), and the omnipresent topic particle は, which turns the whole sentence into the topic of the conversation (L.37).

The sentence marked with は functions just like a noun, that is, it has been nominalized. And what part of speech has been in charge of this? The の, which, as we saw a few pages ago, also has this function. The sentence この星でぜいた
ほし
くな食べ物を食べている (*On this planet they eat*
た　もの　た
sumptuous food), because of a の, becomes a noun like any other, with its same characteristics.

As to the を, it functions as a Direct Object particle in the sub sentence 食べ物を食べて
た　もの　た
いる (*to be eating food*). As you know, if we want to find out which is the DO in a sentence, we ask "what" to the verb. Question: 何を食べているか? (*What is she eating?*)
なに　た
Answer: 食べ物 (*food*). Thus, it is clear that the DO is 食べ物 and that is must be marked
た　もの　　　　　　　　　　　　　　　　　　　　　　　　た　もの
with the particle を. If you always do it this way, you won't go wrong.

b) Possessive and descriptive *no*

J.M. Ken Niimura

> Takeshi: かすみの血の匂い！
> *Kasumi POP blood POP smell!*
> **It's the smell of (I smell) Kasumi's blood!**

In this manga-example, we have two very similar but slightly different usages of the particle の, which will give us the chance for a comparative study. The first の links the words かすみ (*Kasumi*, a girl's name) and 血 (*blood*). In this case, it is usage 1-1), that is, the <u>possessive</u>. The first noun, かすみ, possesses the second one, 血, so we have "Kasumi's blood."

The second の links two nouns, 血 (*blood*) and 匂い (*smell*), and its usage is number 1-2), <u>descriptive</u>. That is, the first noun, 血, describes the second one, 匂い, giving this part the meaning of "smell of blood."

Note: For purely practical and simplifying reasons, we will keep on calling の a possessive particle (PP) every time it appears as a noun modifier.

c) *no* as an end-of-the-sentence particle

In L.17 (book 1) we already saw how の could also be used at the end of a sentence. We have just studied that の acquires different meanings depending on the context when it appears at the end of a sentence. In L.17 we gave a quick explanation and we even saw a manga-example where の is used as an end-of-the-sentence particle to form questions in a collo-

Gabriel Luque

> Nami: 二〇一五年で西暦が終わってしまうの
> *2015 year TP Christian Era SP finish EP*
> **The Christian Era will finish in the year 2015.**

quial register. However, の, as we can see in this example, can also be used to soften a statement (in a "feminine" or "childlike" way). Generally, only women and children use の with this inflection.

d) A new usage of *no*

Toshio: テル坊<ruby>坊<rt>ぼう</rt></ruby>くん、きみのおかみさんをつれてきたのだ！！
Terubō (noun suf) you POP *woman (noun suf)* DOP *bring come* EP!!
Terubō, I've brought your wife!!

If you take a look at the manga-examples we have seen throughout the ten lessons we have already studied in this book, you'll probably find many sentences ending like the one in this bubble: "verb in simple form+のだ." Also possible are のです、んです or んだ－the ん in these last two is a spoken contraction of の. In fact, the の in the previous example would also belong to this group. This construction is used to state something in a soft way: it's a sort of tag many Japanese use so they don't have to finish a sentence categorically. のだ can also give a sentence some "emotion," so that the speaker can share with the interlocutor the interest he has in the conversation topic. **Note:** Notice, too, the usage of the DO particle を and that of the possessive の in the example.

Javier Bolado

e) Two consecutive *o*

Air hostess: <ruby>頭<rt>あたま</rt></ruby>を<ruby>下<rt>さ</rt></ruby>げて<ruby>腰<rt>こし</rt></ruby>をかがめて<ruby>席<rt>せき</rt></ruby>におつきください
head DOP *lower hip* DOP *bend seat* PP *occupy please*
Lower your head, bend forward, and take your seats, please.

Bárbara Raya

We see here a string of three sentences linked by verbs in their *-te* form, one of the functions of the widely used *-te* conjugation which we studied in L.35 The three sentences are 頭<ruby>頭<rt>あたま</rt></ruby>を下<ruby>下<rt>さ</rt></ruby>げる *(lower one's head)*, 腰<ruby>腰<rt>こし</rt></ruby>をかがめる *(bend one's waist)*, and 席<ruby>席<rt>せき</rt></ruby>につく *(take one's seat)*. The sentence ends with the ～てください form *(please)*, which we also studied in L.35. Going back to what concerns us in this lesson, we see how in this sentence there are two DO (頭<ruby>頭<rt>あたま</rt></ruby>, *head*, and 腰<ruby>腰<rt>こし</rt></ruby>, *hip / waist*), and that they are both marked with を.

Finally, notice the に in the last sentence, in its usage #5 (ACP of direct contact) which we studied in L.38.

Studio Kōsen

f) The usage of *mō*

Let's take a little break after so many particles, and end the lesson illustrating "in panels" the time adverbs we saw in the last part of the theory section.

In this first panel we have a good example of the adverb もう *(already)*. Usually, もう indicates "change" and まだ "lack of change." However, both もう and まだ are relatively simple, all you need to know is that you can translate the first one as *already* or *now*, and the second one as *still*.

Maki: もう行くね。お仕事。
already go ep work
I'm going now... To work.

Note: It's worth remarking that the words formed by "もう＋一＋ counter" mean "one more x." Examples: もう一度 *one more time,* もう一杯 *one more drink,* もう一台 *one more (machine),* もう一日 *one more day,* and many others.

g) The usage of *goro*

Man: 十年後にきてくれっ
ten years in TP come
Come back in ten years' time.

Girl: 十年後の何時ごろ？
ten years in POP what time approximately?
At about what time in ten years?

Let's finish the lesson with a funny and absurd example where we can see the adverb ごろ at work.

As we saw in the theory section, ごろ indicates "approximately," "more or less," but it can only be used when it refers to an approximate "period of time," such as hours, days, months... However, in most cases it's used with hours, as in this example. 何時ごろ means *At what time, more or less?* The answer can perfectly be 五時ごろ *(at around five)* or 一時半ごろ *(at around half past one)*, or something similar.

Mary Molina

Notes: In this example we find the construction ～後 *(in x time)* which we already saw in L.34. Besides, the usage of の connecting 十年後 *(in ten years' time)* to 何時 *(at what time?)* corresponds to usage 1-5) which we studied in the theory section, that is, the appositional one.

1. Translate into Japanese the sentence: "The JAL plane is big." (plane: 飛行機, big: 大きい)

2. Translate into Japanese the sentence: "Wait in front of the library, please." (to wait: 待つ, in front of: 前で, library: 図書館)

3. In 暖かいセーターを着てください, replace セーター with a pronoun. (暖かい: warm, セーター: sweater, 着る: to wear)

4. Translate into English 本当に安土の町に住んでいるの? (本当に: really, 安土: Azuchi, 町: town, 住む: to live)

5. Translate: "What is Mari reading?" "She is reading a book by Mishima." (Mari: 真理, to read: 読む, book: 本, Mishima: 三島)

6. Translate into Japanese the sentence: "Yukio's dog got off the bus." (Yukio: 犬, dog: 由紀夫, to get off: 降りる, bus: バス)

7. Translate into English the sentence 修さんはまだ仕事が終わっていないの. (修: Osamu, 仕事: work, 終わる: to finish)

8. Translate: "She walked in the park for about two hours." (she: 彼女, to walk: 歩く, park: 公園, two hours: 二時間)

9. Translate: どうしてコーヒーを飲まないんですか? What do you use んです for? (どうして: why, コーヒー: coffee, 飲む: to drink)

10. Translate into Japanese: "Bring another book, please." (to bring: 持ってくる, book: 本)

第❹課:助詞④と・から・まで

Lesson 41: Particles (4) to/kara/made

With this lesson we will have studied in depth all the particles in Japanese grammar: は, が and も (L.37), に, で and へ (L.38), の and を (L.40), and, finally, と, から and まで, which we are about to study now. We will also study the usages of や and か.

The particle と

と, as most particles, has several different usages which we will have to study carefully and individually.

① Listing things: と is used to link nouns — only nouns or noun phrases (L.40 and 57, book 3) — and to give an exhaustive and complete listing of two or more things.

● 私は映画と音楽とマンガが好きです *I like movies, music and comic-books.*
● 寿司と刺身と味噌汁を食べた *I have eaten* sushi, sashimi *and* miso *soup.*
● 彼は英語と中国語とチェコ語が出来る *He can speak English, Chinese and Czech.*

② Together with / With: と is also used to indicate "with" somebody or something.

● 原さんは大塚さんと囲碁を打っている *Mr. Hara plays* go *with Mr. Ōtsuka.*
● 彼女はジョンと(一緒に)観光をした *She went sightseeing (together) with John.*

The combination (と)一緒に is a frequently used phrase, and means "together with." However, we will find that 一緒に is often omitted from the sentence because we assume it's understood or implied. This is why we have indicated it in parentheses.

On the other hand, these kind of sentences are technically called "reciprocal sentences," because the action indicated by the verb is the same for the two or more "subjects" who perform it. For example, the first sentence could mean both *Mr. Hara plays with Mr. Ōtsuka* and *Mr. Ōtsuka plays with Mr. Hara*. They both have the same role.

There are several kinds of reciprocal sentences in Japanese, and this one indicating "together with" is just one of them. Other verbs, such as 話す *(to talk)*, 結婚する *(to marry)*, 似る *(to look like)*, 違う *(to be different)*, and adjectives, such as 同じな *(the same)*, also use the particle と and, therefore, can be considered reciprocal sentence makers as well.

● 秋成くんはホステスと話している

Akinari is talking with the hostess.

● りんごはなしと違います

Apples and pears are different.

(3) **Quotes:** When we want to quote somebody's words, we will use と. There are two kinds of quotation: indirect — we usually form a subordinate sentence to indicate what was said—, and direct — we explicitly quote what was said, between quotation marks—. (See the table.)

● 博信は君がバカだと言ったよ

Hironobu said you were stupid.

Usages of *to*	
List	太郎とジョンとマリアが来た Tarō, John and Maria came.
(Together) with	ジョンはマリアと映画を見る John watches a movie with Maria
Reciprocity	太郎はマリアと結婚する Tarō marries María
Direct quote	彼は私に「好きだ」と言った He said to me "I like you"
Indirect quote	彼は私が好きだと言った He told me he liked me
Definition	愛とは何でしょう？ What is love?
With *gitaigo/gion*	彼はへなへなと座った He sat down, exhausted
Conditional	映画を見ると分かるよ If you see the film, you'll understand

来 くる: to come｜映画 えいが: film｜見 みる: to see｜結婚 けっこん: to marry
好 すき: to like｜言う いう: to say｜愛 あい: love｜へなへな: weak
座 すわる: to sit｜分 わかる: to understand

● サンドラは「休暇が欲しいなぁ!」と叫んだ *Sandra yelled: "I want holidays!"*

These sentences use verbs such as 言う (*to say*), 叫ぶ (*to yell*), ささやく (*to whisper*), etc. In a like manner, the verbs 思う (*to believe*), 考える (*to think*), 書く (*to write*), and other similar verbs use と. You should commit this to memory, as this combination is extremely common and widely used.

● 大阪は本当に楽しいと思っているよ *I think Osaka is really fun.*

●「さくら」は漢字で「桜」と書く *The word "sakura" is written "桜" in kanji.*

Note: Notice how before と, if we have a -*na* adjective or a noun, we will need the verb to be in its "simple" form (だ). Whereas the -*i* adjective requires no conjugation.

(4) **Definition:** Using the combination とは, or its complete form というのは, we can express the equivalent to a "definition" in a sentence.

●「能験」とは「能力試験」の略です *"Nōken" is the abbreviation for "Nōryoku shiken."*

●「民主主義」というのは何ですか？ *What is (that thing we call) "democracy"?*

Likewise, the expression という is very useful when clarifying a concept or giving more information about something. Notice how in this case we don't write the verb 言う in kanji, due to characteristic conventions of the Japanese language.

●「Monster」というマンガは超面白～い！ *The manga "Monster" is reaaally good!*

●「アゲハ」という女を知ってる？ *Do you know the woman called Ageha?*

⑤ <u>With *gitaigo / giongo*</u>: In L.29 (book 1) we studied the sound symbolisms of the onomatopoeic kind. と is very often used with these words.

● 彼女はしくしくと泣いている *She is sobbing silently.*
● 飛行機がびゅーんと飛んでいた *The plane flew (going byuuun).*

⑥ <u>Conditional</u>: In Japanese there are as many as four ways of expressing the conditional voice, which we will see in depth in L.56 (book 3). For the moment, we will only say for reference that と is used in one of these four ways.

● にんじんを食べると目がよくなります *If you eat carrot, your sight will improve.*

The particle から and other usages

① <u>Origin (from)</u>: The particle から indicates origin or point of departure, be it spatial or temporal.

● パーティは6時からです *The party is from six o'clock.*
● どこから来たんですか？ *Where have you come from? | Where are you from?*
● 学校から家へ歩いていける *I can walk home from school.*
● パンは小麦から作る *Bread is made from wheat.*

Note: This last usage is very similar to the fifth で from L.38. In fact, both particles are practically interchangeable in this context: the only connotation differentiating them is that we use から when the original material is not obvious just by looking at it. In the case of the example, you can't physically "see" that bread is made from wheat and so we use から. When we can determine by sight what the material used is, we use で.

② <u>Cause / Reason</u>: As we saw in L.34, から is used in an answer to a question with どうして *(why?)*, like our "because." However, it can also be used independently with the meaning of "as" or "since."

● 銀座は高いからよそへ行きましょう *Since Ginza is very expensive, let's go somewhere else.*
● 私は大丈夫だから、心配しないで *I'm alright, so don't worry.*
● 日本へ行くから、ちょっと日本語を勉強しよう *Since I'm going to Japan, I'll study some Japanese.*

Note: Just like with point 3 of と, after a *-na* adjective or a noun, you need the verb to be in its "simple" form (だ). Again, this is not necessary with *-i* adjectives.

③ <u>After doing</u>: In L.35 we saw how から is combined with the *-te* form to indicate "after doing..." We will give an example as a reminder, but it is advisable that you review it.

● 日本へ行ってから台湾へ行きたい *After going to Japan, I want to go to Taiwan.*

The particle まで

This particle is easy to use, especially if we learn it together with から, because they have opposite meanings. If から is "from," then まで is "until" or "to."

● 駅まで１０キロぐらいあると思う *I think there are about 10 km to the station.*
● いつまで韓国に残りたいの？ *Until when do you want to stay in Korea?*

Let's see a combination of both から and まで together, a usage we will find very often.

● 授業は３時から４時半までだよ *The class goes from three to half past four.*

Usages of や

We will end this lesson by introducing か and や which, in spite of not being considered "true" particles by Japanese grammar, they have very similar functions in the same position as と has in its first usage (a usage we have studied just a few pages earlier, as you will remember). We use や to make lists of things, just like with と. The difference lies in that, while と is used to make exhaustive lists— where we enumerate everything, without omitting anything from the list—, や is used to make <u>non</u>-exhaustive lists of nouns or noun phrases. (**Note:** や can't be used with verbs or adjectives.) That is, you don't need to specify each and every one of the elements in the list and it gives us the feeling of the phrase "and so on."

● 寿司や刺身を食べた *I have eaten sushi and sashimi (among other things).*
● 彼は英語や中国語やチェコ語が出来る *He can speak English, Chinese, Czech (and others).*
● 東京や岐阜や名古屋に友達がいる *I have friends in Tokyo, Gifu, Nagoya, and so on.*

We also have the expression とか, with practically the same meaning and usage as や. However, や is mainly used in written Japanese, whereas とか is used in colloquial contexts.

● 私は映画とか音楽とかが好きです *I like movies and music (and other things).*

Usages of か

Although か is used in a similar way to と (usage 1), and や, it has a very different meaning, as it indicates a choice between one or several things and something else.

Note: か can be used not only with nouns, but also with verbs and adjectives.

● 寿司か刺身を食べてください *Eat the sushi or the sashimi, please.*
● 電車で行くか歩いていくか決めよう *Let's decide whether we take the train or we walk.*
● 東京か岐阜か名古屋に友達がいる *He has a friend in Tokyo, Gifu, or Nagoya.*

More usages of か

There is a usage of か which is related to the one we have just seen. We are talking about the construction 〜かどうか, used to make questions (direct or indirect) of the "yes or no" kind. We will get a clearer idea with some examples.

The basic sentence is very similar to the ones we saw in the previous point.

● 刺身が好きか嫌いか言ってね *Tell me if you like or dislike sashimi, OK?*

Replacing the second part in the sentence with 〜かどうか, we simplify it, just like we would using "or not" in English.

● 刺身が好きかどうか言ってね *Tell me if you like sashimi or not, OK?*

Let's see some more examples to further clarify:

● 彼がサラリーマンかどうか知らない *I don't know whether he is an office worker or not.*
● 夏美が元気かどうか聞いてもいい？ *Can I ask you if Natsumi is all right (or not)?*
● 大会に出たかどうか分からないな *I don't know if he took place in the competition or not.*

Usages of *kara*	
From	子どもはパリからくる The children come from Paris
Origin	豆腐は大豆から作る Tōfu is made from soybeans
Cause / Reason	宿題は難しいからやらない Since homework is difficult, I won't do it
After doing...	宿題が終わってからテレビを見よう After finishing my homework, I'll watch TV
Usage of *made*	
To / Until	仙台まで新幹線で行ける You can go as far as Sendai by *shinkansen*
Usage of *ya*	
Non exhaustive list	オレンジやレモンを買った I bought oranges, lemons (and others)
Usages of *ka*	
List (disjunctive)	オレンジかレモンを食べてください Eat an orange or a lemon, please
Yes or no? (かどうか)	食べたいかどうか言ってね Tell me if you want to eat or not, OK?
Something (何か)	何か食べたいんですか？ Do you feel like eating something?

こども: child | とうふ: tofu | だいず: soybeans | つくる: to make
しゅくだい: homework | むずかしい: difficult | やる: to do (col.) |
おわる: to finish | テレビ: TV | しんかんせん: shinkansen | いく: to go |
オレンジ: orange | レモン: lemon | かう: to buy | たべる: to eat

Something, some day...

To conclude the lesson, we will have a look at a very similar usage of か to the last usage we studied for the particle も. Let's try to add か to an interrogative pronoun or adverb and let's see what we obtain: 何か (*something, some*), いつか (*some time, some day*), どこか (*somewhere*), 誰か (*someone*), etc. These are certainly very useful words!

● 誰か助けてください！

Someone help me, please!

● 何か問題がありますか？

Do you have any problems?

● どこかで彼女に会いたいな

I'd like to meet her somewhere.

We will complete the lesson with a few examples taken from manga, as usual. Having a look at the theory section, it seems that particle と can be the most problematic, because of its multiple meanings and usages, so we will put a special emphasis on it.

a) Several usages of *to*

Kōsaka: １５日と２０日に出かけるって聞いてピンときたんだ
day 15 CP day 20 TP go out SBP hear "flash" come
When I heard he went out on the 15th and the 20th, I suddenly understood.

This is an intensive example: three diffe-rent usages of と in one sentence!

As you can easily deduce, the first と gives a small "list" of only two elements: the nouns １５日 (*the 15th*) and ２０日 (*the 20th*, be careful with its special pronunci-ation, which we studied in L.6, book 1). This is, indeed, the first usage of と we have learned.

The second と goes with the *gitaigo* ピン. If you don't remember what sound sym-bolisms are, review L.29 (book 1). ピン

J.M. Ken Niimura

indicates something like a "flash," a thought that suddenly strikes you. We usually find ピン in the expression ピンと来る, like in this example: it means "to suddenly realize something."

And now you'll be asking yourself where the third と is. Well, in fact, it's "hidden:" the と of usage #3 (quotes), which we studied a few pages ago, is usually contracted into って in spoken Japanese. Pay careful attention to this special feature, because it happens extremely often. In our example sentence, the contracted と is in 出かけると聞いて (*I heard he went out*). This belongs, then, to usage #3 (quote): と is the connective between the main sentence 聞く (*to hear*) and the subordinate 出かける (*to go out*).

b) Company *to*

Mayumi: あたし ナオヤ先輩と行きたい所があるんですけど…
I Naoya (noun suf) CP go place SP there is but...
I... There is a certain place I'd like to go with Naoya...

Here is a good example of the second usage of と which we studied in the theory section: "together with / with." We said the expression 〜と一緒に (*together with*) can be used in this kind of sentence, but the 一緒に part is very often left out. This is the case in this sentence, which in fact could perfectly be ナオヤ先輩と一緒に行きたい (*I want to go with Naoya*).

Gabriel Luque

Notes: The word 先輩, as we saw in L.15 (book 1), indicates "someone with more experience, who does the same work or study as the speaker, but who started earlier." It is widely used. Notice the tag んです at the end: we explained it in example d) in L.40.

c) Spoken contraction of *to iu*

Sachie: ＯＫだって！街の近くまでのせてくれるって！！
OK says that! Village POP near to take (receive) says that!
He says OK! He's taking us somewhere near the village!

Studio Kōsen

In the a) example of this lesson, we have seen how と can be contracted into って in spoken Japanese. Well, the same happens with the expression という and とは (points 3 and 4). Here we have an example of usage #3 of と: an indirect quote. Sachie quotes twice what they've told her using と plus the verb 言う (*to say*), which gives us という (*says that*), contracted into a simple って. Let's see, now, a usage of this って applied to point #4 (definition): 民主主義」って何？ *What is democracy?* This って, as you know, is the equivalent to とは.

Note: って can be the equivalent both to the contraction of と —like in the example a)— and to the contraction of the full expression という (*says that*) or even to とは (definition), so you should take care to distinguish its usage through the context.

d) The usage of *made* and an idiomatic usage of *kara*

> **Mihoko:** 迎えに来るまで帰ってやんないから。
> *fetch until go back (give) because*
> **I won't go back until he comes to fetch me, huh!**

迎えに来るまで帰ってやんないから。

Javier Bolado

You already know that the particle まで is the equivalent to our *until*. In this example we have a temporal usage of まで (it indicates a point in time): 迎えに来るまで *Until he comes to fetch me.*

In the previous example, there is a spatial usage of まで (it indicates a point in space): 街の近くまで *Somewhere near the village.*

Note: The から at the end of the sentence belongs to usage #2 in the theory section: it indicates cause / reason. This kind of から at the end of a sentence is very common in spoken language, especially when the speaker is angry or in a bad mood (or pretends to be). In such cases, rather than translating it as *because*, it's more adequate to use *huh!*, *there!* or a similar interjection.

e) Cause / Reason

> **Kūkai:** お前には聞かせられないから息子の秀樹をよべ…
> *you IOP TOP hear (passive-reflexive) because son POP Hideki DOP call...*
> **I can't tell you, so call my son Hideki.**

Here is a good example of usage #2 of から: cause / reason. から links the two sentences お前には聞かせられない *I can't tell you* (reason) and 息子の秀樹をよべ *Call my son Hideki* (consequence). This usage of から is extremely useful, so it is worth studying well.

In the sentence we also see the appositive usage of の (L.40, usage 1-5) in 息子の秀樹 (*my son Hideki)*, as well as the imperative よべ

Bárbara Raya

(from the verb 呼ぶ, *to call*), which we studied in L.30 (book 1). The inflection 聞かせられない is a combination of the causative form −a rather complicated form which we'll study in L.60 (book 3)−, and the negative potential form (L.32): it literally means *I can't let you hear,* in other words, I can't tell you.

f) *ka dō ka*

Soldier: な...何を言ってるのかよくわからないが...
w...what DOP say SBP Q? well know but...
Wha...? I don't understand very well what you are saying, but...
とにかくお前の知ってる男かどうか、確かめてみろ！！
anyhow you POP know man "yes or no," check (try)!!
Whatever it is, go and check if you know those men or not!!

Here is a manga-example with a lot of text where we will point out the construction 〜かどうか. We have just seen that this construction is used to form questions of the "yes or no" type. In this case, the sentence we have to take a look at is お前の知ってる男かどうか確かめてみろ *Check if you know those men or not.* 〜かどうか is used to avoid repeating the verb and to simplify: the "extended version" of the sentence would be: お前の知ってる男か知らない男か確かめてみろ *Check if you know those men or if you don't know them.*

J.M. Ken Niimura

Note: In the sentence, we can see a few other things, such as 〜てみる, which we studied in L.35, meaning "try to do something." Notice, too, how 〜てみる is conjugated in the imperative: 確かめてみろ, which would literally mean *try to check,* or *check and see.*

g) Something

Emika: なんか言って徳永君ッ
something say Tokunaga (noun suf)
Say something, Tokunaga!

Our last example shows us a combination of an interrogative adverb or pronoun plus か, which takes the meaning of "something," as we saw in the theory pages.
In this case we have 何か *(something),* but other combinations such as どれか *(some),* いつか *(some time),* どこか *(somewhere),* and other varients are also possible.
Note: We also find in this example the usage of the *-te* form for request, where 〜ください is left out (言って, *say*). This is characteristic of the spoken language, as we saw in L.35.

Studio Kōsen

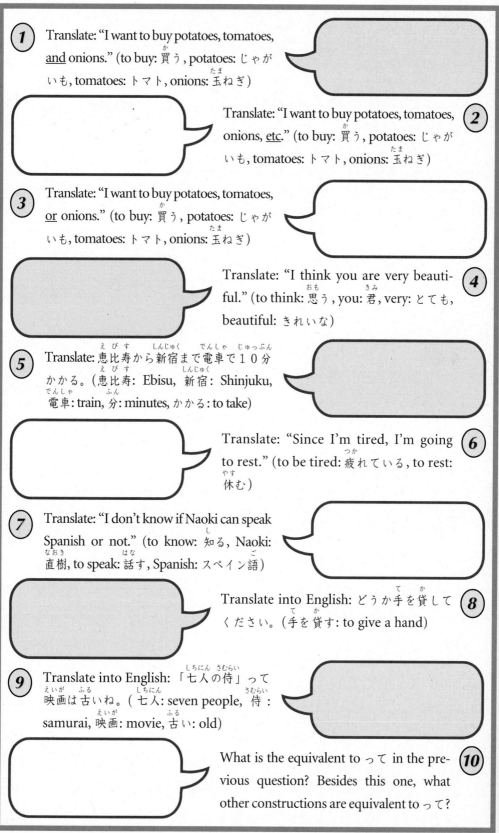

1 Translate: "I want to buy potatoes, tomatoes, <u>and</u> onions." (to buy: 買う, potatoes: じゃがいも, tomatoes: トマト, onions: 玉ねぎ)

2 Translate: "I want to buy potatoes, tomatoes, onions, <u>etc.</u>" (to buy: 買う, potatoes: じゃがいも, tomatoes: トマト, onions: 玉ねぎ)

3 Translate: "I want to buy potatoes, tomatoes, <u>or</u> onions." (to buy: 買う, potatoes: じゃがいも, tomatoes: トマト, onions: 玉ねぎ)

4 Translate: "I think you are very beautiful." (to think: 思う, you: 君, very: とても, beautiful: きれいな)

5 Translate: 恵比寿から新宿まで電車で１０分かかる。(恵比寿: Ebisu, 新宿: Shinjuku, 電車: train, 分: minutes, かかる: to take)

6 Translate: "Since I'm tired, I'm going to rest." (to be tired: 疲れている, to rest: 休む)

7 Translate: "I don't know if Naoki can speak Spanish or not." (to know: 知る, Naoki: 直樹, to speak: 話す, Spanish: スペイン語)

8 Translate into English: どうか手を貸してください。(手を貸す: to give a hand)

9 Translate into English: 「七人の侍」って映画は古いね。(七人: seven people, 侍: samurai, 映画: movie, 古い: old)

10 What is the equivalent to って in the previous question? Besides this one, what other constructions are equivalent to って?

第41課 練習 Exercises

Lesson 42: Shopping

After the hard battle fought against the particles in the last four lessons −with a rest (L.39) in between−, we now deserve a lesson where we can practice everything we've learned so far, and learn a lot of new vocabulary.

We are going shopping!

Let's start satisfying our passion for spending money by first having a look at some sentences which can be helpful whenever we go shopping.

● 何か探しているんですか？ *Are you looking for something?* (L.41)

● はい、Xはありますか？ *Yes, do you have x?*

● いいえ、見ているだけです *No, I'm just looking.*

● あれを見せてください *Could you please show me that?*

● これはいくらですか？ *How much is this?* (L.34)

● お支払いは現金ですか、カードですか？ *Will you pay cash or credit card?* (L.41)

● カードでお願いします *Credit card.* | 現金でお願いします *Cash.*

● これをお願いします *Could I have this, please?*

You have probably noticed we had already seen some of these sentences in L.36. We have included them to refresh your memory.

Buying clothes

The sizes in Japan tend to be rather small, so few people going to Japan (tourists at any rate) will buy clothes, this is why this section is a rather basic one. Nevertheless, take the chance to study the vocabulary related to clothing, as they will be very useful in many other situations: take a look at the table on the following page and study it well.

Shopping	
bag	袋
to bargain	値切る
bill	領収書
cash register	レジ
discount	割引
label (price)	値札
offer	バーゲン
to pay	払う
sales	特売
tax	税
to wrap	包む

Clothes					
belt	ベルト	*kimono*	着物	stockings	ストッキング
blouse	ブラウス	pajamas	パジャマ	suit	スーツ
boots	ブーツ	pants	ズボン	sweater	セーター
bra	ブラ	panties	パンティー	swimming costume	水着
coat	コート	scarf (muffler)	マフラー	tie	ネクタイ
dress	ドレス	shirt	シャツ	T-shirt	Tシャツ
gloves	手袋	shoes	靴	underpants	パンツ
jacket	ジャケット	skirt	スカート	underwear	下着
jeans	ジーンズ	socks	靴下	*yukata*	浴衣

Most Japanese words referring to one's wardrobe come from English, because it wasn't until the Meiji Era (1868) that the Japanese began dressing in Western style. Not having the words, they imported them from the language that was closest at hand: English.

Note: You may have noticed that in Japanese パンツ refers to *underwear* and not to "pants." Also, note that the word ジーパン is an abbreviation of ジーンズパンツ, that is to say *jeans*, and not "G-string panties," as some people may feel inclined to think.

You'll probably appreciate a few traditional vocabulary: 着物 *(kimono)*, 浴衣 *(summer kimono)*, 帯 *(kimono sash)*, はかま *(hakama, a sort of skirt nowadays used almost exclusively in martial arts)*, 下駄 *(geta, Japanese clogs)*, 足袋 *(tabi, socks with the big toe separated)*.

● 自分用の浴衣を探しているんですが... *I'm looking for a yukata for me...* (L.40)

● 女性用のTシャツはありますか？ *Do you have T-shirts for women?*

● 日本のサイズがわかりません *I don't know how sizes in Japan work.*

● このサイズはいくつですか？ *What size is this?*

● もう少し安いものがありますか？ *Do you have something a little bit cheaper?*

● 試着してもいいですか？ *Can I try it on?* (L.32)

Buying manga, books, music, and films

We now enter an area keeping more in touch with what people usually end up buying when they travel to Japan: we are talking about books (which include manga, of course), records of modern and traditional Japanese music, Japanese films (either real image or animation)... And let's not forget, of course, electronic devices of all kinds, and videogames. We will start with books, music, and films.

Warning: Don't expect to find bargains in Japan, unless you are buying second hand in one of the many shops there are: CDs and films are usually quite expensive. Not so much with books, though, which are comparatively cheap and can even be found second-hand at ridiculously inexpensive prices. In spite of what it may seem, Japanese second hand has an amazing quality: the goods seem practically new.

● 「Ｇ　Ｔ　Ｏ」というマンガを探しています *I'm looking for a manga called "GTO."* (L.41)

● 作者か出版社はわかりますか？ *Do you know the author or the publishing company?* (L.41)

● ＩＳＢＮは978-4-88996-186-7です *The ISBN is 978-4-88996-186-7.*

● このビデオはＰＡＬのテレビで見られますか？ *Can I watch this video in an PAL TV set?*

● 浜﨑あゆみの最新作はありますか？ *Do you have Ayumi Hamasaki's new record?*

● このマンガとビデオとＣＤをください *I'll take this manga, this video, and this CD.* (L.41)

● 中古のＤＶＤはどこで買えますか？ *Where can I buy second-hand DVDs?*

Some musical vocabulary: 邦楽 *(Japanese music),* 洋楽 *(Western music),* ロック *(rock),* ポップス *(pop),* ジャズ *(jazz),* クラシック *(classical music),* 演歌 *(enka, traditional Japanese music),* ヒップホップ *(hip hop),* ヘビーメタル *(heavy metal),* ソウル *(soul),* テクノ *(techno),* レゲエ *(reggae).* **And now, movie vocabulary:** 字幕 *(subtitled)* 吹き替え *(dubbed),* 邦画 *(Japanese cinema),* 洋画 *(foreign cinema),* アニメ *(animation),* アクション *(action),* ホラー *(horror),* ドラマ *(drama),* コメディ *(comedy),* スリラー *(thriller),* アドベンチャー *(adventures),* ＳＦ *(science-fiction).*

Buying electronic devices and videogames

Let's now deal with another great receptacle of a very remarkable amount of the yen spent in the Japanese country by foreign visitors: the huge Japanese electronics shops, mainly in the 秋葉原 district, in Tokyo, and the でんでんタウン（日本橋）district in Osaka, where a vast amount of shops are concentrated. Japan is probably the country with the greatest variety of electronic devices in the world: what you don't find in the Land of the Rising Sun most likely doesn't exist.

● あのデジカメを見てもいいですか？ *Can I see that digital camera?* (L.32)

● その電子辞典に英語の説明書は付いているのですか？

Does that electronic dictionary have an English instruction leaflet? (L.40)

● このポータブルＤＶＤプレーヤーはＰＡＬのテレビにつなげますか？

Can you connect this DVD player to a PAL television set? (L.32)

● この機械はアメリカで使えるんですか？それとも、変換機が必要ですか？

Can I use this machine in the USA? Or does it need an electric transformer?

● 英語ＯＳのパソコンはありますか？ *Do you have PCs with an English operating system?*

● あのコンピュータのＨＤはどれくらい大きいですか？

About how big is the hard disk in that personal computer? (L.40)

● このゲームはプレステ2用ですか？ *Can I use this game on Playstation 2?*

Important: In Japan they use 100V electric power, different to most countries in the world, so it might be possible that we need some kind of current converter (変換機) if we wish to use a Japanese appliance in our own country. Likewise, the video system is NTSC, the same as the American continent, but different to the European, which is PAL. Regarding DVDs, they are Zone 2, the same as in Europe but different to America, and most videogames will only work with Japanese systems. Be careful with what you buy, because you could get very upset on returning home and trying to watch that movie you bought during your trip.

Buying souvenirs

To conclude, we will learn how to buy the unavoidable souvenirs and presents.

● この人形は伝統的ですか？ *Is this doll a traditional one?*

● その急須は壊れやすいから、気をつけてくださいね

This teapot is fragile, so please be careful. (L.41)

● プレゼントだから、包んでください *It's a present, so could you wrap it up, please?* (L.41)

● あのせんべいの賞味期限はいつですか？ *When do those rice crackers expire?*

● 安いお土産を売っていませんか？ *Do you sell cheap souvenirs?* (L.40)

Books, music, videos and electronics					
artbook	画集	digital camera	デジカメ	player	プレーヤー
book	本	doll	人形｜フィギュア	poster	ポスター
camera	カメラ	DVD	ＤＶＤ	software	ソフト
(digital) card	カード	electronic agenda	ＰＤＡ	video	ビデオ
CD	ＣＤ	electronic dictionary	電子辞典	video camera	ビデオカメラ
comic-book	漫画｜コミック	merchandise	グッズ	video game	ゲームソフト
computer	コンピュータ	plastic model	プラモデル	watch	時計

文化編：流行狂
Cultural Note: Passion for fashion

It would not be suprising to find out that the word "fashion victim," so much in vogue nowadays, had been invented to describe Japanese urban youth. Or, maybe not. Either way, the truth is that if you walk around the 渋谷 and 原宿 districts (in 東京) or 梅田 and 心斎橋 (in 大阪), you can come across vast numbers of young people whose photograph would perfectly illustrate a dictionary entry for "fashion victim."

Japanese urban fashion is eclectic, colorful, sometimes extreme, and sometimes absolutely outlandish. There are times when you feel you really are before one of those flamboyant fashion shows in Paris or Milan: mega-short skirts, conspicuous accessories, cowboy hats, spike heel boots, pink angora sweaters, hair dyed platinum blonde, terribly expensive designer handbags, knee-long stockings with sports shoes... All this and a lot more rules Japanese ファッション, which varies at a hectic pace being, therefore, extremely difficult to follow.

Shinsaibashi: extreme "fashion-addicts" in their "habitat" (Photo: M. Bernabé)

But not everybody can afford changing their wardrobe completely every two or three months. In fact, this represents one of the urban youth's most urgent problems (basically among girls): how to find money to "be fashionable." Of course, not everybody in Japan is rich enough to be able to afford such frantic spending. Therefore, money is obtained via all kind of scheming: from asking one's parents or simply having an アルバイト (*part-time job for students*) in a コンビニ (*convenience store*), to practically prostituting oneself with the so called 援助交際 (literally, *relationship in exchange of help*), which entails very young girls going out with middle-aged men (generally, 40 or over) in exchange for money. The デート (*dates*) can involve anything: from an innocent afternoon snack or coffee to ending up in bed.

The thing is fashion is like a religion, or rather, pure mimicry: if my neighbor has that Gucci or Cartier handbag, why shouldn't I have it? Thus, it is not in vain that the world's main luxury firms consider 日本 their most important market.

Shopping: irresistible pleasure for some, terrible deadly trap for others. But the truth is nobody can escape it, and much less when visiting a foreign country. The manga-examples will illustrate some common situations in Japanese society.

a) An everyday scene

Customer:	５００円のテレホンカードください	
	500 yen POP telephone card please	
	A 500 yen telephone card, please.	
Woman:	ありがとうございました	はい　お釣り
	thank you very much	*yes, change*
	Thank you very much!	**Here is your change.**

Our first manga-example shows us a very recurrent scene: the hustle and bustle of a newsstand in a station in the height of rush hour. Station newsstands are amazingly small and crammed places where you can find almost anything: chewing gum, candies, fuel drinks, newspapers, all kinds of comic-books... In this example we will point out the customer's sentence: ５００円のテレホンカードください, which is used to ask for some specific thing, in this case a 500 yen telephone card. Although including the DO particle を between カード and ください would be better, it is usually left out in speech.

Notes: Be careful with the の between ５００円 and テレホン: it is usage 1-2 (descriptive) of の, which we saw in L.40. Notice also the clerk's はい: it isn't necessarily a "yes," but a way of calling attention (as in "here you are"). The word はい is extremely common in Japanese, very often with meanings different to "yes."

b) Great bargain

Kazue: おおっ箱ティッシュがバカ安！ブラウス半額！？
wow box tissues SP foolish cheap! Blouse half price!?
Wow! Tissues are dirt cheap! And blouses at half price?!

J.M. Ken Niimura

This is a key example to understand some expressions which will help us find bargains in Japan. In Kazue's bubble, we have the word 半額, which means "half price." Apart from this, take a look at the pamphlets, where you can read バーゲン半額 (*half-price bargains*) and 大安売り (*special bargain sale*). 安売り is a native Japanese word and バーゲン has been imported from English (*bargain*): they both mean "bargain."

Note: ティッシュ are "tissues" and 箱 means "box," therefore, 箱ティッシュ are tissue boxes. These boxes are, according to Kazue, バカ安. If you remember L.23 (book 1), バカ is an insult meaning "silly, stupid." バカ安 would be, in a literal translation, *foolishly cheap:* in other words, *dirt cheap.* **Note 2:** While "tissues" are called ティッシュ, when asking for a "napkin" (outside of the restaurant environment) it is better to ask for a ペーパータオル rather than a ナプキン, as it has the double, and more frequent, meaning of *sanitary napkin*!

c) 2500 yen altogether

Man: しめて２５００円ね
total 2500 yen EP
That's 2500 yen altogether.

Tezuka: に　にせんごひゃく円だー！？
tw...two thousand yen be!?
Tw...two thousand yeeen?!

Here we see how the clerk gives the client the total price: the verb しめる —which is written 締める in kanji— is used here as an adverb (remember verbs in the *-te* form can sometimes function as adverbs, L.22, book 1) with the meaning of "altogether." 締める is

Gabriel Luque

used to give the final figure after adding up the prices of various goods.

Example: 学費は締めて２００万円もかかったよ *School expenses amounted to 2 million yen altogether.* Notice the usage of the particle も: it's used here to emphasize a number (L.37).

d) Brand fever

> **Kojima:** ほら　このバッグなんかヴィトンよ？ヴィトン！
> *look this handbag Vuitton EP? Vuitton!*
> **Look at this handbag. It's a Vuitton, man, a Vuitton!**
> いくらすっと思ってんのよ　20万よ？20万！
> *how much SBP think Q? EP 20 man EP? 20 man!*
> **How much do you think it costs? 200,000, man, 200,000!**

In the cultural note we talked about how obsessed the Japanese are with luxury designer goods, and this example just proves it. The speaker boasts before his friend about having a Louis Vuitton handbag which has been bought for a whopping 20万 (200,000 yen). Since Kojima's second sentence is extremely distorted by his colloquial style of speech, we will transcribe it into "normal" Japanese to analyze it properly: いくらすると思っているの？ The expression いくら

Javier Bolado

する is an alternative way of saying いくらです *(how much is it?)*. It's also worth pointing out the use of the construction と思う *(I think)*, which we studied in usage #3 of と (L.41).

e) To bargain

> **Kishida:** 安くまけろってサインだそうです！
> *cheap bargain SBP sign be seems be!*
> **It looks like the sign for "give me a discount"!**

Bárbara Raya

In Japan bargaining is not paramount, but sometimes, like in flea markets (フリーマーケット) or in some electronics stores, you might obtain some discounts if you insist a little. The standard expression, which would be ちょっとまけてください, *Give me a little discount, please,* uses the verb まける *(to reduce)*, which we see in this example in its imperative form, まけろ (L.30).

Notes: ちょっと means "a little." For obvious reasons, 安い *(cheap)* and 高い *(expensive)* are key words when bargaining and, by extension, when generally buying. Notice って in the sentence: it's a contraction of という (usage #4 of と, L.41).

Shopping ショッピング　−129−

f) A 20% discount

Man: そいつはオメデタイから…
that TOP *"omedetai" because...*
Well, because it's a *"joyous* bream"…

Woman: 2割ほど定価から引いて！
20% approximately price from take out!
(You will) lower the price 20%!

Studio Kōsen

Very often, we will see offers marked with a number plus the word 割引き *(discount)* or, like in the example, just 割. These are, obviously, discounts – the number indicates the percentage–. For example, this 2割 would be a 20% discount, and 5割 would be a 50% discount (notice how the number is multiplied by ten). You will frequently find labels or signs indicating discounts mainly in supermarkets and boutiques. Many use the formula X 割 which we have just seen, and others use the word 半額, which we saw in example b) and which means "half price." A sign in English is also quite frequent: "30 % OFF."

Note: In fact, the shop assistant is talking about sea bream (鯛). Since the pronunciation of the word *sea bream,* たい, coincides with the last part of the adjective おめでたい *(joyous, happy, propitious)*, in Japan, sea bream is eaten on happy occasions.

g) Computer

Kei: ああ…コンピュータ？インターネットでもやる？
oh... computer? Internet or something do?
Oh, the computer? Do you want to connect to the Internet or something?

This example reveals how most computer terms have been introduced into Japanese through English, like in almost all languages in the world. Such is the case of the words コンピュータ and インターネット.

The word "computer" curiously has two Japanese names: the "orthodox" コンピュータ and the more cryptic パソコン, a contraction of the word パーソナル・コンピュータ *(personal computer)*.

Note: Notice the でも in the example. It's the same usage we saw in example g) in L.38.

Gabriel Luque

1. Translate into English the words 包む, 手袋, ベルト, ソフト, 画集, 水着 and セーター.

2. Translate into Japanese the words "suit," "scarf," "discount," "doll," "electronic dictionary," and "tie."

3. You go into a shop to browse around. What do you reply if the clerk asks you if you want anything special?

4. You are looking for a book called "Kimono," and the clerk asks you 何か探しているんですか？ What do you answer?

5. Translate into Japanese the sentence: "Do you have a size 'small' in pants?"

6. Translate into English: あのロックのＣＤとそのホラーのビデオをください。

7. You want to buy a digital camera, but you don't know whether you will be able to use it in your country. Ask the clerk.

8. Translate into Japanese: "Since this pottery piece is fragile, could you wrap it up, please?" (pottery piece: 陶器)

9. You are at a flea market, and you are interested in something. Try to start bargaining in Japanese.

10. Give the three ways of saying "at half price" which we have studied in this lesson.

Lesson 43: Suppositions and conjectures

We have mentioned at some point how the Japanese tend to be ambiguous: they prefer hiding behind vagueness and imprecision, as opposed to risking categorical statements. In this lesson we will study the extremely wide variety of expressions used to indicate supposition and conjecture in Japanese.

Maybe, baby...

Ambiguity in the Japanese language and character is known all over the world, and very often causes confusion and misunderstandings. A Japanese will never say "no" directly; rather, he will let out a rhetorical alternative in the form of "hum, it might be a little difficult," or "I'd have to say that's not quite possible," which will make a Western mind think "he says it's difficult, but he doesn't deny it specifically, therefore, there is the possibility that it could be done," when what the Japanese really means is *no*, even though he doesn't express it unequivocally. Such peculiarity is and ideal breeding ground for annoyance and misunderstandings. Let's now look at the Japanese expressions which might illustrate such characteristic. The Japanese language is very rich in these kinds of structures, and they are used so as not to run risks, to soften sentences, or to take away that nuance of directness found in Western languages.

We already saw the first expression in L.41, it's (と)思う *(I think that)*:

- スピーチを始めたいと思います *(I think) I'd like to start my speech.*
- 論文をもう一度書いてもらいたいと思う *I think I'd like to have you write the thesis again.*

The second expression we will study is かもしれない (かもしれません in its formal form), which means "perhaps," "maybe," "might be." <u>Usage</u>: We add nothing but かもしれない／かもしれません after a verb in its simple form, an *-i* or *-na* adjective, or a noun.

- 彼はフランス人かもしれない *He might be French.*
- 来年、日本へ行くかもしれませんよ *Maybe, I'll go to Japan next year.*
- あのデジカメは高かったかもしれないな *Perhaps, that digital camera was expensive.*

ようだ・みたいだ

From now on, you'll need to concentrate on the expressions we will be seeing, because some of them are very similar and confusing them is easy. We will try to be as clear as possible in our explanations, yet, more often than not, the "borders" of their usages are a bit hazy, so distinguishing their differences can be somewhat of a challenge.

The expression ようだ (in kanji, 様だ) has the meaning of "apparently," and is used when the speaker has direct information (either visual or sensorial) about something. This is information which comes from the speaker's previous knowledge about the subject and his capacity to reason. Therefore, it is a conjecture with a really high degree of certainty: what the speaker is saying is almost certainly true, even though there's always a connotation of ambiguity. <u>Usage</u>: it goes after a verb in its simple form or an *-i* adjective, without adding anything. *-na* adjectives keep な. You must add の between a noun and ようだ.

● 田中さんは気絶したようだ *Apparently, Tanaka has fainted.*

  (Because I can see that he is lying on the floor.)

● その店は花屋さんのようだ *I'd say that shop is (seems like) a flower shop.*

  (Because there are lots of flowers for sale inside.)

● その時計は高いようですね *(I'd say) that watch is expensive, isn't it?*

  (Because I'm familiar with the brand name.)

ようだ is really a *-na* adjective (ような), so it can also go in the middle of a sentence functioning as a comparative ("is like..."). The adverbial form ように is also possible. We will see more on ような and comparatives in L.54 (book 3).

● 徹はＦ１のような車を運転しています *Tetsu drives a car that looks like a F1.*

ようだ is usually used in written or formal Japanese. On informal occasions, みたいだ is preferred. This is, theoretically, an equivalent to ようだ, that is, an expression based on direct information, with a very high degree of certainty. However, in practice, みたいだ is used in multiple occasions, not always with a high degree of certainty. <u>Usage</u>: We add nothing but みたいだ after a verb in its simple form, an *-i* or *-na* adjective, or a noun.

● トム君はひげを生やしたみたいだよ！ *It looks like Tom has grown a beard!*

● あの公園は静かみたいだ *That park looks quiet.*

みたいだ is also a *-na* adjective (みたいな) and it works just like its formal synonym ようだ:

● 徹はＦ１みたいな車を運転しているぞ *Tetsu drives a car that looks like a F1.*

だろう

Here is an expression we know very well, the verb "to be" (です) in the -ō form (L.34): だろう. This だろう is slightly different to other verbs in the -ō form, because it doesn't have the meaning of "let's...," but is used at the end of a sentence and has two different meanings. The first one involves expressing a pure conjecture (not necessarily based on previous information). <u>Usage:</u> We add nothing except for だろう after a noun, an -*i* or -*na* adjective, or a verb in its simple form. **Note:** the formal version of だろう is でしょう.

- あのパソコンは古いだろう *That computer is probably old.*
- 正子ちゃんは多分来ないだろうね *I suppose Masako (probably) won't come.*
- 木村さんの娘さんはきれいでしょう *(I imagine) Kimura's daughter is probably beautiful.*

The second meaning of だろう is that of a "tag" asking for a reply to the speaker's statement, similar to "isn't it?" or "right?" It's usage is very similar to ね (L.17, book 1).

- おい、木村！あんたの娘、きれいだろう？ *Hey, Kimura! Your daughter is beautiful, isn't she?*
- このケーキはおいしいでしょう？ *This cake is delicious, isn't it?*

Note: It is worth learning these adverbs which are very often used in expressions of supposition: 多分 *(perhaps)*, おそらく *(probably)*, もしかすると / もしかして *(possibly)*, どうやら *(likely)*, ひょっとすると / ひょっとして *(by chance)*, and きっと *(surely)*.

らしい

Another expression to express supposition. らしい perhaps expresses an in-between, because it's used to express something the speaker knows because he has heard or read (it repeats information which is no longer firsthand). It's not as certain a conjecture as ようだ, nor such a "loose" one as だろう. <u>Usage:</u> We add nothing except for らしい after a noun, an -*i* or -*na* adjective, or a verb in its simple form.

- ドイツ人は頑固らしいよ *(From what I've read / heard) the Germans are stubborn.*
- ジムはアメリカに帰らないらしい *(Apparently) Jim will not be going back to the USA.*

In addition, らしい is an -*i* adjective meaning "worthy of," "as is expected from," or "becoming," and followingly it can be conjugated like any -*i* adjective. Negative: らしくない | Past: らしかった | Past negative: らしくなかった.

- 愛ちゃんは日本人らしいですね *Ai is so Japanese-like.*

  (Ai is just like what you'd expect a Japanese girl to be.)
- おい、お前！男らしく振舞え！ *Hey, you! Behave manly! (Act like a man would do!)*

そうだ (1)

Let's have a look now at the two そうだ expressions. The first works in a very similar way to the other expressions we have seen so far: you simply add そうだ to a verb, adjective or noun. However, with the second one you must "conjugate" verbs and adjectives.

The first そうだ means exactly the same as らしい: we use it to pass on information the speaker has obtained directly from another source, either through a conversation with someone else, or because he has read it or seen it on TV, for example. The differences between そうだ (1) and らしい are that そうだ (1) is completely based on "hearsay," whereas らしい is based on what we've heard, seen, read, or reasoned to be so. <u>Usage</u>: it goes after a verb in its simple form or an *-i* adjective, without adding anything. だ must be added between そうだ and *-na* adjectives or nouns.

● 奈良で電車事故があったそうだ *(I've heard / read that) in Nara there was a train accident.*
● 学校の制服は高かったそうだ *(From what I heard) the school uniform was expensive.*
● ジムさんは先生だそうですね *(From what I've been told) Jim is a teacher, isn't he?*

そうだ (2)

The second そうだ, which has nothing to do with the first one, is used to express conjecture about the state of something, a conjecture

Inflections for そうだ (2)		
Verbs	〜ます＋そう	倒れる⇒倒れます⇒倒れ⇒倒れそうだ To fall ⇒ it looks like it's falling (it's about to fall)
-i adj.	〜い＋そう	寒い⇒寒⇒寒そうだ cold ⇒ it looks like it's cold
-na adj.	〜な＋そう	元気な⇒元気⇒元気そうだ cheerful ⇒he looks cheerful

based on what the speaker sees or has seen (visual information). そうだ (2) can't be used in the past because it is only used when talking about things that are probably true in the present or might be true in a foreseeable future. Words conjugated with そうだ (2) become *-na* adjectives and function as such. <u>Usage</u>: see the inflection table for そうだ (2) above. **Note:** そうだ (2) is not used with nouns.

● あのバイクはとても古そうだ *That motorcycle looks very old.*
● この仕事は君に出来そうだと思う *I think you can (probably) do that job.*
● 今日は元気そうな顔をしているね *You look (your face looks) cheerful today, don't you?*

When used with verbs, そうだ (2) sometimes adds the connotation of "to be about to:"

● 雪が降りそうですね *It looks like it's about to snow, doesn't it?*
● 父は怒りそうになった *My father looked like he was going to get angry.*

はずだ・にちがいない

And here is yet another expression for conjecture, はずだ, which is used to express that the speaker hopes that what he expects is real, therefore はずだ expresses more an event or state which is practically assumed rather than a supposition. It is equivalent to "supposed to..." <u>Usage</u>: it goes after a verb in its simple form or an *-i* adjective, without adding anything. *-na* adjectives keep な. You must add の between a noun and ようだ.

- ● ヴェロニカさんは家にいる**はずだ** *(I imagine) Veronica is supposed to be home.*
- ● 彼女は歌が上手な**はずです** *(I'm almost sure that) she is supposed to sing very well.*

Another expression is にちがいない, which is the clearest and most categorical in this lesson, as it expresses something which is practically certain: "without doubt." <u>Usage</u>: We add nothing but にちがいない after a noun, an *-i* or *-na* adjective, or verb in its simple form.

- ● ヴェロニカさんは家にいる**にちがいない** *There is no doubt Veronica is home.*
- ● 彼女は歌が上手**にちがいありません** *She undoubtedly sings very well.*

Finally, here is a summary table of the whole lesson, with the formal versions of each one of the expressions, in brackets.

Suppositions: general summary table		
かもしれない	Pure supposition	その男は日本人かもしれない（かもしれません） That man might be Japanese (but I'm not sure)
ようだ	Supposition based on something directly perceived and qualified by the speaker's reason or knowledge	その男は日本人のようだ（のようです） (Considering what I see now and what I knew before about the Japanese in general) that man seems to be Japanese
みたい	Informal version of ようだ	その男は日本人みたい（みたいです） (Considering what I see now and what I knew before about the Japanese in general) that man seems to be Japanese
だろう	Pure supposition (not necessarily based on something)	その男は日本人だろう（でしょう） That man is probably Japanese
らしい	Supposition based on something the speaker has heard, seen, or read	その男は日本人らしい（らしいです） (From what I've heard) that man might be Japanese
らしい (2)	Adjective indicating "worthy of" or "to be expected of"	その男は日本人らしくない（らしくありません） That man doesn't behave like a Japanese (although he probably is)
そうだ	Similar usage to らしい. Supposition based on something read or heard	その男は日本人だそうだ（だそうです） (From what I've heard) that man might be Japanese
そうだ (2)	Supposition based on what the speaker sees or feels, but with not much of a basis (medium probability)	その男は日本語を話しそうだ（話しそうです） That man (so it looks to me) probably speaks Japanese
はずだ	Supposition the speaker almost considers as a fact	その男は日本人のはずだ（のはずです） That man is (supposed to be) Japanese
にちがいない	Very high probability, almost considered as a fact: "there is no doubt"	その男は日本人にちがいない（にちがいありません） That man is undoubtedly Japanese
おとこ: man	にほんじん: Japanese (person)	にほんご: Japanese (language)	はなす: to speak		

We imagine you must be pretty confused after being exposed to such a massive amount of suppositions and conjectures. Let's take a look now at some examples to help clarify the fine lines between each of the types of conjectures.

a) A typical greeting

Yajirō: お元気そうで何よりです 先生
(honorif.) cheerful (look) what more be teacher
I'm glad to see you (look like you) are well, teacher.

Our first example belongs to the expression そうだ (2) which, you will remember, is used when making a conjecture based on visual information. The characteristic of そうだ (2) is that it works inflecting verbs or adjectives. In this case, the *-na* adjective 元気な *(healthy, cheerful)* becomes 元気そうな *(look healthy or cheerful)*.

The expression in this manga-example, 元気そうで何よりです, is used quite often to greet someone you haven't seen for a long time. より means "more than..." and we will have a better look at it when we study the comparatives (L.54, book 3). The literal translation of this expression would be *You look well and there is nothing better than that.*

A note on the negative: The *-sō* form of the negative ない is なさそう, and the negative (of adjectives, not verbs) is formed replacing the い in "normal" negatives (L.13 and 14, book 1) with ～さそう. *-i* adj.: 青い | neg: 青くない | *sō* neg: 青くなさそう *(it doesn't look blue).* *-na* adj.: 元気な | neg: 元気ではない | *sō* neg: 元気ではなさそう *(it doesn't look cheerful).*

Note: かわいそう and えらそう are exceptions. They don't mean *it looks cute* (from かわいい, *cute*) nor *it looks important* (from えらい, *important*), but *pitiful* and *self-important*, respectively. **Attention:** the *-sō* form of いい *(good)* is よさそう *(looks good)*.

b) Perhaps: a colloquial contraction

> **Sawada:** 早_{はや}くしないと死人_{しにん}が出_でちゃうかもよ｜クス
> *quickly do (cond.) dead SP come out perhaps EP? | (coy snicker)*
> **If you don't hurry up, someone might end up dying. | Hu...**

The first expression studied in the theory section was かもしれない *(perhaps, maybe, might...)*, maybe the most common of all suppositions, and the easiest to use, since all you must do is place it at the end of the sentence.

In this case we see the most colloquial usage of かもしれない, shortened to a

Gabriel Luque

simple かも. かも is most often used by young people. **Notes:** 出_でちゃう is the colloquial contraction of 出_でてしまう (L.35), which literally would mean *something comes out (and then one might regret it)*. The と is used to indicate conditional. We already glanced at this usage of と in L.41, but we will study it in depth in book 3.

c) Qualified supposition: *yō da*

> **Matsuda:** ここに オレより強_{つよ}い力_{ちから}をもった人間_{にんげん}はいねぇようだ
> *here PP I more than strong strength DOP have human TOP no there is looks like*
> **It appears that there's no one here stronger than me.**

J.M. Ken Niimura

The expression to highlight here is ようだ. As we know, ようだ comes very often at the end of a sentence. Here, since what comes before ようだ is a verb in its simple form －いねぇ, a vulgar and rough contraction of いない *(there isn't)*－ we don't add anything between it and ようだ. (Check the rules for usage in the theory section for more information.) ようだ has the meaning of "apparently," and is used when the speaker makes a conjecture based on what he sees, on the one hand, and what he already knows about the situation, on the other. Thus, there's a high probability that what is being said is close to the truth. In this panel, the character could have perfectly used みたいだ, a more colloquial and relaxed expression with a very similar meaning. **Note:** like in example a), we have here a より *(more than...)*, which we will see in book 3.

d) An almost certain conjecture: *hazu*

Takada: 田辺さん...あなたはそんな人間じゃないはずだ...
Tanabe (noun suf.)... you TOP *such human no be look like*
Mr. Tanabe... You're not supposed to be that type of a person.

We have seen in the theory section how はずだ, more than a conjecture, is almost a veiled statement or a statement "disguised" as a conjecture. As we see in the example, the character uses はずだ to suppose something which is almost assumed as true. This expression is very common in Japanese.

J.M. Ken Niimura

Note: There are two ways to express the negative of はずだ. The first one, as in here, is conjugating the verb in the negative (そんな人間じゃないはずだ). For the second one, you negate the だ in はずだ: そんな人間のはずでは(じゃ)ない. Keep this in mind, because you could encounter either of the two.

e) A "youthful" expression: *ppoi*

Aya: 競争でもしてるのかな？ **Emi:** なんかかーちゃんとアニキはマジっぽいな...
competition or do Q? EP? *I don't know mom* CP *brother* TOP *seriously (look)* EP...
They're competing? **I'd say mom and my brother are serious...**

Generally, the expression っぽい after an adjective means "looks..." (赤っぽい, *reddish* | まじめっぽい *looks serious*), and after verbs like 怒る (*to get angry*) or 忘れる (*to forget*) it's more or less like our "-ish" or "-ful" (怒りっぽい, *peevish,* 忘れっぽい, *forgetful*). Traditionally, っぽい has essentially negative connotations. However, there is a growing tendency among the young to use っぽい indiscriminately with non-negative connotations replacing other conjectural expressions, such as らしい or みたいだ — like in the example. Whether or not this usage is just a passing vogue, only time will tell. Inflections:
Verbs: add っぽい to the verbal root. 忘れる ⇒ 忘れ ⇒ 忘れっぽい (*forgetful*) | **-*i* adj.:** remove い and add っぽい: 安い ⇒ 安っぽい (*cheapish*) | **-*na* adj.:** remove な and add っぽい: 元気な ⇒ 元気っぽい (*livelish*).

Studio Kōsen

f) The *mitai-na* adjective as a comparative

Some of the expressions we have seen can not only go at the end of the sentence, but also in the middle, because they are really -*na* adjectives. These are ような, みたいな and 〜そうな (usage (2) of そうだ). ような and みたいな are comparatives and mean "to be like..." We will carefully study the comparatives in L.54

Bárbara Raya

Ami: あたしみたいな女をなぜ守るの！？
I like woman dop why protect Q? !?
Why are you protecting a woman like me?!

(book 3), but in this panel we have a very good example. Placing みたいな after あたし (*I*, fem.), we obtain あたしみたいな (*like me*). Therefore, あたしみたいな女 = *a woman like me*. Regarding verbs and adjectives inflected in the -*sō* form −そうだ (2)−, they become normal -*na* adjectives which, in turn, work like this: 元気な (*cheerful*) ⇒ 元気 そうな (*looks cheerful*) ⇒ 元気そうな男 (*cheerful looking man*) | 高い (*expensive*) ⇒ 高そ うな (*looks expensive*) => ⇒ 高そうな本 (*expensive looking book*).

g) As is expected from...

Nobuhito: マコトくん　もっと男らしく入りたまえ
Makoto (noun suf) more man like come in
Makoto, you must come in more like a man.

Bárbara Raya

And last, an example of the usage of らしい as an -*i* adjective. As we have seen, when らしい functions as an adjective it has the meaning of "as is expected from" or "worthy of." Here, we have 男らしい (*as is expected from a man, like a man*), but here らしい has been transformed into an adverb: 男らしく would be something like *manly*. らしい can also go in the negative (男らしくない, *not manly*), in the past (男らし かった, *was manly*), and in the past negative (男らしく なかった, *was not manly*).

Note: We already saw the imperative 〜たまえ in L.30 (book 1). It is used by a speaker who is or feels in a position which is superior to his interlocutor. It is quite "authoritarian."

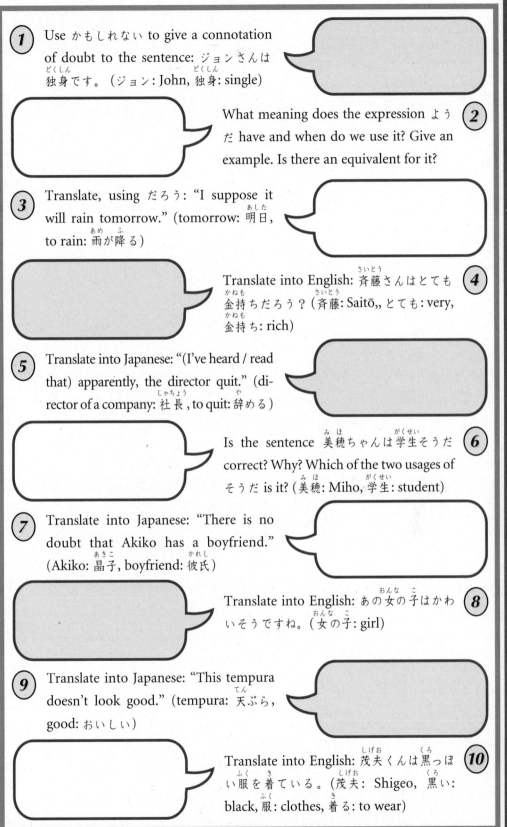

1 Use かもしれない to give a connotation of doubt to the sentence: ジョンさんは独身です。（ジョン: John, 独身: single)

2 What meaning does the expression ようだ have and when do we use it? Give an example. Is there an equivalent for it?

3 Translate, using だろう: "I suppose it will rain tomorrow." (tomorrow: 明日, to rain: 雨が降る)

4 Translate into English: 斉藤さんはとても金持ちだろう？（斉藤: Saitō,, とても: very, 金持ち: rich)

5 Translate into Japanese: "(I've heard / read that) apparently, the director quit." (director of a company: 社長, to quit: 辞める)

6 Is the sentence 美穂ちゃんは学生そうだ correct? Why? Which of the two usages of そうだ is it? (美穂: Miho, 学生: student)

7 Translate into Japanese: "There is no doubt that Akiko has a boyfriend." (Akiko: 晶子, boyfriend: 彼氏)

8 Translate into English: あの女の子はかわいそうですね。（女の子: girl)

9 Translate into Japanese: "This tempura doesn't look good." (tempura: 天ぷら, good: おいしい)

10 Translate into English: 茂夫くんは黒っぽい服を着ている。（茂夫: Shigeo, 黒い: black, 服: clothes, 着る: to wear)

第43課 練習

Exercises

Lesson 44: Transitive and intransitive verbs

This next lesson will be a little bit more difficult, not so much because it is complicated, but more because you will need to learn a large number of verb pairs. Now let's begin to fine-tune our Japanese by studying transitive and intransitive verbs.

A memory exercise

You probably remember what transitive and intransitive verbs are, from what you studied in grammar lessons at school, but, just in case, we will give you a quick reminder. In outline, a transitive verb is constructed with direct object (DO), and an intransitive one is constructed without DO. As a simple example, *to remove, to put* or *to take out* are transitive, and *to arrive, to swim* or *to run away* are intransitive: one can *remove «something»* (the DO) but *can't swim "something."*

In Japanese there are also transitive and intransitive verbs, just as we know them. For example, 殺す *(to kill)* is transitive, while 死ぬ *(to die)* is intransitive. But, obviously, this subject would not deserve a full lesson if it were that easy.

The peculiarity in Japanese are the so-called "pairs of transitive-intransitive verbs." Sometimes, there are two similar but essentially different verbs for one type of action, a transitive one (it needs DO), and an intransitive one (without DO). For example, take a look at the pair 始める and 始まる. Both mean *to begin*, but the first one is transitive and the second one isn't. With the first one, a subject needs to perform the action, whereas with the second one, the action is performed "by itself." Look at the example:

- 香里さんは試験を始めた *Kaori began the exam.*
- 6時に試験が始まる *The exam begins at six.*

The basic structure for these pairs of verbs would be something like this:

<u>Transitive Verb:</u>　　YがXをV trans.　Ex: 香里が試験を始める *Kaori begins the exam.*

<u>Intransitive Verb:</u>　X がV intrans.　Ex: 試験が始まる *The exam begins.*

Y: performs the action | X: receives the action

Some recommendations

This in particular gives rise to many errors among Japanese students whose mother tongue is European: since Western languages don't have a similar structure, mistaking the verb is very easy. Unfortunately, there is no easy solution to learn how to use the transitive-intransitive pairs of verbs: all we can do is learn them by heart. In page 144 you have an extensive table where the most frequent pairs of verbs are specified. We have tried to make it as easy as possible, marking the most basic verbs in bold type: those are the first you must learn. Further on, when you have mastered the essential ones, you can memorize the rest.

Also, take note of how we have divided the verbs according to the changes they undergo when changing from intransitive into transitive (some change from *-aru* to *-eru*, others from *-reru* to *-su*, etc.)

You will see how in almost all cases, the kanji reading doesn't vary: only the ending changes. The only three exceptions are 消える *(to be put out / to disappear)* −消す *(to put out, to erase),* 出る *(to go out)* − 出す *(to take out)* and 入る *(to go in)* − 入れる *(to put in)*. Very often, the meaning of each pair of verbs is identical, but when translating here we use the passive form *(the door is opened, the child is found, the light is put out)*. This is a trick to memorize and better understand how these verbs work.

聞こえる and 見える

In manga-example d) of L.32, we saw the verbs 聞こえる *(to hear)* and 見える *(to see),* and said they were different to 聞く *(to hear)* and 見る *(to see)* because the first ones indicate "one can see or hear something unconsciously or passively," while the second ones indicate "one can see or hear something because that is what one expressly wants to do." In this lesson we have more knowledge than when we began studying this book, so you can probably see the differences we are trying to point out. Indeed, they are two pairs of transitive-intransitive verbs: 聞こえる and 見える are intransitive, whereas 聞く and 見る are transitive. Let's see some examples:

● 波の音が聞こえる *You can hear the sound of the waves.* (intransitive)
● 純子さんは波の音を聞いている *Junko is listening to the sound of the waves.* (transitive)
● ここからは富士山が見える *You can see Mount Fuji from here.* (intransitive)
● 私は富士山を見るのは初めてです *This is the first time I see Mount Fuji.* (transitive)

Pairs of transitive and intransitive verbs

Intrans.	Translation	Trans.	Translation	Intrans.	Translation	Trans.	Translation
-aru		**-eru**		残(のこ)る	to be left	残(のこ)す	to leave
上(あ)がる	to rise	上(あ)げる	to raise	回(まわ)る	**to turn round**	回(まわ)す	**to turn**
集(あつ)まる	to be gathered	集(あつ)める	to gather	戻(もど)る	to go back	戻(もど)す	to give back
終(お)わる	to end	終(お)える	to finish	**-eru**		**-asu**	
変(か)わる	to change	変(か)える	to change	遅(おく)れる	to be late	遅(おく)らす	to make late
決(き)まる	to be decided	決(き)める	to decide	逃(に)げる	to escape	逃(に)がす	to let escape
下(さ)がる	to go down	下(さ)げる	to lower	冷(ひ)える	to get cold	冷(ひ)やす	to cool
閉(し)まる	**to be closed**	閉(し)める	to close	増(ふ)える	to be increased	増(ふ)やす	to increase
かかる	**to be hung**	かける	to hang	燃(も)える	to be on fire	燃(も)やす	to burn
締(しず)まる	to calm down	締(しず)める	to calm	**-u**		**-asu**	
高(たか)まる	to rise	高(たか)める	to raise	動(うご)く	to move	動(うご)かす	to move
助(たす)かる	to be saved	助(たす)ける	to save	飛(と)ぶ	to fly	飛(と)ばす	to make fly
捕(つか)まる	to be caught	捕(つか)まえる	to catch	泣(な)く	to cry	泣(な)かす	to make cry
伝(つた)わる	to be transmitted	伝(つた)える	to convey	**-u**		**-eru**	
止(と)まる	to stop	止(と)める	to stop	開(あ)く	**to be open**	開(あ)ける	**to open**
始(はじ)まる	to begin	始(はじ)める	to begin	片付(かたづ)く	to be tidy	片付(かたづ)ける	to tidy up
曲(ま)がる	to be bent	曲(ま)げる	to bend	育(そだ)つ	to grow up	育(そだ)てる	to bring up
見(み)つかる	**to be found**	見(み)つける	to find	立(た)つ	to stand	立(た)てる	to erect
-reru		**-su**		付(つ)く	**to stick to**	付(つ)ける	**to attach**
現(あらわ)れる	to appear	現(あらわ)す	to show	続(つづ)く	**to continue**	続(つづ)ける	**to continue**
壊(こわ)れる	**to be broken**	壊(こわ)す	to break	届(とど)く	to arrive	届(とど)ける	to deliver
離(はな)れる	to separate	離(はな)す	to separate				

Other verbs

Intrans.	Translation	Trans.	Translation
倒(たお)れる	to fall	倒(たお)す	to throw dwn.
汚(よご)れる	to be stained	汚(よご)す	to stain
生(う)まれる	to be born	生(う)む	to give birth
起(お)きる	to get up	起(お)こす	to raise
落(お)ちる	**to fall**	落(お)とす	**to drop**
降(お)りる	to get off	降(お)ろす	to drop off
下(お)りる	to get down	下(お)ろす	to take down
消(き)える	**to be put out**	消(き)す	**to put out**
聞(き)こえる	**to be heard**	聞(き)く	**to hear**
出(で)る	**to go out**	出(だ)す	**to take out**
脱(ぬ)げる	to come off	脱(ぬ)ぐ	to take off
乗(の)る	to ride in	乗(の)せる	to carry
入(はい)る	**to go in**	入(い)れる	**to put in**
見(み)える	to be seen	見(み)る	to see
分(わ)かれる	to divide	分(わ)かる	to understand

Left-column additional groups:

Intrans.	Translation	Trans.	Translation
-reru		**-ru**	
売(う)れる	to sell	売(う)る	to sell
折(お)れる	to be folded	折(お)る	to fold
割(わ)れる	to be broken	割(わ)る	to break
-ru		**-su**	
写(うつ)る	to be reflected	写(うつ)す	to reflect
返(かえ)る	to return	返(かえ)す	to give back
帰(かえ)る	to go back	帰(かえ)す	to let go back
通(とお)る	**to pass**	通(とお)す	**to pass**
直(なお)る	to be mended	直(なお)す	to correct
治(なお)る	to recover	治(なお)す	to cure

More examples

Let's see now a few examples with some of the pairs of verbs we have seen in the table in the previous page:

- 人々が会場に集まった *People gathered in the hall.* (intransitive)
- 僕は書類を全部集めました *I gathered all the documents.* (transitive)
- 私の家が燃えました *My house was burnt.* (intransitive)
- その葉っぱを燃やしてください *Burn those leaves, please.* (transitive)
- マイクはレストランに入りました *Mike went into the restaurant.* (intransitive)
- ママは卵を冷蔵庫に入れた *Mom put the eggs in the fridge.* (transitive)

Notice how the particles for subject が (or topic は, depending on the case), and direct object を are used in the sentences. Notice, too, how in many cases, when we translate intransitive sentences, we use the passive form. You might use this as a hint.

A last and very clear example could be given with the pair 落ちる *(to fall)* and 落とす *(to drop)*. Imagine you are carrying a vase, and it falls on the floor. If you use 落ちる, you are just saying the vase fell, but if you use 落とす, you are implying you or somebody let the vase drop on the floor. This example should help you get a better understanding of the subtle differences between transitive and intransitive verbs.

Compound verbs

Let's put aside the pairs of transitive-intransitive verbs, and have a look at another characteristic which can really increase the nuances we give our sentences. We are talking about forming compound verbs with connotations such as "easy to...," "hard to...," "start doing...," etc.

Compound verbs in Japanese are formed with the verbal root (the -*masu* form without the final ます of any verb), plus the ending which will give the connotation we want. For example, ending ～やすい adds the connotation of "easy to..." to a verb.

<u>An example</u>: 分かる *(to understand)* ⇒ -*masu* form: 分かります ⇒ Root: 分かり ⇒ We add ～やすい: 分かりやすい *(easy to understand)*.

<u>Another example</u>: 汚れる *(to be stained)* ⇒ -*masu* form: 汚れます ⇒ Root: 汚れ ⇒ We add ～やすい: 汚れやすい *(easily stained)*.

- 内田先生の授業は分かりやすいです *Professor Uchida's classes are easy to understand.*
- この服はとても汚れやすいね *These clothes are very easily soiled, aren't they?*

Easy to and hard to

We have just seen how to form verbs with the connotation of "easy to..." by adding ～やすい to the verb. Its opposite, "hard to...," is formed by adding ～にくい.

Note: Verbs to which we add ～やすい and ～にくい function like *-i* adjectives, so they are conjugated in the same way.

● この音楽は聞きにくい *This music is hard to listen to.*

● あのマンガはとても読みやすかったです *That manga was very easy to read.*

● 日本は住みにくくない国だ *Japan is a country where it isn't hard to live.*

Start doing, finish doing and keep on doing

We can also form compound verbs adding the auxiliary verbs ～始める *(start doing)*, ～終わる *(finish doing)*, and ～続く *(keep on doing)* to a verbal root.

Note: Here, the resultant verb functions like any other verb, so you can conjugate it in the *-te* (L.24 [book 1] and L.35), *-ō* (L.34), and *-tai* (L.31) forms, as well as many others.

● 先生は急に話し始めました *The teacher suddenly started talking.*

● レポートを書き終わってください *Finish writing that report, please.*

● 彼は来ないから、飲み続けよう！ *Since he's not coming, let's keep on drinking!*

● カラオケで歌を歌い始めたいです *I want to start singing songs at the karaoke.*

Other auxiliary verbs to create compounds

There are other auxiliary verbs to create compound verbs, which function just like ～始める, ～終わる and ～続ける (the resultant verb being conjugated as any other verb):

～かかる and ～かける: nearly, half. (See adjunctive table.)

～出す: begin to. 走り出す, *break into a (begin to) run.*

～回る: go around. 歩き回る, *walk about.*

～込む: put in (suddenly). 聞き込む, *ask directly, very openly.*

Compound verbs with 食(た)べる *(to eat)*		
～やすい	easy to...	食べやすい Easy to eat
～にくい	hard to...	食べにくい Hard to eat
～始める	to start doing...	食べ始める To start eating
～終わる	to finish doing...	食べ終わる To finish eating
～続ける	to keep on doing...	食べ続ける To keep on eating
～かける	nearly, half (intrans.)	食べかける To leave something half-eaten
～かかる	nearly, half (trans.)	食べかかる Something is half-eaten

The truth is transitive and intransitive verbs are really difficult to master perfectly. You must always be aware so that you know which verb to use depending on the occasion and the subject. You might make mistakes, but keep on trying and learn from your errors: this is the only way to improve.

a) Pair of transitive-intransitive verbs

Yōichi: ただの砂糖を入れるんじゃ風味が出ない...
normal POP sugar DOP put in then flavor SP go out...
Adding normal sugar won't bring out the flavor...
野菜を使ってかくし味の甘味を出してやるんだ...！
vegetables DOP use hidden flavor POP sweetness DOP take out do...!
You must use vegetables to bring out the sweet hidden flavor!

Leaving aside all gourmet terms, which fascinate Japanese readers, in this example we will focus on the pair of verbs 出る (conjugated here in the negative, 出ない) and 出す (in the *-te* form, 出して) which, as we have already seen, form a pair of transitive-intransitive verbs.

The transitive verb is 出す *(to take out)*. 出す requires a subject to perform the action (in this case the subject is "the vegetables") and a DO, which receives the action (in this case, 甘味, *sweet taste, sweetness*). Therefore, this sentence expresses *The vegetables bring out the sweet flavor*. In the case of the intransitive verb 出る *(to go out)*, it only needs a subject, 風味 *(flavor, essence)* and there is no DO. Here, the sentence expresses something like *the flavor does not (or won't) come out*. Notice, too, that we have another transitive verb, 入れる *(to put in)*. The subject is most likely "I," and the DO is 砂糖 *(sugar)*. Therefore: *I put in sugar*. To conclude, the intransitive version of 入れる is 入る *(to go in)*. 私が入る means *I go in*. The pairs of verbs 出る—出す and 入る—入れる are often used and so you must learn their usages carefully.

b) "To decide," transitive version

> **Jirō:** そういえば...名前まだ決めてなかったな...
> *that say... name still decide EP...*
> **Speaking of which... I still haven't decided the name...**

Gabriel Luque

It might be useful for you to know that, in Japanese, the word that names transitive verbs is 他動詞 (他: *other*, 動詞: *verb*), literally "verb whose action is performed by some other subject."

The meaning of the transitive verb we see in this example, 決める, is *to decide*.

Since it's a transitive verb, it requires "another" subject (it's omitted, but it would be "I") to perform the action indicated by the verb *(to decide)* on a DO (here, 名前, *name*). Therefore, 私は名前を決める means *I decide the name*.

Notes: In spoken Japanese, certain particles are sometimes left out, を in this case (名前を決める *to decide the name*). Notice also the まだ *(still)*, which we saw in L.40.

c) "To be decided," intransitive version

> **Hideki:** あと一本！あと一本のドライブシュートできまるんだ！
> *after one (counter)! After one (counter)! POP drive shoot IP can be!*
> **One more! This will be decided with one more drive shoot!**

Intransitive verbs are know in Japanese as 自動詞 (自: *oneself*, 動詞: *verb*), that is, "verb whose action is performed by oneself." We have just seen the transitive verb 決める in the previous example, and we are now to study its "intransitive partner," 決まる. The verb 決まる means *to be decided,* and here the action is performed by "oneself," there is no DO. In the example, the subject (the one per-

Bárbara Raya

forming the action), is left out, but it could be ゴールが決まる *a goal will be decided (be entered)* or 試合が決まる *(the match will be decided)*. Notice how in English we very often use the passive form to translate intransitive verbs.

Note: Take a look at the counter used to count shots: 本, which is usually used to count long and thin things, such as pencils, trees, toothpicks... (L.25, book 1).

d) Something "gets cold" (intransitive)

> **Yoneda:** 帰りましょう...風が冷えてきたようだ
> *go back... wind SP cool down come looks like*
> **Let's go back... It looks like the wind has cooled down.**

First of all, take a look at the verb in this example: 冷える. It's an intransitive verb, whose action is performed by "itself," as we mentioned in the previous example. In this manga-example, the *wind* (風) *cools down* (冷える) by itself, no one cools it down. If we wanted to say *God cools down the wind*, we

Javier Bolado

would have to use 冷やす, the equivalent transitive verb: 神様は風を冷やす, because it would be "someone else" (神様, God) who would perform the action of cooling down. **Note:** Take a look at the other grammatical structures in this sentence, which will be very helpful for you to review. We have a formal -ō form (帰りましょう, L.34), a ～て くる construction (L.35), and even a conjecture with ～ようだ (L.43).

e) Someone "conveys" something (transitive)

> **Sano:** 女房と娘に...「パパは最後までがんばった」と伝えてくれ
> *wife CP daughter IOP... "dad TOP end until hold out" SBP convey (imp.)*
> **Tell my wife and my daughter... that, "dad held out till the end."**

J.M. Ken Niimura

The verb 伝える in this sentence means *to convey / to tell*, and is a transitive one. Its intransitive counterpart, with the same meaning, is 伝わる. In our manga-example, the speaker asks someone to convey a certain message to another person. If we were to summarize the sentence, we would get something like あなたはメッセージを伝える *you convey the message*. On the other hand, if the message were to be conveyed by itself, we would have to use the intransitive form: メッセージが伝わる *the message is transmitted*.
Notes: ～てくれ is the imperative form of ～てくれる (somebody else does you a favor), which we glanced at in book 1 and which we will study in depth in L.45. Besides, notice the second と: it's usage #3 (quote), which we studied in L.41.

Transitive and intransitive verbs 自動詞と他動詞 −149−

f) An intransitive compound verb

Bárbara Raya

> **Man:** きてくれーっ 倉が燃えだしたあっ
> *come (imp.) warehouse* SP *burn (go out)*
> **Come! The warehouse is burning!**

Although transitive and intransitive verbs might be somewhat tiring, it is an essential grammar point and so you should study them carefully. Memorize the verbs in the table in page 144, at least the most basic ones. In this example we have yet another intransitive verb: *(the warehouse) is burning / has caught fire* (倉が燃える). If there were a subject responsible for the fire (let's say a 泥棒, *thief*), we would have to use its transitive counterpart 燃やす: 泥棒が倉を燃やす, *The thief burns the warehouse.* Going onto a different area, notice how the compound verb 燃え出す has been formed. We have already seen that adding 〜出す to a verb, we obtain a connotation of "begin to" or "burst out doing" (we will add that it also gives it a "violent" or "rapid" connotation). 燃え出す indicates something like *begin to burn (quickly, suddenly)*.

g) More compounds

> **Nishida:** だから差別は無くしがたい
> *therefore discrimination* TOP *lose (hard to)*
> **I'm telling you discrimination is hard to eradicate.**

In the last example we have a new ending used to form compounds, 〜がたい, which means something like 〜にくい (*hard to...*), but it's much more formal and has a stronger meaning. The formation of compound verbs with 〜がたい is identical to 〜にくい and 〜やすい: you add 〜がたい to the verbal root (*-masu* form without ます).
Example: 許す *(to forgive)* ⇒ *-masu* form:

Studio Kōsen

許します ⇒ we remove ます ⇒ 許し ⇒ We add 〜がたい: 許しがたい *(hard to forgive)*. The resultant verb functions like an *-i* adjective.
There are a few more endings or auxiliary verbs, such as 〜合う *(mutually)* or 〜きる *(to cut abruptly)*. However, for the moment, those we have studied will be sufficient.

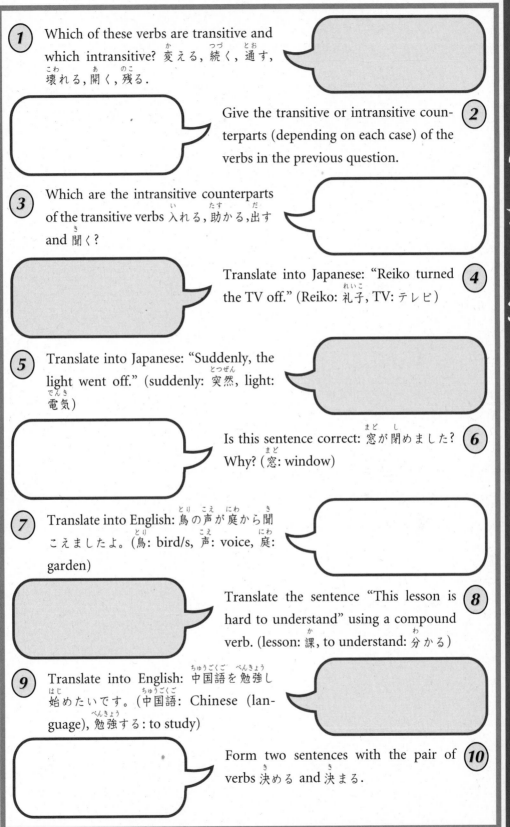

1. Which of these verbs are transitive and which intransitive? 変える, 続く, 通す, 壊れる, 開く, 残る.

2. Give the transitive or intransitive counterparts (depending on each case) of the verbs in the previous question.

3. Which are the intransitive counterparts of the transitive verbs 入れる, 助かる, 出す and 聞く?

4. Translate into Japanese: "Reiko turned the TV off." (Reiko: 礼子, TV: テレビ)

5. Translate into Japanese: "Suddenly, the light went off." (suddenly: 突然, light: 電気)

6. Is this sentence correct: 窓が閉めました? Why? (窓: window)

7. Translate into English: 鳥の声が庭から聞こえましたよ。(鳥: bird/s, 声: voice, 庭: garden)

8. Translate the sentence "This lesson is hard to understand" using a compound verb. (lesson: 課, to understand: 分かる)

9. Translate into English: 中国語を勉強し始めたいです。(中国語: Chinese (language), 勉強する: to study)

10. Form two sentences with the pair of verbs 決める and 決まる.

第44課 練習 Exercises

Lesson 45: To give and to receive

In L.28 (book 1) we had a quick look at the usage of the three verbs meaning to give and to receive, あげる, もらう and くれる. At that time we just skimmed through them, because these are essential verbs in Japanese and it was advisable for you to know about them at a relatively early stage in your learning. Now the time has come to study them in depth.

The concept of *uchi* and *soto*

We will start by explaining two of the most particular concepts in Japanese society: 内 (*inside*) and 外 (*outside*). These seemingly have no relationship with the subject of giving and receiving, but trust us when we say that this will help you to better understand the lesson, as well as the Japanese mind. The Japanese clearly distinguish between what is "inside" their circle *(uchi)* and what is "outside" it *(soto)*, and this distinction is present in all aspects of everyday life, including, of course, language. Let's see some examples:

Everyday life. *Uchi:* me, my closest family. | *Soto:* any other person (family which is not so close would be in the middle, closer to *uchi* than to *soto*). **Work.** *Uchi:* me, my workmates (including my bosses). | *Soto:* anybody belonging to another company, a client or a supplier. **School.** *Uchi:* me, my classmates, my course tutor, my club. | *Soto:* any other teacher, people from other classes, clubs, and schools.

There are gradations, of course: for instance, one can get closer to the *uchi* circle of another person if they establish a deep and lasting relationship: the deeper the relationship, the closer to *uchi*. For example, a boy and a girl meet (a completely *soto* relationship), become friends (they are still *soto* to each other, but less so), they fall in love and start going out (at this point they start being more *uchi* than *soto*) and they finally marry (they become 100% *uchi* to each other).

The point of view is also essential: which part of the sentence carries the most weight, who is speaking, and who performs a certain action. It is very important that all these aspects are very clear.

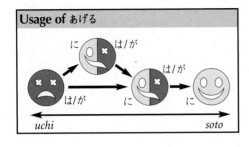

Usage of あげる

uchi ← → soto

The verb あげる

We will now go on to study the subject we are dealing with: the usage of the three verbs expressing "giving" and "receiving" relationships. These verbs, あげる, もらう and くれる, have an unusual usage and usually give the Western student of Japanese much trouble, so we will study them very carefully.

Take a look at the diagram of the usage of あげる. The bottom arrow expresses the *uchi-soto* relationship. The more to the left, the more *uchi* is the character; the more to the right, the more *soto* it is. A smiling face indicates the character "receives" something. Whereas a surly face means the character "gives" something (the half-half faces indicate they are, on the one hand, receiving, and on the other, giving). Regarding color, dark faces represent the main point of view, that is, the dark gray character is responsible for the action. The particles used by each character are also shown.

あげる, then, is used with the meaning of "give," and is not very difficult.
- 私 は友達 に薬 をあげる *I give my friend some medicine.*
- 妻 は井口 さんにサーカスの切符 をあげた *My wife gave Mr. Iguchi a ticket for the circus.*
- 警察官 はおじいさんに新聞 をあげた *The policeman gave the old man a newspaper.*
- 先生 は来客 にお土産 をあげました *The teacher gave the visitor a souvenir.*

Very important: the verb あげる is <u>never</u> used in sentences such as *Hanako gave me (me or someone in the* uchi *circle) a flower.* In this case, we use the verb くれる.

The verb もらう

もらう means "to receive," and is used to express: "I or someone in the *uchi* circle receives something." The usage of this verb is not very difficult either, as you will see in the examples.

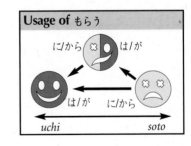

Usage of もらう

uchi ← → soto

Note: The giver can take particles に or から alike.
- 私 は息子 にケーキをもらう *I receive a cake from my son.*
- 僕 は同僚 にいいアドバイスをもらった *I received a good piece of advice from a colleague.*
- 娘 は友達 からプレゼントをもらいました *My daughter received a present from a friend.*
- 高 い時計 をもらって、うれしい *I have received an expensive watch and I am happy.*

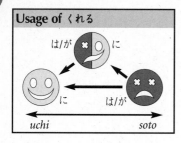

Usage of くれる

The verb くれる

Here is the tough nut in the lesson: the verb くれる, which is like a mixture of あげる and もらう, is hard to master if we don't quite understand who is performing the action and what role the *uchi-soto* relationship plays in the context. くれる is used when the "giver" is someone from soto (he can also be from *uchi*, but it is not common), and the "receiver" is, <u>compulsorily</u> someone in the *uchi* circle. The point of view is placed on the <u>giver</u>, never on the receiver. The sentence *Hanako gave me a flower must*, then, use くれる. Take a look at the diagram to understand this better: "I" *(uchi)* am the smiling light gray face in the left, and "Hanako" (soto) is the surly dark gray face in the right.

- 花子は私に花をくれた *Hanako gave me a flower | I received a flower from Hanako.*
- 友達は娘にアドバイスをくれた *A friend gave my daughter some advice.*
- ジョンは(私に)その本をくれると思うよ *I think John will give me that book.*
- 彼はいい人だから、お金をくれた *As he is a good person, he gave me (or* uchi*) some money.*

The concept of *tate*

The other axis that is the basic tenet of the Japanese social structure is the "vertical" axis or 縦. The society is hierarchically divided: relevant to oneself, there are those in superior positions, there are those in equivalent positions, and, finally, there are those in inferior positions. This is also unavoidably reflected in language, as we will see in L.52 (book 3), where we will talk about formal language.

Verbs あげる, くれる and もらう don't escape hierarchy, and have "families" of verbs with the same meaning and usage. We will use one or the other depending on whether the speaker is in a superior, equal, or inferior position (see diagram).

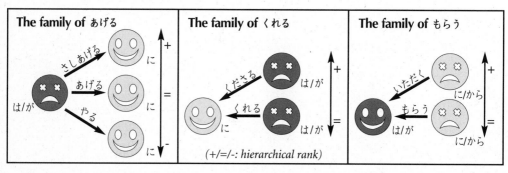

The family of あげる

The family of くれる

(+/=/-: hierarchical rank)

The family of もらう

Therefore, we will use あげる when we give something to somebody in our same position, but if his or her position is superior to ours, we will then use さしあげる. Whereas, if we are giving something to someone in an inferior position we will use やる. もらう and くれる have no versions for "inferior," only for neutral and superior, which are いただく and くださる, respectively. Let's see some sentences for a clearer understanding.

- 私は先生にプレゼントをさしあげたい *I want to give the teacher a present.*
- 僕は弟にお金をやった *I gave my younger brother some money.*
- 彼は犬におもちゃをやった *He gave the dog a toy.*
- 私は井上さんに１万円をいただいた *I received 10,000 yen from Mr. Inoue.*
- 井上さんは私に１万円をくださった *Mr. Inoue gave me 10,000 yen.*
- お客様は微笑をくださいました *The client gave (offered) me a smile.*

Note: We don't usually show "superiority" before anybody, so the usage of やる is rather limited to family usage (sentence 2), very close friends, or relationships between a human being and an animal (sentence 3). Avoid using it, as it sounds quite arrogant.

あげる, もらう and くれる as auxiliary verbs

The three verbs we have just studied, including their formal and informal versions, can function as auxiliary verbs following verbs in the *-te* form. For example, the sentence 私は花子に花を買ってあげた literally means *I bought (and, in doing so, I did her a favor) a flower for Hanako.*

The usage of あげる, くれる and もらう (and their respective "families") as auxiliary verbs is identical to their usage as the verbs themselves – that is, the same explanatory diagrams in the previous pages are valid here–, and they add the connotations of "doing and being done a favor" to sentences. These constructions appear over and over in all registers of the language, so it is very advisable to learn their usage well.

- 友達に英語を教えてあげたい *I want to teach my friend English.*
- 私は妹にケーキを焼いてやる *I bake a cake for my younger sister.*
- 先生に本を貸してさしあげました *I leant my teacher a book.*
- 昨日、りんごをもらってきた *Yesterday, I went (and came back) to receive some apples.*
- 先生は娘に親切してくださっています *The teacher is kind to my daughter.*
- 友達は彼女にマンガを買ってくれた *My friend bought my girlfriend a comic book.*
- 説明していただきたいんですけど... *I would like you to explain this (to me), but...*

Way of: 〜方

Let's now briefly forget about the group of giving and receiving verbs, and devote this last theory page to seeing two characteristics of the Japanese language, the explanation of which we have postponed until now for several reasons. The first is how to form nouns from verbs meaning "way of."

<u>Usage</u>: We will need a verbal root (*-masu* form without the final ます, L.31), to which we add 〜方. Example: 書く *(to write)* ⇒ *-masu* form: 書きます ⇒ root: 書き ⇒ we add 〜方: 書き方 *(way of writing)*.

● 焼きそばの作り方は簡単です *(The way of) making yakisoba is very simple.*
● この漢字の書き方を忘れた *I have forgotten how (the way) to write this kanji.*
● 洗濯のし方を教えてください *Please, teach me how (the way) to do the washing.*

With *suru* verbs you must place の between the noun and the する verb: 洗濯のし方.

Not much: あまり

The second expression we will study is あまり, a very common adverb meaning "not much." Be very careful, because this adverb means "not much" only with verbs and adjectives in the negative.

● サラは日本語があまり上手ではない *Sarah is not very good at Japanese.*
● 寿司はあまり好きじゃない *I don't like sushi much.*
● 今日はカラオケであまり歌いたくない *Today, I don't feel very much like singing at karaoke.*

Sometimes, あまり, when adding に, is used with non-negative verbs and adjectives, and it then means "so much" or "very much."

● あまりに眠かったので授業で寝てしまった *I was so tired I fell asleep in class.*
● あまりに失礼だったから殴ってしまった *He was so rude, I hit (punched) him.*

You have probably already seen in in this or other lessons the uagse of adverbs とても, 非常に, or 大変 to indicate "very." Of these, you should at least learn, for now, とても.

● ダンは日本語がとても上手です *Dan is very good at Japanese.*
● 数学の授業は非常に難しいよ *The math class is extremely difficult.*
● あの道は大変危険です *That road is horribly dangerous.*

Pay attention to the distinction between とても *(very)* and たくさん *(a lot)*.

● 漢字はとても難しいです *Kanji are very difficult.*
● 漢字はたくさんあります *There are a lot of kanji.*

Mastering the three giving and receiving verbs is difficult for a Westerner, but we hope this lesson has enabled you to at least to understand the way they work. We will now go on to see a few examples that should help to set these new concepts in.

a) The verb "to give:" *ageru*

Kani: そうかそうかごくろうさんじゃったな
that Q? that Q? good job be EP
Well, well… You have done a good job.

Kudō: プレゼント？
present?
A present?

Kani: では お礼にステキなプレゼントをあげてしまおう.
well gratitude for nice present DOP give going to
Well then, I shall give you a nice present to thank you.

We will start having a look at an example of the usage of あげる, which, as you know, is used to indicate "give." Be careful, because when someone "gives" something to somebody in the *uchi* circle we must use くれる, and not あげる. In all other cases, we use あげる.

Here, Kani is going to "give" Kudō a present. The point of view is placed on the speaker himself, who is also the performer of the action of giving: therefore, あげる is used. Notice how the verbs to give and to receive are normal verbs, and, as such, can be conjugated. Here, あげる is in the *-te* form and with the ～しまう construction (L.35), indicating "to finish doing something completely." ～しまう is conjugated in the *-ō* form (L.34), which gives the whole sentence the sense of "I'm going to give you (completely)."

Notes: ごくろうさん is the informal version of ご苦労様 (L.27, book 1), literally "thank you for getting tired." じゃった is the version of だった *(was)* used by elder men.

b) *Kureru* as an auxiliary verb

> **Phoebe:** あんたはあたしを助けてくれました
> *you* TOP *I* DOP *save (favor)*
> **You saved me.**

Gabriel Luque

Notice how くれる functions as an auxiliary verb in this example. The verbs of giving and receiving appear very often combined with other verbs conjugated in the *-te* form. This sentence is very clear: we perfectly see how あんた *(you)* is who performs the action of "giving," and is also in the point of view (it is marked with the particle は). Receiving the action is あたし *(I)*, someone in the *uchi* circle: therefore, くれる is the logical option. くれる as an auxiliary verb adds the nuance of "doing a favor." Thus, 助けてくれる would literally mean something like "someone does the favor of saving somebody in the uchi circle."

c) The usage of *yaru* and the imperative *-kure*

> **Walter:** いいとも、会わせてやるぜ。そのまえにこれを飲んでくれ。
> *all right (emph), put together (allow to)* EP. *that before this* DOP *drink (order)*
> **All right, I'll fix you up with her. But before that, take this (pill).**

In this example, there are two forms to highlight. First, we have the usage of ～てやる, that is, やる as an auxiliary verb. Remember やる belongs to the family of あげる and is used when speaking to people in an "inferior" position. In this example, Walter uses やる to get his inter-

J.M. Ken Niimura

locutor to understand his supposed superiority, or simply to "act cool:" this usage often appears in manga, but in real life is hardly ever used because it is too rude and arrogant. The second form is ～てくれ. くれ, the imperative form (L.30, book 1) of くれる, is used very often to give orders, although not as strong as the pure imperative. In this case, we have 飲んでくれ, which literally means "do me (me or someone in the *uchi* circle) a favor and drink." The imperative version 飲め *(drink)* is a much stronger command.

Note: Walter gives his interlocutor a pill, and asks him to 飲んでくれ *(drink it)*. Curiously enough, in Japanese one doesn't "take" medicine, but "drinks" it.

d) *Morau* as an auxiliary verb

Ieyasu: 花子 今夜は秀忠の相手をしてもらいたいのじゃ
Hanako tonight TOP *Hidetada* POP *the other* DOP *do receive* POP *be*
Hanako, I want you to entertain Hidetada tonight.

Here we have もらう functioning as an auxiliary verb. Notice how Ieyasu tells Hanako
he *wants to receive* (もらいたい) from her
something (in this case an action) for Hidetada. Remember もらう is used to say "I or
someone in the *uchi* circle <u>receives</u> something." Hidetada is Ieyasu's son and, there-

Javier Bolado

fore, belongs to his *uchi* circle, which justifies the usage of もらう. The basic sentence would
be 秀忠は花子に相手をしてもらう (*Hidetada receives the fact of Hanako entertaining him*).
Note: 相手 means *interlocutor, opponent,* etc., but the expression 相手をする means *to keep
company, take care of,* or *entertain.* のじゃ is a distortion of のだ (L.40), used by elder men.

e) The formal version of *kureru: kudasaru*

Man: この方達トオルのお友達でわざわざ東京からたずねて来て下さったのよ
this people Tooru POP *friend expressly Tokyo from visit come (favor)* EP EP
**These people are Tooru's friends and have taken the trouble
to come from Tokyo to visit him.**

Studio Kōsen

Formality levels are very important in
Japanese society, as we will see in L.52
(book 3). This also affects giving and
receiving verbs, which have formal and
informal "versions" depending on the
occasion. Here we have a 下さる –
formal version of くれる –, functioning

as an auxiliary verb. It literally means "I or someone in the *uchi* circle receives something from or is done a favor by someone I respect and treat with formality." As a
curiosity, the expression 〜てください (*please*) comes from just this 〜てくださる.
Notes: 方 is a formal word meaning the same as 人 (*person*), and is used to show respect
(L.52). 達 is sometimes used to indicate plural: 子ども達 (*children*), 先生達 (*teachers*),
陽一達 (*Yōichi and the others*). わざわざ is an adverb indicating "expressly" or
"(somebody other than me) takes the trouble to do something."

f) Way of: *-kata*

> **Takeo:** 父ちゃんコマ買ったんだよ まわし方 教えてー
> *Dad spinning top buy be EP spin (way of) teach*
> **I have bought a spinning top, Dad. Teach me how to make it spin!**

Let's leave aside now the giving and receiving verbs, and go on to study the usage of the suffix 〜方, which we use to form nouns from verbs meaning "way of."

In our manga-example we have the word まわし方, which means *way of spinning* and obviously comes from the transitive verb 回す *(to spin)*: *-masu* form ⇒ 回します, root ⇒ 回し, we add 〜方 ⇒ 回し方 *(way of spinning)*.

Takeo says, literally, (コマの)回し方を教えて *teach me the way of spinning (the spinning top)*, but we have chosen a more natural form: *teach me how to make (the spinning top) spin*.

Note: Notice the usage of the "softening" or "assertive" tag んだ at the end of the first sentence. (L.40, manga-example d)).

g) Not much: *amari*

> **Emi:** ママ　おトイレへ行ったし... 　お肉あんまり食べなかったしー
> *Mom toilet DP go besides... meat not much eat besides*
> **Mom has gone to the toilet... And she hasn't eaten much meat...**

In this last example we will study the usage of あまり, which means "not much." In the panel we see the word あんまり, which is just a small colloquial distortion of the word あまり. The sentence we want to highlight is お肉をあまり食べなかった *she hasn't eaten much meat*. Notice how the verb that goes with あまり (when this means "not much") must always be conjugated in the negative, or you would be saying something completely different. If you say 肉をあまり食べた, that is, with the verb 食べる *(to eat)* in the affirmative, we indicate *I ate a lot of (too much) meat*.

J.M. Ken Niimura

Notes: Sometimes (mainly in women and children's speech) the honorific prefix お〜 is placed before some words: おトイレ *(toilet)*, お肉 *(meat)*, etc. Notice, too, the usage of 〜し as a "softener" of sentences. We we will study this in L.46 (book 3).

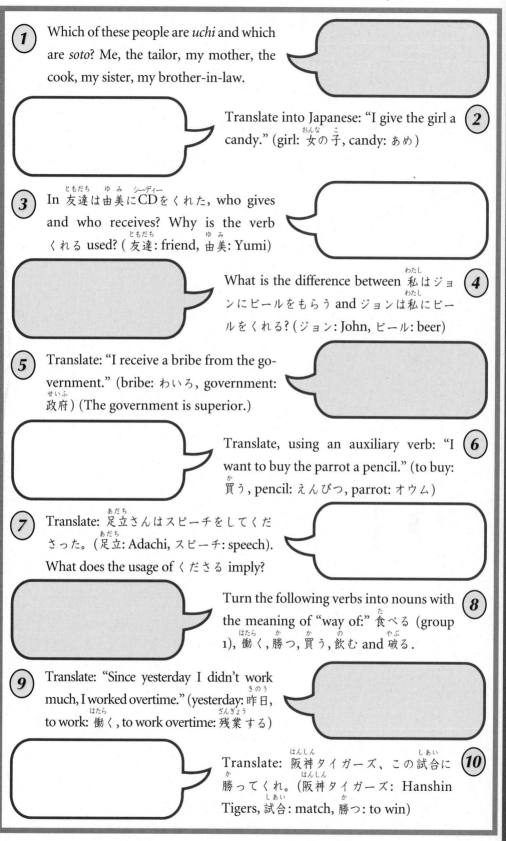

1 Which of these people are *uchi* and which are *soto*? Me, the tailor, my mother, the cook, my sister, my brother-in-law.

2 Translate into Japanese: "I give the girl a candy." (girl: 女の子, candy: あめ)

3 In 友達は由美にCDをくれた, who gives and who receives? Why is the verb くれる used? (友達: friend, 由美: Yumi)

4 What is the difference between 私はジョンにビールをもらう and ジョンは私にビールをくれる? (ジョン: John, ビール: beer)

5 Translate: "I receive a bribe from the government." (bribe: わいろ, government: 政府) (The government is superior.)

6 Translate, using an auxiliary verb: "I want to buy the parrot a pencil." (to buy: 買う, pencil: えんぴつ, parrot: オウム)

7 Translate: 足立さんはスピーチをしてくださった。(足立: Adachi, スピーチ: speech). What does the usage of くださる imply?

8 Turn the following verbs into nouns with the meaning of "way of:" 食べる (group 1), 働く, 勝つ, 買う, 飲む and 破る.

9 Translate: "Since yesterday I didn't work much, I worked overtime." (yesterday: 昨日, to work: 働く, to work overtime: 残業する)

10 Translate: 阪神タイガーズ、この試合に勝ってくれ。(阪神タイガーズ: Hanshin Tigers, 試合: match, 勝つ: to win)

APPENDIXES

Answers to the exercises
Compilation of kanji
Vocabulary index

Appendix I: Answers to the exercises

In this first appendix you will find the answers to the exercises in each of the 15 lessons that constitute this book, arranged according to lesson and question number.

How to use this appendix

At the end of each lesson, small exercises haven been set out with the aim of improving your overall comprehension of the subjects dealt within those lessons. The exercises offer, as well, the tools you need to acquire practice in forming sentences in Japanese and they stimulate you to study the grammar points covered in the lessons in greater depth.

This book is designed for autodidactic study, which means you are meant to learn without the help of a teacher (although it is always much better if you do have one, of course). To make things as easy as possible, we enclose this appendix with the answers to the exercises.

In this appendix you will find suggestions for possible answers to the exercises that have been given, but we must mention that some exercises have more than one correct answer. Whenever possible, we have tried to provide all possible variations, although sometimes you might come upon an option which won't be in this appendix, though it may be perfectly valid. Therefore, we encourage you to use the suggested answers in this appendix as an approximate guide more than a set of unbreakable rules etched in stone.

It goes without saying that the idea is to first do the exercises (looking up the theory explanations whenever you need to) and, then, to check this section to see whether your answers are right, or if, on the contrary, you have made some mistakes. Now remember to be fair to yourself by not checking this section before you have done the exercises, for, as we all know, when cheating, we only cheat ourselves.

Lesson 31

1- 買いたい

2- 見たくなかった

3- 私は酒を飲みたい ｜ 私は酒が飲みたい. (Add です at the end of the sentence to make a formal sentence.)

4- *Last year I wanted to go to Taiwan.*

5- 靴がほしくないです

6- *I want her to bring tea.*

7- *(It looks like) Mr. Kobayashi doesn't want to go on a business trip.*

8- Use the constructions と思う or と言う, or with another kind of approach, the constructions みたい, ようだ or らしい (L.43).

9- 日本語を習うつもりです

10- Sometimes, な at the end of a sentence turns it into a sentence in the negative imperative.

Lesson 32

1- うばえる ｜ おどれる ｜ 泳げる ｜ できる ｜ 考えられる

2- If you can't find out (after looking up the Vocabulary index, dictionaries, etc.), you can always turn to the practical expression "sentence + ことができる." Thus: 見ることができる and 切ることができる. By the way, 見る belongs to group 1 – and, therefore, we would have 見られる in the potential form– and る belongs to group 2 – so its potential form is 切れる.

3- あなたは飛べません (formal form) ｜ 君は飛べない (colloquial form). Usually, あなた is not used with the verb conjugated in its simple form and 君 is not used with the verb in its formal version. Another solution is: あなたは飛ぶことができません or 君は飛ぶことができない.

4- *Can Sonia speak English?*

5- Any of these sentences are valid: 私は学校へ行かなければならない ｜ 私は学校へ行かなくてはならない ｜ 私は学校へ行かなければいけない ｜ 私は学校へ行かなければだめだ. However, this being an informal sentence, it would be better to replace 私 with 僕 (masc.), 俺 (masc.) あたし (fem.), or any other first person pronoun of the colloquial kind. Look up L.7 (book 1) for more information.

6- *She has to eat spaghetti.*

7- If we interpret the sentence as *Is he able to read the newspaper?*, you can use any of these two: 彼は新聞を読めますか？ or 彼は新聞を読むことができますか？. However, if we interpret it as *Is he allowed to read the newspaper?*, then we must use 彼は新聞を読んでもいいですか？, 彼は新聞を読んでもよろしいですか？ or 彼は

新聞を読んでもかまいませんか？.

8- It can be any of these sentences: 彼は新聞を読んではいけない, 彼は新聞を読んでは ならない or 彼は新聞を読んではためだ.

9- *Don't write on the blackboard!* ちゃ is the contraction of ては in ～てはだめ.

10- ここから富士山が見える. The verb 見える *(can see)* has been chosen because we can see the mountain in a passive way, without intentionally trying to. That is, we see it "because it's there" not because "we want to see it." In this case, using the potential form of the verb 見る *(to see)* would be very strange.

Lesson 33

1- 予約 | 出発 (departure) or 出口 (exit from a place) | トイレ | 飛行機

2- Aisle | airport | seat belt | arrival

3- 英語が話せますか？| 英語ができますか？

4- *I don't understand Japanese.*

5- Any of these: ドイツ | アンドラ | スペイン | フランス | イタリア | ポルトガル | イギ リス | ロシア

6- すみませんが、通してください

7- すみません、オレンジジュースのおかわりをください | すみません、オレンジジュー スのおかわりをお願いします

8- If I'm coming as a tourist, I answer 観光です, if on business ビジネスです, if to study 留学です.

9- Tourism | bank | euro | visa | nationality.

10- シートベルトを締めてください or much more formal シートベルトをお締めになっ てください

Lesson 34

1- Translation: *His wife is beautiful.* Question: あなたの奥さんはきれいですか？

2- あれは何ですか？| あれはヘリです

3- *How much is that over there?* | *That is ten dollars.*

4- 何個(いくつの)りんごを買うつもりですか？

5- *Why don't you want to watch television?* | *Because it isn't interesting.*

6- 将来、マレーシアに行くつもりです

7- 拝もう | 壊そう | 出よう | 行こう | 走ろう

8- 映画館まで歩きましょう

9- *I think I'm going to buy a new computer.*

10- *I have decided to study History in a year's time.*

Lesson 35

1- Infinitive: うばって｜おどって｜泳いで｜考えて / Negative:うばわないで｜おどらないで｜泳がないで｜考えないで

2- この料理はおいしくて栄養があります

3- *The kitchen door is open.*

4- Formal: 食べてから、散歩しましょう｜Informal: 食べてから、散歩しよう

5- *I'm dying to (see how it is / try to) go to Mongolia | I really feel like (seeing how it is / trying to) going to Mongolia*

6- Literal: *We are going to read this book through, in case it is necessary later on.* Not literal: *We are going to completely read this book through.*

7- Formal: テレビを消さないでください Colloquial: テレビを消さないで

8- The 1st sentence means *I went to Tokyo (and I have already come back).* The 2nd one means *I went to Tokyo (it might be useful later on / just in case),* and the 3rd one means *I went to Tokyo (something I regret doing / I don't like at all / I consider a mistake).*

9- 私たちは論文を書かなくてもいいです

10- 札幌に来てよかった（です）

Lesson 36

1- Price : 宿泊料｜to cancel: キャンセルする｜rooms available: 空室あり｜breakfast included: 朝食 付き

2- 署名: signature｜バス: bath｜階段: stairs｜クレジットカード: credit card｜レストラン: restaurant｜〜泊 x nights (stay)

3- 一泊、いくらですか？

4- *Will you pay cash or credit card?*

5- You can use any of the words in the table for "Room."

6- すみませんが、朝 7 時にモーニングコールをお願いします

7- すみません、ちょっと困っていますが... 部屋がうるさくて眠れません

8- A 浴衣 is a kind of summer kimono, quite light, used after the bath, or just to relax (in summer). Many girls wear 浴衣 in summer to go for a walk, specially during summer festivals.

9- *Come in! Welcome to the Kyoto Ryokan. Take your shoes off, please.*

10- 好きなお風呂に入ってもいい(です)

Lesson 37

1- Topic: bread | Subject: I (it's not in the sentence, it's taken for granted).

2- （私は）パンはすぐ食べます

3- 亀はのろいです

4- *I can eat cheese, but I can't eat tomato.*

5- It acquires the meaning of *It looks like he wants to drive the car*, emphasizing "to drive" and implying that what he wants to do is drive the car, he doesn't want to do anything else with it (such as get in it, clean it, whatever…)

6- 彼<ruby>は<rt></rt></ruby>明日は、車を運転したがっている (he wants to do it tomorrow, not another day)
かれ あした くるま うんてん
彼は明日、車を運転したがっている (he wants to drive a car, not another vehicle)
かれ あした くるま うんてん
彼は明日、車の運転はしたがっている (see question 5)

7- あなたは一万 円が必要だ / です｜あなたは一万 円が要る / 要ります

8- 時間はあるが、お金がない

9- 私も日本へ行きたくない

10- *I like her, she always wears clothes that are neither conspicuous nor discreet.*

Lesson 38

1- 大学に本屋がある / あります

2- 私は店に入る / 入ります

3- It's not correct, because time adverbs that can't be determined with a specific date or time (as in 来年, "next year") never take に. The correct sentence would be 来年、経済を勉強するつもりだ.

4- 太郎さんは花子さんに花をあげる / あげます

5- The first, with に, indicates I'm drawing "on" the road, that is, directly on it (like drawing on the asphalt or the sidewalk, for example). It is usage #4 (direct contact) of に. Whereas, the second one, with で, simply indicates I'm on the road drawing, for example, I'm painting a picture on a canvass, or a sketch on a piece of paper or a notebook, while I'm standing (or sitting, it doesn't matter) on the road. It's usage #1 (place) of で.

6- 直子さんはケーキをナイフで切った

7- メキシコに帰りたい（です）

8- 大学には本屋がある / あります

9- *Anybody can read this sentence.*

10- でも has 3 usages: a) Mere combination of the particles で (adverbial complement) and も (also / neither).｜b) With the meaning of "even"｜c) With the meaning of "or something" (manga-example g))

Lesson 39

1- Ship: 船｜bus stop: バス乗り場｜ticket: 切符｜ordinary express train: 普通 電車｜crossing: 交差点

2- 空車: vacant (taxi)｜自動車: car｜指定席: reserved seat｜禁煙席: non-smoking seat｜

両替 : (loose) change | ホーム : platform

3- 鎌倉 旅館までお願いします

4- *Does this bus go to the Hiroshima Atomic Bomb Dome?*

5- You can use any word in the table for "Transport" in the first page of the lesson.

6- ここから一番 近い JR の駅はどこですか？

7- 新宿 行きのホームはここですか？

8- すみません。切符をなくしてしまいました

9- *The train going to Osaka will shortly arrive at platform 2.*

10- It would cost 190 yen for adults, and 100 yen for children.

Lesson 40

1- JALの飛行機は 大きいです

2- 図書館の前で待ってください

3- 暖かいのを着てください *(Put a warm one on)*

4- *Do you really live in the town of Azuchi?*

5- 真理さんは何を読んでいますか？真理さんは三島の本を読んでいます

6- 由紀夫さんの犬はバスを降りました／降りた

7- *Osamu hasn't finished his work yet.*

8- 彼女は公園を二時間ぐらい歩きました／歩いた

9- Why don't you drink your coffee? This んです is a contraction of のです and is used to soften the question.

10- もう一冊の本を持ってきてください

Lesson 41

1- じゃがいもとトマトと玉ねぎを買いたい(です)

2- じゃがいもやトマトや玉ねぎ(など)を買いたい(です)

3- じゃがいもかトマトか玉ねぎを買いたい(です)

4- 君はとてもきれいだと思います

5- *It takes about 10 minutes from Ebisu to Shinjuku by train.*

6- 疲れているから休みましょう／休もう

7- 直樹さんがスペイン語が話せるかどうか知りません／知らない

8- *Please, give me a hand (somehow).*

9- *The film (called) "The Seven Samurai" is old, isn't it?*

10- It's the equivalent to という. って can also replace the particle と (in its usage as a marker for "quote") and the construction とは.

Lesson 42

1- 包む: to wrap | 手袋: gloves | ベルト: belt | ソフト: software | 画集: artbook | 水着: swimming costume | セーター: sweater

2- Suit: スーツ | scarf: マフラー | discount: 割引 | doll: 人形 , フィギュア | electronic dictionary: 電子辞典 | tie: ネクタイ

3- いいえ、見ているだけです

4- 『着物』という本を探しています

5- 小さいサイズのズボンはありますか？

6- *I want that rock CD over there, and that horror video.*

7- このデジカメは私の国で使えますか？

8- この陶器は壊れやすいから、包んでください

9- すみません、これをちょっとまけてください

10- 半額 | 5割 | 50% OFF

Lesson 43

1- ジョンさんは独身かもしれない

2- ようだ has the meaning of "apparently." It is used when the speaker has direct information (either visual or sensorial) on some subject. To this information the speaker's previous knowledge and his capacity for reason are added. It has a high degree of certainty: what the speaker is saying is based on actual fact. An example: あの人はレゲエのファンのようだ *(That person looks like a reggae fan)*. An equivalent expression, but a little bit more colloquial, is みたいだ.

3- 明日は雨が降るだろう

4- *Mr. Saitō is very rich, isn't he?*

5- 社長が辞めたらしい

6- No, it's wrong. The correct sentence would be 美穂ちゃんは学生だそうだ, because you must add だ after a noun (like 学生) or a *-na* adjective. This is the first usage of そうだ (supposition based on something read or heard).

7- 晶子さんは彼氏がいるに違いない

8- *That girl is wretched, isn't she? (I feel sorry for that girl, don't you?)*

9- この天ぷらはおいしくなさそうです

10- *Shigeo wears blackish clothes.*

Lesson 44

1- Transitive: 変える , 通す | Intransitive: 続く , 壊れる , 開く , 残る

2- 1: 変わる , 通る | 2: 続ける , 壊す , 開ける , 残す

3- 入る , 助ける , 出る , 聞こえる

4- 礼子さんはテレビを消した

5- 突然、電気が消えた

6- It's not correct because 閉める is a transitive verb and needs a subject to perform the action. If the subject is 窓 *(window)*, then we must use the intransitive verb 閉まる *(to be closed)*: 窓が閉まりました *(The window closed)*. If we want to use 閉める, we will need a subject to perform the action, and then 窓 will become a Direct Object (marked with the particle を). For example: 私は窓を閉めました *(I closed the window)*.

7- *I could hear the bird's voices (song) from the garden.*

8- この課は分かりにくい(です)

9- *I want to start studying Chinese.*

10- For example: 私は作文のテーマを決める *(I decide the subject of the composition)* | 試合の結果が決まる *(The result of the match is being decided)*.

Lesson 45

1- *Uchi:* me, my mother, my sister, my brother-in-law | *Soto:* the tailor, the cook (Although this will depend on the relationship with the family. For example, if the relationship with "my brother-in-law" is very distant, it is even possible he may be considered more *soto* than *uchi*.)

2- 私は女の子にあめをあげる

3- Gives: Yumi | Receives: I

The verb くれる is used because the point of view is placed on the receiver, a receiver who must belong to the *uchi* circle ("I" is *uchi*, of course).

4- Both sentences have very similar meanings. The first one is *I receive beer from John* and the second one is *John gives me beer*. The main difference is in the point of view: while in the first sentence the point of view is placed on "I," in the second one it's placed on "John:" that is why different verbs are used.

5- 私は政府に/からわいろをいただきます

6- 私はオウムにえんぴつを買ってやりたい

7- *Mr. Adachi made a speech (and in doing this he did us a favor).* The usage of くださる implies that the fact that Mr. Adachi has made a speech is a honor for us, he has done us some kind of "favor" making it. Besides, using くださる instead of the less formal verb もらう we show respect towards Mr. Adachi.

8- 食べ方 | 働き方 | 勝ち方 | 買い方 | 飲み方 | 破り方

9- 昨日、あまり働かなかったので(から)、残業した

10- *Hanshin Tigers, you must win this match (it's an order).*

Appendix II: Compilation of kanji

Just like we did in the first book, we will complete the lessons with a short appendix devoted to kanji. However, since learning kanji is not this method's main aim, in this second book we will only go over about one hundred characters.

The importance of *kanji*

By now, you should have a very clear idea of what kanji are and why they are essential in the study of Japanese. You should study kanji with all your might, both their reading as well as their writing, if you want to be able to read and write in Japanese. There is no way to truly learn the language without muddling through them. In this method, however, we have preferred to give priority to the learning of grammar and vocabulary, as well as to the practice of fast reading in Japanese. For this, we used the many example sentences written in kana and kanji, with the *furigana* reading for the later, to make the task easier. This is why we have chosen to give you an in-depth description of only the really essential kanji.

Which kanji are essential?

Ideally, when the student finishes studying a basic course in Japanese, he / she should know how to read and write about 600 kanji. However, the 日本語 能力 試験, the Japanese Language Proficiency Test (more information about it in book 3), only requires 100 kanji for level 4 (elementary), and another 200 for level 3 (basic). That is, the basic level student is only required to know 300 characters, of which 245 are compulsory and the rest are random. In *Japanese in MangaLand 1* we saw 160 characters; this time, we will only see 100. Still, between the 260 kanji gathered in books 1 and 2 in the method, we will find all the 245 compulsory ones for levels 3 and 4 of the Japanese Proficiency Test. We have compiled a list with the 260 kanji we have studied and we have indicated with a 4 or a 3 the level to which they belong, so that you can have the most complete possible guide.

Usage of the index

The kanji in this index are ordered according to their frequency of usage, and to the ease with which we can relate one character to another (or more) when their meanings and/or writing are similar. This time, however, we have not given each kanji's stroke order, because we prefer to focus more on their reading than their writing. A good exercise, though, is trying to guess their right stroke order, following the instructions in the first book, and then looking up a kanji dictionary to check whether you've done it correctly.

Following usual conventions in kanji dictionaries, the *on'yomi* reading is shown in katakana, and the *kun'yomi* reading in hiragana. However, we have always used hiragana in the *furigana* indicating the reading of each compound word.

Regarding the example compound words, we have tried to choose simple and common terms, as well as words with kanji you have previously studied, to make their study and the association of ideas easier.

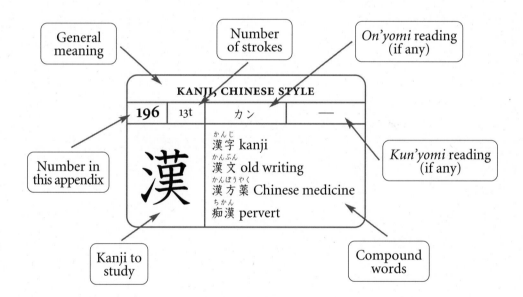

However...

However, besides studying in depth these 260 characters, we recommend using some method or dictionary to learn more kanji on your own, and become more fluent in the writing and stroke order of each character. Ideally, after studying all three books of *Japanese in MangaLand* (including book 3), you would reach 600 or 700 kanji before embarking upon a still more advanced study of the language.

4 一 1	4 二 2	4 三 3	4 四 4	4 五 5	4 六 6	4 七 7	4 八 8	4 九 9	4 十 10
4 百 11	4 千 12	4 万 13	4 円 14	4 人 15	4 日 16	4 月 17	4 火 18	4 水 19	4 木 20
4 金 21	4 土 22	3 口 23	3 目 24	3 手 25	3 足 26	3 心 27	耳 28	4 東 29	4 西 30
4 南 31	4 北 32	4 男 33	4 女 34	4 子 35	4 父 36	4 母 37	4 弟 38	3 兄 39	姉 40
3 妹 41	4 山 42	4 川 43	4 田 44	石 45	朝 46	3 昼 47	夜 48	4 大 49	4 小 50
3 多 51	3 少 52	3 分 53	4 年 54	4 前 55	後 56	3 今 57	4 午 58	4 時 59	上 60
4 下 61	4 右 62	4 左 63	4 中 64	3 方 65	3 元 66	4 気 67	4 文 68	4 出 69	4 入 70
4 白 71	3 赤 72	3 青 73	4 本 74	3 店 75	3 学 76	4 校 77	4 先 78	4 生 79	3 会 80
3 社 81	3 私 82	4 高 83	3 安 84	太 85	3 春 86	夏 87	3 秋 88	3 冬 89	4 半 90
間 91	3 道 92	4 車 93	3 自 94	3 動 95	近 96	遠 97	暑 98	寒 99	行 100
4 来 101	3 名 102	4 友 103	3 新 104	古 105	強 106	弱 107	力 108	3 立 109	3 若 110
3 広 111	悪 112	3 重 113	3 早 114	3 持 115	待 116	3 買 117	3 売 118	3 開 119	閉 120
3 始 121	終 122	帰 123	3 休 124	3 体 125	3 言 126	4 話 127	4 聞 128	3 書 129	3 読 130
4 見 131	3 思 132	3 作 133	3 教 134	習 135	3 使 136	3 知 137	雨 138	3 病 139	仕 140
3 事 141	3 者 142	3 地 143	所 144	4 外 145	好 146	変 147	3 着 148	3 物 149	3 食 150
3 飲 151	3 国 152	4 語 153	3 空 154	3 花 155	4 字 156	楽 157	4 電 158	4 明 159	3 家 160
4 何 161	4 天 162	海 163	洋 164	風 165	野 166	犬 167	牛 168	魚 169	鳥 170
3 肉 171	茶 172	3 味 173	飯 174	3 館 175	工 176	場 177	駅 178	3 室 179	屋 180
町 181	院 182	3 堂 183	図 184	3 銀 185	寺 186	特 187	以 188	業 189	3 有 199
同 191	毎 192	3 週 193	曜 194	夕 195	漢 196	英 197	映 198	黒 199	色 200
4 長 201	止 202	3 正 203	度 204	3 台 205	代 206	研 207	究 208	試 209	験 210
世 211	界 212	問 213	題 214	答 215	急 216	注 217	意 218	写 219	真 220
回 221	転 222	料 223	理 224	不 225	用 226	品 227	質 228	員 229	貸 230
借 231	勉 232	京 233	都 234	旅 235	族 236	親 237	主 238	住 239	考 240
死 241	別 242	計 243	画 244	集 245	歌 246	発 247	切 248	去 249	歩 250
3 走 251	起 252	3 運 253	送 254	3 通 255	建 256	音 257	医 258	紙 259	3 服 260

WHAT?

161	7t	ナン / ナニ	—

何

なに
何 what?
なんにん
何人 how many people?
なんまい
何枚 how many sheets?
なんかい
何回 how many times?

SKY, HEAVEN

162	4t	テン	あま

天

てんき
天気 weather
てんさい
天才 genius
てんもんがく
天文学 astronomy
あま がわ
天の川 Milky Way

SEA

163	9t	カイ	うみ

海

うみ
海 sea
かいがん
海岸 beach, coast
かいすい
海水 sea water
ほっかいどう
北海道 Hokkaidō

OCEAN, WEST

164	9t	ヨウ	—

洋

たいへいよう
太平洋 Pacific Ocean
せいよう
西洋 the West
ようふく
洋服 Western clothes
ようしき
洋式 Western style

WIND, STYLE

165	9t	フウ｜フ	かぜ

風

かぜ
風 wind
かみかぜ
神風 *kamikaze* (divine wind)
わふう
和風 Japanese style
ふぜい
風情 elegance, appearance

FIELD, PLAIN

166	11t	ヤ	の

野

の
野 field
やきゅう
野球 baseball
ぶんや
分野 field (of study)
やさい
野菜 vegetables

DOG

167	4t	ケン	いぬ

犬

いぬ
犬 dog
のらいぬ
野良犬 stray dog
あいけん
愛犬 pet dog
ばんけん
番犬 watchdog

COW, BULL, CALF

168	4t	ギュウ	うし

牛

うし
牛 cow, bull
ぎゅうにく
牛肉 beef
ぎゅうにゅう
牛乳 cow's milk
ぎゅうどん
牛丼 beef bowl

FISH

169	11t	ギョ	さかな

魚

さかな
魚 fish
さかなや
魚屋 fish shop
きんぎょ
金魚 goldfish
ぎょらい
魚雷 torpedo

BIRD

170	11t	チョウ	とり

鳥

とり
鳥 bird
や とり
焼き鳥 chicken shish kebab
とりはだ
鳥肌 goose bumps
ちょうるい
鳥類 birds, fowl

MEAT

| 171 | 6t | ニク | — |

肉 meat
豚肉 pork meat
肉体 body
肉眼 the naked eye

TEA

| 172 | 9t | チャ｜サ | — |

お茶 tea
紅茶 black tea
緑茶 green tea
茶道 tea ceremony

TASTE

| 173 | 8t | ミ | あじ(わう) |

味 taste
味わう to taste
味見 sampling, tasting
味方 ally, friend

BOILED RICE

| 174 | 12t | ハン | めし |

ご飯 boiled rice, meal
炊飯器 rice cooker
焼き飯 fried rice
飯屋 eatery

MANSION, BUILDING

| 175 | 16t | カン | やかた |

館 mansion
図書館 library
博物館 museum
館内 within the museum

TO BUILD, TO MODEL

| 176 | 3t | コウ｜ク | — |

工場 factory
工業 industry
人工 artificial
工夫 invention, device

PLACE

| 177 | 12t | ジョウ | ば |

場所 place, spot
場合 situation
道場 dōjō, gymnasium
サッカー場 soccer stadium

TRAIN STATION

| 178 | 14t | エキ | — |

駅 train station
駅前 in front of the station
石橋駅 Ishibashi station
駅員 station employee

ROOM, HALL

| 179 | 9t | シツ | — |

教室 classroom
入室 entering the hall
室内 inside the hall
王室 Royal family

SHOP

| 180 | 9t | オク | や |

パン屋 bakery
薬屋 chemist
八百屋 greengrocery
屋上 roof

TOWN, SUBURB			
181	7t	チョウ	まち

町

まち
町 town
まちいしゃ
町医者 medical practitioner
かたくらちょう
片倉町 suburb of Katakura
ちょうちょう
町 長 mayor (of a town)

BUILDING, INSTITUTION			
182	10t	イン	—

院

びょういん
病 院 hospital
いんちょう
院 長 hospital director
だいがくいん
大学院 postgraduate school
じいん
寺院 Buddhist temple

TEMPLE, HALL			
183	11t	ドウ	—

堂

しょくどう
食 堂 dinning room
どうどう
堂々 imposing, magnificent
でんどう
殿堂 shrine, temple
にんてんどう
任天堂 Nintendō

DIAGRAM			
184	7t	ズ｜ト	はか(る)

図

はか
図る to plan, to try
ず
図 drawing, diagram
ずぼし
図星 bull's-eye
としょかん
図書館 library

SILVER			
185	14t	ギン	—

銀

ぎん
銀 silver
ぎんこう
銀行 bank
すいぎん
水 銀 mercury
ぎん
銀メダル silver medal

BUDDHIST TEMPLE			
186	6t	ジ	てら

寺

てら
お寺 Buddhist temple
てらまち
寺町 Teramachi (in Kyōto)
じいん
寺院 temple
りょうあんじ
竜安寺 Ryōanji temple

SPECIAL			
187	10t	トク	—

特

とく
特に specially
とくべつ
特別 special
どくとく
独特 special, different
とっか
特価 special price

TO USE			
188	5t	イ	—

以

いか
以下 below
いじょう
以上 over/end
いない
以内 included
いがい
以外 except

INDUSTRY, TRADE, KARMA			
189	13t	ギョウ｜ゴウ	わざ

業

わざ
業 business
ごう
業 karma
さんぎょう
産 業 industry, manufacture
ぎょうむ
業務 duties, business

TO EXIST, TO HAVE			
190	6t	ユウ｜ウ	あ(る)

有

あ
有る to exist, to have
ゆうりょう
有 料 fee-charging
ゆうがい
有害 harmful
うむ
有無 whether there is or isn't

SAME

191	6t	ドウ	おな(じ)

同

おな
同じ same
どうかん
同感 same sentiment
どうるい
同類 same kind
どうい
同意 agreement

EACH, EVERY

192	6t	マイ	—

毎

まいかい
毎回 every time
まいにち
毎日 every day
まいつき
毎月 every month
まいとし
毎年 every year

WEEK

193	11t	シュウ	—

週

しゅうかん
週間 week
しゅうまつ
週末 weekend
しゅうきゅう
週休 weekly holiday
まいしゅう
毎週 every week

DAY OF THE WEEK

194	18t	ヨウ	—

曜

ようび
曜日 day of the week
げつようび
月曜日 Monday
きんようび
金曜日 Friday
どようび
土曜日 Saturday

EVENING, NIGHT

195	3t	—	ゆう

夕

ゆう
夕 evening, night
ゆうがた
夕方 evening
ゆうや
夕焼け sunset
ゆうしょく
夕食 supper

KANJI, CHINESE STYLE

196	13t	カン	—

漢

かんじ
漢字 kanji
かんぶん
漢文 old writing
かんぽうやく
漢方薬 Chinese medicine
ちかん
痴漢 pervert

ENGLAND, ENGLISH, BEAUTIFUL

197	8t	エイ	—

英

えいこく
英国 England
えいご
英語 English language
えいやく
英訳 English translation
えいさい
英才 great talent

TO REFLECT

198	9t	エイ	うつ(る/す)

映

うつ
映す to reflect, to project
えいが
映画 film, movie
はんえい
反映 reflection
えいぞう
映像 image

BLACK

199	11t	コク	くろ(い)

黒

くろ
黒い black
しろくろ
白黒 black and white
こくばん
黒板 blackboard
こくじん
黒人 black person

COLOR, SENSUALITY

200	6t	シキ	ショク	いろ

色

ちゃいろ
茶色 brown
いろ
色っぽい sensual
しきさい
色彩 coloring
いしょく
異色 unusual, original

LONG, BOSS			
201	8t	チョウ	なが(い)

長
なが
長い long
ながの
長野 Nagano (city)
しゃちょう
社 長 company director
てんちょう
店 長 shop manager

TO STOP			
202	4t	シ	と(まる/める)

止
と
止まる to stop
ていし
停止 suspension
ちゅうし
中止 to cancel
しゅうし
終 止 an end

CORRECT			
203	5t	ショウ｜セイ	ただ(しい)

正
ただ
正しい correct
せいかい
正解 correct answer
せいしき
正式 official
しょうがつ
正月 New Year

TIME, DEGREE			
204	9t	ド	たび

度
たび
この度 this time, now
ど
2度 twice
ど
40度 40°
どきょう
度胸 courage, pluck

STAND, COUNTER FOR MACHINES			
205	5t	ダイ｜タイ	—

台
くるま だい
車3台 three cars
どだい
土台 foundation
だいどころ
台所 kitchen
たいわん
台湾 Taiwan

GENERATION			
206	5t	ダイ	か(える/わる)

代
か
代える to substitute
せだい
世代 generation
じだい
時代 era, period
ねんだい
70年代 the seventies

TO SHARPEN, TO POLISH			
207	9t	ケン	と(ぐ)

研
と
研ぐ to sharpen
きゅうきょく
究極 finality
けんきゅうじょ
研究所 laboratory
けんしゅう
研 修 study and training

TO RESEARCH, THOROUGHLY			
208	7t	キュウ	きわ(める)

究
きわ
究める to study thoroughly
けんきゅう
研 究 research
きゅうめい
究 明 exhaustive research
がっきゅう
学 究 scholar

TO TEST, TO TRY			
209	13t	シ	ため(す)｜こころ(みる)

試
ため
試す to test
こころ
試みる to try
し あい
試 合 match, game
ししょく
試食 to taste

TO TEST			
210	18t	ケン	—

験
しけん
試験 exam
けいけん
経験 experience
たいけん
体験 experience (physical)
じっけん
実験 experiment

Compilation of kanji 漢字集 −179−

GENERATION, WORLD

211	5t	セ | セイ	よ

世

あの世 the other world
世界 world
世代 generation
ルイ１４世 Louis xiv

LIMIT, WORLD

212	9t	カイ	—

界

世界 world
限界 limit
境界 border
政治界 political world

QUESTION

213	11t	モン	と(い/う)

問

問い question
問う to ask
問答 questions & answers
質問 question

TITLE

214	18t	ダイ	—

題

問題 problem
題名 title
話題 subject of conversation
課題 subject

ANSWER

215	12t	トウ	こた(え/える)

答

答え answer
答える to answer
応答 reply
正答 right answer

TO HURRY

216	9t	キュウ	いそ(ぐ)

急

急ぐ to hurry
特急 limited express train
至急 quickly
救急車 ambulance

TO POUR

217	8t	チュウ	そそ(ぐ)

注

注ぐ to pour (liquid)
注意 attention
注射 injection
注文 order

FEELING, MEANING

218	13t	イ	—

意

意味 meaning
注意 attention
意志 will
意外 unexpected

TO COPY

219	5t	シャ	うつ(す/る)

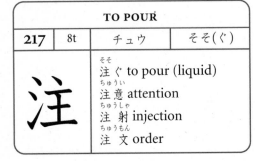

写

写す to copy
写真 photograph
複写 a copy
描写 description

TRUTH

220	10t	シン	ま

真

真ん中 in the middle
真夏 midsummer
写真 photograph
真実 truth

ROTATION, TIME

221	6t	カイ	まわ(る/す)

回

まわ
回す to send around
かいてん
回転 rotation
かい
3回 three times
かいしゅう
回収 collection

TO FALL, TO MOVE

222	11t	テン	ころ(ぶ/がる)

転

ころ
転ぶ to fall
かいてん
回転 rotation
てんしょく
転職 change of occupation
じてんしゃ
自転車 bicycle

TO MEASURE, PRICE

223	10t	リョウ	—

料

りょうり
料理 cooking
りょうきん
料金 price
はいたつりょう
配達料 delivery charge

REASON, LOGIC

224	11t	リ	—

理

りょうり
料理 cooking
りろん
理論 theory
ぶつり
物理 physics
りゆう
理由 reason, cause

NO, NEGATION

225	4t	フ	ブ	—

不

ふよう
不要 unnecessary
ふまん
不満 frustration
ふあん
不安 uneasiness
ぶきみ
不気味 strange, unusual

TO USE

226	5t	ヨウ	もち(いる)

用

もち
用いる to use
ようい
用意 preparation
しんよう
信用 trust
がくせいよう
学生用 for students

ARTICLE, GOODS

227	9t	ヒン	しな

品

しなもの
品物 goods
ひんしつ
品質 quality
ようひん
洋品 foreign articles
げひん
下品 vulgar

CONTENTS, QUALITY

228	15t	シツ	シチ	—

質

ひんしつ
品質 quality
しつもん
質問 question
すいしつ
水質 water quality
しちや
質屋 pawnshop

MEMBER, EMPLOYEE

229	10t	イン	—

員

しゃいん
社員 employee
てんいん
店員 shop clerk
かいいん
会員 club member
いいんかい
委員会 committee

TO LEND

230	12t	タイ	か(す)

貸

か
貸す to lend
か　　きん
貸し金 loan
か
貸しボート hired boat
たいしゃく
貸借 debit and credit

TO BORROW

231	10t	シャク	か(りる)

借

借りる to borrow
借り物 a borrowed thing
借地 leased land
借金 debt

TO MAKE AN EFFORT

232	10t	ベン	—

勉

勉強 study
勤勉 diligent

CAPITAL, KYOTO, TOKYO

233	8t	キョウ｜ケイ	—

京

京都 Kyoto
東京 Tokyo
上京 to move to Tokyo
京阪 Kyoto and Osaka

CAPITAL

234	11t	ト	みやこ

都

都 capital
首都 capital of a country
都市 city
京都 Kyoto

TO TRAVEL

235	10t	リョ	たび

旅

旅 trip
旅行 travel
旅費 traveling expenses
旅館 ryokan inn

FAMILY, FELLOW GROUP

236	11t	ゾク	—

族

家族 family
親族 relatives
民族 race, nation
貴族 the nobility

FAMILIAR, PARENTS

237	16t	シン	おや｜した(しい)

親

親子 parents and children
親しい intimate
両親 parents
親族 relatives

MAIN, OWNER

238	5t	シュ	おも｜ぬし

主

主に mainly
持ち主 owner, possessor
主人 my husband
主食 main meal

TO LIVE, TO INHABIT

239	7t	ジュウ	す(む)

住

住む to live, to inhabit
住民 resident
住所 mail address
住宅 dwelling

TO THINK

240	6t	コウ	かんが(える)

考

考える to think
思考 thought
考古学 archeology

TO DIE			
241	6t	シ	し（ぬ）

死

死ぬ to die
死体 corpse
死刑 death penalty
死語 dead language

TO SEPARATE, DIFFERENT			
242	7t	ベツ	わか（れる）

別

別れる to break up
別々 separately
別名 nickname
別世界 different world

TO COUNT, TO CALCULATE			
243	9t	ケイ	はか（る）

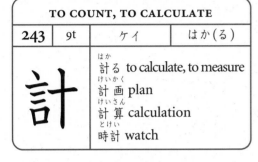

計

計る to calculate, to measure
計画 plan
計算 calculation
時計 watch

DRAWING, TO LIMIT			
244	8t	カク｜ガ	—

画

画家 painter (artist)
漫画 comic book, manga
絵画 painting, drawing
計画 plan

TO GATHER			
245	12t	シュウ	あつ（める/まる）

集

集まる to gather
集中 concentration
集会 meeting
画集 artbook

SONG			
246	14t	カ	うた｜うた（う）

歌

歌 song
歌う to sing
歌手 singer
和歌 *waka* poem

TO LEAVE, TO GO AWAY			
247	9t	ハツ	—

発

発売 to put on sale
神戸発 departing from Kōbe
出発 departure, starting
発音 pronunciation

TO CUT			
248	4t	セツ	き（る/れる）

切

切る to cut
切手 stamp
切ない sad, distressing
切腹 *seppuku (harakiri)*

TO GO AWAY, TO PASS			
249	5t	キョ	さ（る）

去

去る to go away, to leave
去年 last year
死去 to die

TO WALK			
250	8t	ホ	ある（く）/ あゆ（む）

歩

歩く to walk
歩む to walk (poetic)
2歩 two steps
歩行者 pedestrian

漢字集

TO RUN, TO ESCAPE			
251	7t	ソウ	はし(る)

走

はし
走る to run
そうこう
走行 to move fast
とうそう
逃走 to escape running
だっそう
脱走 escape, flight

TO GET UP, TO HAPPEN			
252	10t	キ	お(きる)|お(こる)

起

お
起きる to get up
お
起こる to happen
きどう
起動 to start (an engine)
きりつ
起立 to stand up

TO TRANSPORT, TO OPERATE			
253	12t	ウン	はこ(ぶ)

運

はこ
運ぶ to transport
うんそう
運送 transport
うんえい
運営 administration
うんこう
運行 movement

TO SEND			
254	9t	ソウ	おく(る)

送

おく
送る to send, to see out
うんそう
運送 transport
ゆうそう
郵送 mail
ほうそう
放送 broadcast (TV, radio)

TO PASS, TO INFORM			
255	10t	ツウ	とお(る/す)|かよ(う)

通

とお
通る to pass
かよ
通う to commute
つうこう
通行 to pass
こうつう
交通 traffic

TO BUILD			
256	9t	ケン	た(つ/てる)

建

た
建てる to build (a building)
たてもの
建物 building
けんちく
建築 architecture
さいけん
再建 to rebuild

SOUND			
257	9t	オン|イン	おと|ね

音

おと
音 sound
ほんね
本音 real intention
はつおん
発音 pronunciation
ぼいん
母音 vowel (phonetic)

MEDICINE, TO CURE			
258	7t	イ	—

医

いしゃ
医者 doctor
いがく
医学 medicine (studies)
いいん
医院 doctor's office
いやくひん
医薬品 medicine

PAPER			
259	10t	シ	かみ

紙

かみ
紙 paper
てがみ
手紙 letter
お がみ
折り紙 origami
しへい
紙幣 bank note

CLOTHES, DRESS			
260	8t	フク	—

服

ようふく
洋服 Western clothes
わふく
和服 Japanese clothes
せいふく
制服 uniform
ふくそう
服装 clothes

Appendix III: Vocabulary index

In this third and last appendix we offer a systematic list of all the words that have appeared in this book, with their respective translations.

How to use this index

Take a look now at each of the columns in the vocabulary appendix. In the first column you have the hiragana version of each of the terms (ordered in the Japanese syllabic order, see next page for explanation), and then its "usual" version in kanji, hiragana or katakana, as appropriate. Next, in brackets, you are given its morphological category (see below), the lesson where it first appeared, and, sometimes, the lesson where this term has an important role. To conclude, in the last column, you will find the English translation of each word.

Morphological categories

N:	nouns
V:	verbs
V1:	verbs ending in *-eru* or *-iru* from group 1
V2:	verbs ending in *-eru* or *-iru* from group 2
Virr:	verbs with an irregular conjugation
Vn:	nouns that become verbs when adding する
iAdj:	*-i* adjectives
naAdj:	*-na* adjectives
Adv:	adverbs
Ph:	phrases, set phrases
PN:	pronouns
C:	counters
T:	toponyms, geographical proper nouns

● The sign "|" separates the different meanings that one word can have.

Very important: the order of the kana

If you haven't yet mastered the established order among the different kana, you won't be able to use this index, nor, by extension, any Japanese dictionary. This means that you must make the effort now to learn the order of the kana, which we could say is the Japanese version of our alphabetical order.

The kana follow this order: *a-ka-sa-ta-na-ha-ma-ya-ra-wa-n*, and so, for example, the た line goes after さ and before な. Within each line, the order to follow is *a-i-u-e-o*. That is, within the か column, we first have か, then き, followed by く, then け, and finally こ. If we keep going in the dictionary order, we will have さ, then し, and so on and so forth until the end...

The "voiced" forms (in which two strokes or a circle are added to a kana, i.e.: が, じ, ぺ and so on), are ordered without taking into account their "vocalization." This means that, for example, we will have the word ごうもん before こうや and after こうかん, inside the same column of こ.

Hiragana and katakana are mingled together. This means that we can have the word ヒステリー before ひな and after ひくい wheter the word is written in hiragana or in katakana.

Whatever you do, you must make an effort to remember the order *a-ka-sa-ta-na-ha-ma-ya-ra-wa-n*: it is absolutely necessary when using a dictionary and, having reached this far in your studies, it is now essential.

The complete order would be:

あ, い, う, え, お, か(が), き(ぎ), く(ぐ), け(げ), こ(ご), さ(ざ), し(じ), す(ず), せ(ぜ), そ(ぞ), た(だ), ち(ぢ), つ(づ), て(で), と(ど), な, に, ぬ, ね, の, は(ば)(ぱ), ひ(び)(ぴ), ふ(ぶ)(ぷ), へ(べ)(ぺ), ほ(ぼ)(ぽ), ま, み, む, め, も, や, ゆ, よ, ら, り, る, れ, ろ, わ, を, ん.

あ A

い I

いきる	生きる	(V1)	34	to live
いく	行く	(V)	31	to go
いくつ	いくつ	(Adv)	34	who many?
いくら	いくら	(Adv)	34	how much (money)?
いくらする	いくらする	(Adv)	34	how much is it?
いけ	池	(N)	37	pond
いご	囲碁	(N)	41	*go* (game)
いざかや	居酒屋	(N)	38	bar, tavern
いす	いす	(N)	36	chair
いすらえる	イスラエル	(T)	33	Israel
いそぐ	急ぐ	(V)	31	to hurry
いたす	致す	(V)	33	to do
いたずらっこ	いたずらっ子	(N)	38	mischievous, naughty
いたりあ	イタリア	(T)	33	Italy
いちご	いちご	(N)	38	strawberry
いちにち	一日	(N)	39	one day
いちばん	一番	(Adv)	39	the first
いつ	いつ	(Adv)	34	when?
いつか	いつか	(Adv)	41	some day
いっしょに	一緒に	(Adv)	37, 41	together with | with
いつでも	いつでも	(Adv)	38	any time
いってん	一点	(N)	40	one point
いつも	いつも	(Adv)	37	always
いぬ	犬	(N)	38	dog
いもうと	妹	(N)	38	younger sister
いりぐち	入口	(N)	39	entry
いる	要る	(V2)	37	to need
いるか	イルカ	(N)	37	dolphin
いれる	入れる	(V1)	39, 44	to put in
いんたーねっと	インターネット	(N)	42	Internet
いんど	インド	(T)	33	India

う U

ういすきー	ウイスキー	(N)	33	whisky
うえ	上	(Adv)	40	upside
うおっか	ウオッカ	(N)	37	vodka
うけとる	受け取る	(V2)	33	to receive
うごかす	動かす	(V)	44	to move
うごく	動く	(V)	44	to move
うしなう	失う	(V)	34	to lose
うた	歌	(N)	43	song
うたう	歌う	(V)	44	to sing
うち	内	(V)	45	inside | *uchi* | while
うちがわ	内側	(N)	39	the inside
うつ	打つ	(V)	41	to hit
うつす	写す	(V)	44	to copy, to reflect
うつる	映る	(V2)	34	to be reflected | to record (video)
うつる	写る	(V2)	44	to be copied
うばう	奪う	(V)	32	to rob | to snatch
うまれる	生まれる	(V1)	44	to be born
うむ	生む	(V)	44	to give birth
うめだ	梅田	(T)	39	Umeda (in Osaka)
うりば	売り場	(N)	39	counter (for sales)
うる	売る	(V2)	44	to sell
うるさい	うるさい	(Adj.i / L)	31	noisy | Silence!
うれる	売れる	(V1)	44	to be sold
うんちん	運賃	(N)	39	price (of a ticket)
うんてん	運転	(Vn)	37	driving
うんてんしゅ	運転手	(N)	39	driver

え E

え	絵	(N)	38	drawing, illustration
えあこん	エアコン	(N)	36	air conditioning
えいが	映画	(N)	40	movie
えいがかん	映画館	(N)	34	cinema
えいご	英語	(N)	32, 33	English (language)
えいよう	栄養	(N)	35	nutrition
えがく	描く	(N)	38	to draw, to paint
えき	駅	(N)	35, 39	train station
えさ	餌	(N)	32	feed, bait
えすえふ	SF	(N)	42	science fiction
えっちでぃー	HD	(N)	42	hard disk
えびす	恵比寿	(T)	41	Ebisu (in Tokyo)
えふわん	F1	(N)	43	Formula 1
えらい	偉い	(iAdj)	31	important (somebody)
えらそうな	偉そうな	(naAdj)	43	self-important, patronizing
えれべーた	エレベータ	(N)	36	elevator
えん	円	(N)	33	yen
えんか	演歌	(N)	42	*enka* (Japanese music)
えんじょこうさい	援助交際	(N)	42	relationship in exchange for help
えんぴつ	えんぴつ	(N)	45	pencil

お O

おいしい	おいしい	(iAdj)	35	good, delicious
おうむ	オウム	(N)	45	parrot
おえる	終える	(V1)	44	to finish
おーえす	OS	(N)	42	operating system
おおきい	大きい	(iAdj)	40	big
おおさか	大阪	(T)	33	Osaka
おーすとらりあ	オーストラリア	(T)	33	Australia
おおぜい	大勢	(N)	38	many people
おーぶん	オーブン	(N)	38	oven
おかし	お菓子	(N)	31, 40	candy, cookie
おかね	お金	(N)	37	money
おかみさん	女将さん	(N)	36	landlady of a *ryokan*
おがむ	拝む	(V)	34	to pray
おかわり	おかわり	(N)	33	another serving (of food)
おきなわ	沖縄	(T)	38	Okinawa
おきる	起きる	(V1)	31, 44	to get up
おく	置く	(V)	33	to leave, to place
おくさん	奥さん	(N)	34	wife (somebody else's)
おくらす	遅らす	(V)	44	to be late
おくれる	遅れる	(V1)	44	to be late
おこす	起こす	(V)	44	to wake somebody up
おこなう	行う	(V)	33	to perform
おこる	怒る	(V2)	43	to get angry
おしえる	教える	(V1)	31	to teach
おそう	襲う	(V)	38	to attack
おそらく	おそらく	(Adv)	43	probably
おちつく	落ち着く	(V)	35	to calm down
おちゃ	お茶	(N)	31, 33	tea
おちる	落ちる	(V1)	44	to fall
おっと	夫	(N)	32	my husband
おつまみ	おつまみ	(N)	33	snack
おつり	お釣り	(N)	39	change
おと	音	(N)	44	sound
おとうさん	お父さん	(N)	37	father
おとうと	弟	(N)	45	younger brother
おとく	お得	(N)	42	offer, sale

おとす	落とす	(V)	44	to drop
おとな	大人	(N)	37	adult
おどる	踊る	(V2)	32	to dance
おなじ	同じ	(Adv)	42	the same
おび	帯	(N)	42	*obi*, kimono belt
おふぃす	オフィス	(N)	38	office
おふろ	お風呂	(N)	34, 36	bath (Japanese style)
おみやげ	お土産	(N)	42	souvenir
おもいだす	思い出す	(V)	35	to remember
おもう	思う	(V)	31	to think, to believe
おもしろい	面白い	(iAdj)	34	interesting | funny
おもちゃ	おもちゃ	(N)	38, 45	toy
おゆ	お湯	(N)	36	hot water
およぐ	泳ぐ	(V)	32	to swim
おりる	下りる	(V2)	44	to come down
おりる	降りる	(V2)	39, 44	to get off
おる	折る	(V2)	44	to fold | to break
おれ	俺	(PN)	31	I (vulgar)
おれる	折れる	(V1)	44	to be folded
おれんじ	オレンジ	(N)	33	orange
おろす	下ろす	(V)	44	to take down
おろす	降ろす	(V)	44	to drop off
おわる	終わる	(V2)	38, 44	to finish
おんがく	音楽	(N)	34	music

か KA

か	課	(N)	44	lesson
かーと	カート	(N)	33	cart
かーど	カード	(N)	36	card
～かい	～階	(C)	36	(counter for floors)
かいいんしょう	会員証	(N)	36	membership card
かいさつ	改札	(N)	39	ticket gate
かいじょう	会場	(N)	44	a site
がいしょく	外食	(Vn)	37	eating out
かいだん	階段	(N)	36	stairs
かいほう	解放	(Vn)	37	to free
かいもの	買い物	(N)	37	shopping
かう	買う	(V)	31	to buy
かうんたー	カウンター	(N)	33	counter
かえす	帰す	(V)	44	to send home
かえす	返す	(V)	44	to return, to give back
かえる	帰る	(V2)	31, 44	to come back, to go back
かえる	替える	(V2)	33	to exchange (money)
かえる	変える	(V1)	31, 44	to change
かえる	返る	(V2)	44	to return to
かお	顔	(N)	43	face
かかる	かかる	(V2)	39	to take (time)
かかる	かかる	(V2)	44	to be hung
かがくしゃ	科学者	(N)	38	scientist
かがめる	かがめる	(V1)	40	to bend, to bow
かき	柿	(N)	34	persimmon
かぎ	鍵	(N)	36	key
かく～	各～	(Adv)	39	each...
かく	書く	(V)	31	to write
がくせい	学生	(N)	37	student
がくひ	学費	(N)	42	school expenses
かける	かける	(V1)	44	to hang, to put
がしゅう	画集	(N)	42	artbook
かす	貸す	(V)	31	to lend

きめる	決める	(V1)	41, 44	to decide
きもの	着物	(N)	42	kimono
きゃく	客	(N)	45	client, visitor
きゃべつ	キャベツ	(N)	34	cabbage
きゃんせる	キャンセル	(Vn)	36	cancellation
きゃんばす	キャンバス	(N)	38	canvas
きゅうか	休暇	(Vn)	41	holidays
きゅうこう	急行	(N)	39	express train
きゅうす	急須	(N)	42	teapot
きゅうに	急に	(Adv)	44	suddenly
ぎゅうにゅう	牛乳	(N)	33	cow's milk
きゅーば	キューバ	(T)	33	Cuba
きょう	今日	(Adv)	38	today
きょうかしょ	教科書	(N)	35	textbook
きょうそう	競争	(Vn)	43	competition
きょうと	京都	(T)	38	Kyoto
きょうふ	恐怖	(N)	37	terror, fear
きょうみぶかい	興味深い	(iAdj)	40	interesting
きょうよう	共用	(Adv)	36	common use, shared
きょねん	去年	(Adv)	34	last year
きらいな	嫌いな	(naAdj)	37	dislike, hate
きる	切る	(V2)	32	to cut
きる	着る	(V1)	36	to wear, to put on
きれいな	きれいな	(naAdj)	34	pretty, clean, pure
きろ	キロ	(N)	32	kilometer
きんえんしゃ	禁煙車	(N)	39	non-smoking car
きんかくじ	金閣寺	(T)	39	Kinkaku-ji temple (in Kyoto)
きんこ	金庫	(N)	36	safe, vault
ぎんこう	銀行	(N)	33	bank
ぎんざ	銀座	(T)	41	Ginza (in Tokyo)

く　KU

くう	食う	(V)	35	to eat (vulgar)
くうこう	空港	(N)	33	airport
くうしつ	空室	(N)	36	vacant rooms
くうしゃ	空車	(N)	39	vacant (taxi)
くすり	薬	(N)	33	medicine
くださる	くださる	(Virr)	45	somebody gives (formal)
くだらない	くだらない	(iAdj)	34	nonsensical, absurd
くち	口	(N)	31	mouth
くつ	靴	(N)	31	shoe
くつした	靴下	(N)	42	sock
ぐっず	グッズ	(N)	42	merchandising, goods
くつろぐ	くつろぐ	(V)	36	to make oneself comfortable
くもる	曇る	(V2)	37	to become cloudy
くら	倉	(N)	44	warehouse
くらしっく	クラシック	(N)	42	classical (music)
ぐりーんしゃ	グリーン車	(N)	39	first class car
くる	来る	(Virr)	31	to come
くるま	車	(N)	34, 39	car
くれじっと	クレジット	(N)	36	credit
くれる	くれる	(V)	45	receive (somebody gives)
くろい	黒い	(iAdj)	43	black

け　KE

けいざい	経済	(N)	34	economy
けいさつかん	警察官	(N)	45	police officer
けいむしょ	刑務所	(N)	38	prison
けいやく	契約	(Vn)	38	contract

さいご	最後	(Adv)	44	the last one
さいず	サイズ	(N)	42	size
さいん	サイン	(N)	42	sign | signature
さがす	探す	(V)	42	to search
さかな	魚	(N)	33	fish
さがる	下がる	(V2)	39, 44	to come down, to go down
さくしゃ	作者	(N)	42	author
さくら	桜	(N)	41	cherry tree | cherry blossom
さけ	酒	(N)	31	*sake*
さけぶ	叫ぶ	(V)	41	to shout
さげる	下げる	(V1)	44	to lower
ささやく	ささやく	(V)	41	to whisper
さしあげる	差し上げる	(V1)	38, 45	to give (formal)
さしみ	刺身	(N)	35	*sashimi*
ざせき	座席	(N)	33	seat
さそう	誘う	(V)	34	to invite
さっかー	サッカー	(N)	37	soccer
ざっし	雑誌	(N)	33	magazine
さつじんしゃ	殺人者	(Vn)	45	murderer
さっぽろ	札幌	(T)	35	Sapporo
さとう	砂糖	(N)	33	sugar
さべつ	差別	(N)	44	discrimination
さむい	寒い	(iAdj)	35	cold
さらりーまん	サラリーマン	(N)	35	company employee, office worker
ざんぎょう	残業	(Vn)	45	overtime
ざんびあ	ザンビア	(T)	33	Zambia
さんぽ	散歩	(Vn)	35	a walk

し SHI

しあい	試合	(N)	44	match | tournament
しあわせ	幸せ	(N)	32	happiness
しーつ	シーツ	(N)	36	sheet
しーと	シート	(N)	33	seat
しーとべると	シートベルト	(N)	33	seat belt
じーんず	ジーンズ	(N)	42	jeans
じかん	時間	(N)	33	time
しく	敷く	(V)	36	to spread
しくしく	しくしく	(Vn)	41	sob
しけん	試験	(N)	44	exam
じこ	事故	(N)	43, 45	accident
じこく	時刻	(N)	33	time
じこくひょう	時刻表	(Adv)	39	timetable, schedule
しごと	仕事	(N)	38	work
じさ	時差	(N)	33	time difference
じしょ	辞書	(N)	31	dictionary
しずかな	静かな	(naAdj)	43	quiet, silent
した	下	(Adv)	40	under
したぎ	下着	(N)	34	underwear
しちゃく	試着	(Vn)	42	trying clothes on
しつれいな	失礼な	(Adv.na)	45	rude
していせき	指定席	(N)	39	reserved seat
じてんしゃ	自転車	(N)	39	bicycle
じどうしゃ	自動車	(N)	31, 39	car
しない	市内	(N)	36	in the city
しにん	死人	(N)	43	dead
しぬ	死ぬ	(V)	31	to die
しはつ	始発	(N)	39	first train
しはらう	支払う	(V)	36	to pay
じはんき	自販機	(N)	39	vending machine

す　SU

すいーと	スイート	(N)	36	suite
すいえい	水泳	(N)	40	swimming
すうがく	数学	(N)	38	mathematics
すーつ	スーツ	(N)	42	suit
すかーと	スカート	(N)	42	skirt
すきな	好きな	(naAdj)	37	like
すくない	少ない	(iAdj)	38	a few
すこし	少し	(Adv)	36	a little
すごす	過ごす	(V)	40	to pass, to spend
すし	寿司	(N)	41	*sushi*
すてきな	素敵な	(Adv.na)	45	wonderful, fantastic
すぱげってぃ	スパゲッティ	(N)	32	spaghetti
すぴーち	スピーチ	(N)	43	speech
すぺいん	スペイン	(T)	33	Spain
すべて	全て	(Adv)	34	everything
ずぼん	ズボン	(N)	42	trousers
すみません	すみません	(Ph)	36	I'm sorry | excuse me
すむ	住む	(V)	38	to live, to inhabit
すりっぱ	スリッパ	(N)	36	slippers
すりらー	スリラー	(N)	42	thriller (movie)
する	する	(Virr)	31	to do
すわひりご	スワヒリ語	(N)	32	Swahili
すわる	座る	(V2)	32	to sit

せ　SE

せ	背	(N)	37	back
ぜい	税	(N)	42	tax
せいかく	性格	(N)	31	character
ぜいかん	税関	(N)	33	customs
ぜいきん	税金	(N)	31	tax
せいさんき	清算機	(N)	39	fare adjustment machine
ぜいたくな	贅沢な	(naAdj)	40	luxurious
せいと	生徒	(N)	31	pupil
せいふ	政府	(N)	45	Government
せいふく	制服	(N)	43	uniform
せいれき	西暦	(N)	40	A.D. (Anno Domini)
せーたー	セーター	(N)	34, 42	sweater
せーふ	セーフ	(N)	36	safe, vault
せき	席	(N)	40	seat
せつめい	説明	(Vn)	45	explanation
せつめいしょ	説明書	(N)	42	instruction book
せわ	世話	(Vn)	36	care
せんしゅ	選手	(N)	38	player, athlete
せんだい	仙台	(T)	39	Sendai
せんたく	洗濯	(Vn)	35	washing
せんぱい	先輩	(N)	41	senior
ぜんぶ	全部	(Adv)	34	everything
せんべい	せんべい	(N)	42	*senbei* rice cracker

そ　SO

ぞう	象	(N)	37	elephant
そうじ	掃除	(Vn)	35, 36	cleaning
そうじゅう	操縦	(Vn)	32	to pilot
そうる	ソウル	(N)	42	soul music
そだつ	育つ	(V)	44	to grow
そだてる	育てる	(V1)	44	to bring up
そつぎょう	卒業	(Vn)	40	graduation
そふぁ	ソファ	(N)	34, 36	sofa

つ TSU

て TE

でっき	デッキ	(N)	33	deck, platform
てつづき	手続き	(Vn)	33	proceedings
てぶくろ	手袋	(N)	42	gloves
でる	出る	(N)	34, 44	to go out
てれび	テレビ	(N)	31	television
てれほんかーど	テレホンカード	(N)	42	telephone card
てをかす	手を貸す	(Ph)	41	to give a hand
てんいん	店員	(N)	37	store clerk
でんき	電気	(N)	36	light, electricity
てんごく	天国	(N)	35	heaven, paradise
でんしじしょ	電子辞書	(N)	42	electronic dictionary
でんしゃ	電車	(N)	35, 39	train
でんでんたうん	でんでんタウン	(T)	42	DenDen Town (in Osaka)
でんとうてきな	伝統的な	(naAdj)	42	traditional
てんぷら	天ぷら	(N)	43	*tenpura*
てんぼう	展望	(Vn)	33	view
でんわ	電話	(N)	36	telephone

と　TO

どあ	ドア	(N)	36	door
どいつ	ドイツ	(T)	33	Germany
といれ	トイレ	(N)	31, 33	toilet, WC
どう	どう	(Adv)	34	how about?
とうえき	当駅	(N)	39	this station
とうき	陶器	(N)	42	ceramics
とうきょう	東京	(T)	35	Tokyo
どうして	どうして	(Adv)	34	why?
とうじょう	搭乗	(Vn)	33	boarding
とうしょうぐう	東照宮	(T)	39	Tōshōgū shrine (Nikkō)
とうちゃく	到着	(Vn)	33	arrival
とうふ	豆腐	(N)	41	*tōfu*
どうやら	どうやら	(Adv)	43	apparently
どうりょう	同僚	(N)	45	comrade, colleague
とおい	遠い	(iAdj)	34	far
とおす	通す	(V)	33, 44	to let pass
どーむ	ドーム	(N)	39	dome
とおる	通る	(V2)	40, 44	to pass
どくしん	独身	(N)	43	unmarried, single
とけい	時計	(N)	42	watch, clock
どこ	どこ	(Adv)	34	where?
どこか	どこか	(Adv)	41	somewhere
どこでも	どこでも	(Adv)	38	anywhere
ところ	所	(N)	41	place
としょかん	図書館	(N)	40	library
とっきゅう	特急	(N)	39	limited express train
とつぜん	突然	(Adv)	44	suddenly
とても	とても	(Adv)	32, 45	very | not nearly
とどく	届く	(V)	44	to reach
とどける	届ける	(V1)	44	to send
どなた	どなた	(Adv)	34	who? (formal)
とにかく	とにかく	(Adv)	41	anyhow
どの	どの	(Adv)	34	which?
とばす	飛ばす	(V)	44	to make fly
とびら	扉	(N)	39	door
とぶ	飛ぶ	(V)	40, 44	to fly
とまと	トマト	(N)	33	tomato
とまる	止まる	(V2)	44	to stop
とめる	止める	(V1)	39, 44	to stop, to put a stop to
ともだち	友達	(N)	32	friend

ぽすたー	ポスター	(N)	42	poster
ほすてす	ホステス	(N)	41	hostess
ぽっぷす	ポップス	(N)	42	pop (music)
ほてる	ホテル	(N)	36	hotel
ほほえみ	微笑み	(N)	45	smile
ほらー	ホラー	(N)	42	horror (movie)
ぽるとがる	ポルトガル	(T)	33	Portugal
ほれる	惚れる	(V1)	32	to fall in love
ぼろい	ぼろい	(iAdj)	38	in pieces, crumbling
ほん	本	(N)	32	book
ほんとうに	本当に	(Adv)	40	really
ほんや	本屋	(N)	38	bookstore
ほんやく	翻訳	(Vn)	35	translation

ま MA

まいる	参る	(V2)	39	to come
まえに	前に	(Adv)	40	in front of
まがる	曲がる	(V2)	39, 44	to turn, to bend
まくら	まくら	(N)	33	pillow
まける	まける	(V1)	42	to lower the price
まげる	曲げる	(V1)	44	to bend
まご	孫	(N)	35	grandchild
まじ	マジ	(Adv)	43	seriously, in earnest
まだ	まだ	(Adv)	44	still
まち	街	(N)	40	suburb
まち	町	(N)	40	town
まちあわせ	待ち合わせ	(Vn)	38	appointment
まちがえる	間違える	(V1)	39	to make a mistake
まつ	待つ	(V)	31	to wait
まっすぐ	まっすぐ	(Adv)	39	straight ahead
まど	窓	(N)	33, 36	window
まにあう	間に合う	(V)	33	to be in time
まふらー	マフラー	(N)	42	scarf
まま	ママ	(N)	45	mommy, mom
まもなく	まもなく	(Adv)	33, 39	briefly
まもる	守る	(V2)	43	to protect
まれーしあ	マレーシア	(T)	34	Malaysia
まわす	回す	(V)	44	to turn about
まわる	回る	(V2)	44	to go round
まんいん	満員	(Adv)	39	crowded
まんが	漫画	(N)	31	comic book
まんしつ	満室	(N)	36	full (hotel)

み MI

みえる	見える	(V1)	32, 44	can see (unconsciously)
みぎ	右	(Adv)	39	right
みずぎ	水着	(N)	42	swimming costume
みせ	店	(N)	38	shop
みせる	見せる	(V1)	42	to show
みそしる	味噌汁	(N)	41	*miso* soup
みち	道	(N)	38	road
みつかる	見つかる	(V2)	33, 44	to find
みつける	見つける	(V1)	44	to find
みなみ	南	(Adv)	33	south
みなみあふりか	南アフリカ	(T)	33	South Africa
みやざき	宮崎	(T)	43	Miyazaki
みやじま	宮島	(T)	39	Miyajima
みる	見る	(V1)	31, 44	to see, to look
みんしゅしゅぎ	民主主義	(N)	41	democracy

む MU

むかえる	迎える	(V1)	38	to go to meet
むずかしい	難しい	(iAdj)	40	difficult
むすこ	息子	(N)	41	son
むすめ	娘	(N)	43	daughter
むだな	無駄な	(naAdj)	40	useless | waste

め ME

め	目	(N)	41	eye
めーたー	メーター	(N)	39	taximeter
めきしこ	メキシコ	(T)	33	Mexico
めざましどけい	目覚まし時計	(N)	36	alarm clock
めっせーじ	メッセージ	(N)	44	message
めでたい	めでたい	(iAdj)	42	joyous

も MO

もうふ	毛布	(N)	33	blanket
もえる	燃える	(V1)	44	to burn, to be in flames
もくてき	目的	(N)	33	aim
もしかして	もしかして	(Adv)	43	possibly
もしかすると	もしかすると	(Adv)	43	possibly
もちあげる	持ち上げる	(V1)	38	to raise
もつ	持つ	(V)	40	to have, to hold
もどす	戻す	(V)	44	to return, to give back
もどる	戻る	(V2)	44	to return, to go back
ものれーる	モノレール	(N)	39	monorail
もやす	燃やす	(V)	44	to burn
もらう	もらう	(V)	45	to receive
もんげん	門限	(N)	36	closing time, curfew
もんごる	モンゴル	(T)	35	Mongolia
もんだい	問題	(N)	41	problem

や YA

やくざ	ヤクザ	(N)	45	*yakuza*
やさい	野菜	(N)	33	vegetable
やさしい	優しい	(iAdj)	37	kind, gentle
やすい	安い	(iAdj)	35	cheap
やすうり	安売り	(N)	42	sales
やすむ	休む	(V)	38	to rest
やつ	奴	(PN)	34	guy | he (vulgar)
やっぱり	やっぱり	(Adv)	31	of course, I thought so
やぶる	破る	(V2)	45	to break
やる	やる	(V2)	45	to give (vulgar)
やる	やる	(V2)	35	to do

ゆ YU

ゆうしょう	優勝	(Vn)	38	victory
ゆうしょく	夕食	(N)	36	supper
ゆーすほすてる	ユースホステル	(N)	36	youth hostel
ゆーろ	ユーロ	(N)	33	euro
ゆかた	浴衣	(N)	36, 42	*yukata*
～ゆき	～行き	(Adv)	33	going to..., bound for...
ゆき	雪	(N)	43	snow
ゆるす	許す	(V)	44	to forgive | to allow

よ YO

ようが	洋画	(N)	42	Western cinema
ようがく	洋楽	(N)	42	Western music

索引